Edwin S, Wallace

Jerusalem the Holy

a brief history of ancient Jerusalem

Edwin S, Wallace

Jerusalem the Holy
a brief history of ancient Jerusalem

ISBN/EAN: 9783337286354

Printed in Europe, USA, Canada, Australia, Japan

Cover: Foto ©Lupo / pixelio.de

More available books at **www.hansebooks.com**

Jerusalem the Holy

A Brief History of Ancient Jerusalem; with an Account of the Modern City and its Conditions Political, Religious and Social

BY

EDWIN SHERMAN WALLACE
Late United States Consul for Palestine

With Fifteen Illustrations from Photographs and Four Maps

NEW YORK   CHICAGO   TORONTO
FLEMING H. REVELL COMPANY
M DCCC XCVIII

To My Mother
At Rest in the Heavenly Jerusalem,
and
To My Wife
Who Shared with Me the Varied Experiences
of Five Years' Residence in the
Jerusalem of Earth

Preface

BOOKS about Jerusalem are sufficiently numerous. Many volumes within recent years have recorded the impressions of tourists with such adequacy for their purpose as a few days' sojourn in the city permits. These, while generally too long for the careless, are too superficial for those really interested in the past and present of the Holy City. Some fifty years ago the appearance of Williams' "Holy City" and Barclay's "City of the Great King" gave the English public two real histories of Jerusalem. But the great length of these excellent treatises has confined them in great measure to the shelves of large libraries, while the flight of time and the growth of knowledge is, slowly but surely, rendering them antiquated.

In the present volume the author has sought to combine completeness with brevity, and thus to place in the hands of those who are interested in this city of sacred memories and holy sites a book of such facts as are ascertainable. The opinions expressed are based upon careful study of recognized authorities, supplemented by diligent personal investigation, carried on during a residence of five years in Jerusalem. In many conversations with travellers the writer has learned what is of greatest interest to those who have but limited time for their own observation. The attempt is here made to give the benefit of his studies to those who are interested, to answer as briefly as possible the questions that have been so often asked, and thus to prepare intending visitors for an intelligent comprehension of what they shall see when they arrive in the Holy City. At the same time the work, it is hoped, will benefit those whom circumstances prevent from beholding the present remnant of the once great city, by giving them a picture of what it is and narrating the experiences through which it has reached its present condition.

For the historical parts of the work I must acknowledge my indebtedness to many, but especially to Professor Sayce's "Patriarchal Palestine"; Edersheim's "Jesus the Messiah"; Doctor Robinson's "Biblical Researches"; Williams' "Holy City," and Barclay's "City of the Great King." So many books have been consulted that it would be useless to mention all. I have not hesitated to draw from every source, and those who are acquainted with the publications of the Palestine Exploration Society will find that these papers have assisted me very materially. The illustrations are from photographs taken by Rev. Putnam Cady and Prof. E. Warren Clark.

EDWIN SHERMAN WALLACE.

United States Consulate, Jerusalem, 1898.

Contents

CHAPTER		PAGE
I.	THE CITY OF THE CANAANITES	13
II.	THE CITY OF DAVID AND SOLOMON	27
III.	JERUSALEM AS CHRIST SAW IT	47
IV.	THE CITY AS IT IS TO-DAY	69
V.	THE NEW JERUSALEM	89
VI.	THE WALLS AND GATES	101
VII.	THE HILLS ROUND ABOUT	115
VIII.	THE VALLEYS	129
IX.	THE TEMPLE HILL	147
X.	CHURCH OF THE HOLY SEPULCHRE	171
XI.	THE NEW, OR GORDON'S, CALVARY	199
XII.	SOME PLACES OF SPECIAL INTEREST	215
XIII.	EXCAVATIONS IN JERUSALEM	231
XIV.	CLIMATE AND HEALTH	247
XV.	PASSION WEEK AND EASTER	261
XVI.	THE JEWS	287
XVII.	CHRISTIANS IN JERUSALEM	311
XVIII.	THE MOSLEMS	329
XIX.	THE FUTURE OF JERUSALEM	349

LIST OF ILLUSTRATIONS.

THE MOSQUE OF OMAR		*Frontispiece*
ROBINSON'S ARCH		*Facing page* 60
NATIVE WATER CARRIERS STREET MARKET SCENES		" " 79
UNITED STATES CONSULATE CONSULAR GUARDS		" " 94
INTERIOR OF DAMASCUS GATE GATE OF ST. STEPHEN EAST WALL AND MOSLEM CEMETERY THE GOLDEN GATE		" " 106
MOUNT OF OLIVES AND GARDEN OF GETHSEMANE		" " 118
OLD OLIVE TREE IN GARDEN OF GETHSEMANE		" " 139
THE CITY AS SEEN FROM THE SUMMIT OF THE NEW CALVARY	"	" 199
SOUTHERN VIEW OF THE NEW CALVARY		" " 209
SYRIAN BISHOP OF JERUSALEM		" " 320
MAPS	*following*	" 359

THE CITY OF THE CANAANITES

Jerusalem—The Name—Its Origin—Salem—Testimony of Egyptian Monuments—Tel-el-Amarna Tablets—Melchizedek—Ebed-Tob—Abraham in Canaan—Civilization of the Canaanites—Debir—Modern Explorations—Jerusalem always a Sacred City—Jebusites—Hittites—The Confederates—Adoni-Zedek—Victories of Joshua—Division of the Land—Judah and Benjamin—Moral and Religious Degeneracy—Jebusite Supremacy—Judges—Samuel—Founding of the Monarchy—David—Conquest of Jerusalem.

I

THE CITY OF THE CANAANITES

JERUSALEM as a name and as a place has given students of archæology much concern. The origin of the name and of the people who first employed it to describe their city has been a fruitful source of speculation. Diligent questioning of the monuments of Egypt and the tablets of Babylonia has succeeded in making these long silent witnesses give up their secrets. Periods of time, the history of which conjecture has supplied, are now positively known. Fact has taken the place of supposition. The inquirer as to the origin of the word *Jerusalem* is no longer told that the word was coined at the time of David; he learns that it was in existence centuries before, that it was known as the name of a city of importance in the days when Babylonish influence was felt as far west as the shores of the Mediterranean.

Until within very recent years one might have accepted any of several definitions of the word *Jerusalem*. The rabbis in their zeal to connect the founding of the city with Abraham asserted that he, the father of their faith, first called the place Jireh and that Shem contributed the latter half of the name; in order that there might be no unpleasantness between these two worthies, God himself combined the two words into the one by which the city has since been known. Reland and Ewald derived it from two Hebrew words meaning "the inheritance of peace." Gesenius translated it "foundation of peace." Others have held the opinion that originally there were here two separate cities, one known as Jebus, the other Salem; that eventually they were united and their names resolved into one, which, for the sake of euphony, became Jerusalem instead of Jebussalem. A similar view was held by those who give the Hebrew dual form to the word, reading it Jerushalaim, a form that occurs in five places in the Old Testament. When the Greek influence predominated, a Greek derivation made it mean "the holy place of Solomon."

All these hypotheses had their value when no positive information was at hand: now the facts are before us. In the cuneiform documents the city is called Uru-Salim, the city of Salim. In the early language of Canaan as we learn from a Nineveh tablet "uru" was equivalent to the Babylonish "alu," a city. The Semitic "uru" represents the "eri," "a city," of the pre-Semitic language of Babylonia. As to "Salim" there has never been a doubt: it means "peace," and was the name of the God of Peace. So we have Uru-Salim, Jerusalem, the city of the God of Peace.

The information furnished by the monuments and tablets makes us reasonably certain as to another long-disputed subject. When Abraham returned after defeating the kings who had despoiled Sodom and carried Lot away captive, he was met "in the valley of Shaveh, which is the King's dale" by "Melchizedek, king of Salem," and "priest of the most High God." This Melchizedek was king of Jerusalem. From the history of Absalom we know that the "King's dale" was near Jerusalem. Salem was frequently used for the longer name, and so appears several times on the Egyptian monuments. One of the victory-inscriptions of Rameses II. on the walls of the Rameseum at Thebes, describing that monarch's conquests in Southern Palestine, mentions Salem. Rameses III. at Medinet Habu, tells us that he conquered "the district of Salem" between "the country of Hadashah" and "the district of the Dead Sea" and "the Jordan."

Salim, the God of Peace, was the patron deity of Jerusalem, the city of peace. Melchizedek, priest of the most high God, officiating in the city of peace, came out to welcome and bless the returning conqueror Abraham, who had routed the enemies of the land and restored peace to its inhabitants. The offerings of bread and wine made by the priest were tokens, the one that peace had been established, the other of gratitude to him whose prowess had effected this desirable consummation. The story of Melchizedek can no longer be subject to critical doubts. The Tel-el-Amarna tablets give their corroborative testimony of illustration and explanation. Salem was Jerusalem.

Among the Tel-el-Amarna tablets are found letters written by a king of Jerusalem to Amenophis, the then reigning Pharaoh in Egypt. This king, Ebed-Tob, was not a governor appointed from Egypt, but, as he himself says, was a tributary ally of the empire of the Nile. There are some striking points of resemblance between this king, Ebed-Tob, and the royal priest Melchizedek. He claims his kingdom not by human appointment, nor by succession from royal progenitors, but through the oracle of the "Mighty King." The Pharaoh is called "the Great King," so that when "the Mighty King" is spoken of we see in Him "the Most High God" of Melchizedek. In this early day, fifteen centuries before our era, Jerusalem had a religious monarch who confesses that he owes the honor of his appointment and the dignity of his royal position to his God.

When Abraham journeying from Ur of the Chaldees, came to Canaan, he found a people not entirely strange to him. The civilization of his native land had preceded him; in the cities of Canaan the people worked and worshipped as in his own country. Babylonia was the predominant power in "the land of the Amorites." In the cities of the West the language of Babylon was commonly known; there were schools for the study of it, and scribes who copied on tablets of clay the records that were to be preserved. With two or three notable exceptions the cuneiform characters were used in all diplomatic and polite correspondence.

It has been taken for granted that the land to which Abraham came as an immigrant was sparsely settled by barbarous people; the Tel-el-Amarna tablets show us that this assumption was far from the truth. And yet the real condition of the land and the people might have been inferred from the Old Testament, in the names by which some of the cities of Canaan were known: for example, Debir—"the sanctuary" was known by two other names, Kirjath-Sannah, "the city of instruction," and Kirjath-Sepher, "the city of books." It is more than probable that in these names we receive a characterization of the place according to the employment of its inhabitants. Debir was situated in the mountainous parts of Judah; if its exact location ever be discovered, a library of information about these early times may be given to the world.

The results of modern exploration in Palestine, while they have disappointed expectations in some respects, have been of great value in assisting in the formation of correct opinions of the early periods of history. As each discovery corroborates the Biblical narrative, the hope grows that the labors of explorers may be rewarded by some great "find." Professor Petrie and Doctor Bliss in their work at Tel-el-Hesi demonstrated the possibility of such a hope being realized. If Tel-el-Hesi could reveal the work of men's hands wrought from 3,000 to 1,500 years B. C., and one letter in cuneiform character of the same date as the Tel-el-Amarna tablets, there is no limit to the hopes that those interested in such discoveries may be permitted to entertain. Palestine is a land of mounds, or tels, the sites of ancient cities. They are waiting for the pick of the excavator to disclose their hidden treasures of information concerning the pre-Israelite dwellers in this land.

The excavations made under the direction of the Palestine Exploration Fund, by Conder and Bliss have settled some disputed questions of topography, but, carefully and industriously as the work has been done, have added little to our knowledge of the city's builders and inhabitants previous to the Jewish conquest under David. Our information, limited as it is, has been derived from other sources, the discovery of which warrants the belief that, when existing obstacles to excavations within the present city walls and near the Holy Places of the Moslems are removed, discoveries equal in importance to that of Tel-el-Amarna will be made.

This much is now positive knowledge, that when Abram, the Chaldean sheikh, pitched his tents in the land of Canaan he was in a country that was settled and reasonably well governed, that the Babylonish culture and civilization predominated, that Jerusalem was a city whose ruler was recognized as king over a district, probably the lord of Canaan, to whom the neighboring princes paid homage, and that Jerusalem was already a sacred city. We cannot yet say to which of the numerous Canaanitish tribes Melchizedek, the king of Righteousness, belonged. From the Book of Numbers[1] we learn that "the Hittites and the Jebusites and the Amorites dwell in the mountains." It can further be inferred with reason that the dwellers in the city in Abram's time were either Hittites or Amorites, or both, for the Jebusites were a local tribe, in possession of the city at the time the Israelites under Joshua entered Canaan, and were either Amorite or Hittite in origin.[2] Ezekiel[3] confirms this opinion when in charging the Jerusalem of his day with inconsistency, he says: "Your mother was an Hittite and your father an Amorite." The two nations occupied the entire land at one time, Kadesh on the Orontes being the stronghold of the Hittites. Hittites and Amorites dwelt together at Hebron, and Kadesh-barnea was "in the mountains of the Amorites."

Knowing this much generally about these two large tribes, or nations, does not enable us, however, to say which one of them occupied the rocky summit of Zion, nor when the Jebusite took possession. A theory as to time, based upon the records of the Tel-el-Amarna tablets, has much in its favor. In

---

[1] Num. xiii. 29.   [2] Sayce's "Patriarchal Palestine," pp. 50, 51.
[3] Ezekiel xvi. 45.

the list there given no mention is made of the Jebusites. The name Jebus further does not appear. The fact that Urusalim is the common appellation leads to the conclusion that the Jebusitic occupation was of later date. At the time the tablets were written, the king, Ebed-Tob, was being hard pressed by enemies, whom he calls Khabiri, or "Confederates." To assist him against those who were seeking to conquer his territories and to dethrone him, he writes in urgent terms to the reigning Pharaoh to send him help. But affairs in Egypt were in a critical condition and no forces could be spared. The result Ebed-Tob feared actually happened, as one of the tablets informs us. Jerusalem was finally assaulted and taken, and the king captured. There is no record that informs us who these early enemies of Jerusalem were. Among the Khabiri, or "Confederates," was a Bedouin chief, Labai, and his sons. These confederates overran and took all of southern Canaan. When next we hear of Jerusalem it is a Jebusite stronghold. Doubtless in the partition of the spoils of their combined victories the city was allotted to this new tribe, or, following the suggestion given by Ezekiel, we may say that the Jebusites were a tribe formed by a union of part of the Hittite and part of the Amorite tribes.

All this, however, is in the nature of conjecture based upon the correspondence of time of the appearance of these Confederates and the change of the city's name. The Khabiri were in possession of Hebron at this time and philologists tell us that the words Khabiri and Hebron have the same origin. Other explanations as to who the "Confederates" were and whence they came are offered, but to follow them would lead us from our present purpose. Enough that they succeeded in taking the city and making themselves complete masters of it and the surrounding country. Here we find them, secure in their possession and boastful of their security for some centuries.

Five centuries after Abraham made his offering to Melchizedek, at that time King of Jerusalem, his descendants, after generations of servitude in the land of the Pharaohs and forty years of wilderness wandering, entered Canaan as conquerors. The name of the king of Jebus who opposed them suggests that the city still retained its sacred character, and his calling upon the neighboring princes of Hebron, Jarmuth, Lachish and Eglon to come and help him to resist the invaders indicates that they were in some sense subservient to him. These five kings are all called Amorites in Joshua x, 5. Adoni-zedek, the righteous lord, was this king's name, and from it we infer that he, too, combined in his person the office of king and priest. The alliance of the kings was, however, unable to resist the invaders under Joshua. They gave battle at Gibeon, about three miles northwest of Jerusalem and were completely routed. The victory of the Israelites was decisive. Adoni-zedek and his four vassal princes were taken and paid the penalty of their resistance with their lives.

Following up his victory at Gibeon Joshua immediately took the cities, whose kings he had hanged near the cave of Makkedah,[1] and slaughtered all their inhabitants. Of Jerusalem no mention is made at this time. It was not assailed; or the assault was not successful. It was then, no doubt, being the capital city, a much more strongly fortified place than any of the other cities and regularly to invest it would have consumed more time and required more formidable enginery of war than the Israelites had at their disposal. It was left for a more opportune season. In the meantime other alliances of the native princes commanded the attention of Joshua and his men-at-arms.

In the division of the land made subsequently by Joshua the northern boundary of Judah's allotted territory ran "south of the Jebusite";[2] and so Jebus was counted in Benjamin's portion. However, the Benjamites seem to have permitted the forces of Judah to do the fighting necessary to obtain possession.

[1] Joshua x. 15, etc.   [2] Joshua xv. 8.

Doubtless for this reason many passages in the Bible speak of Jerusalem as a city of Judah. At any rate Judah did successfully assail Jebus,[1] with the assistance of the forces of Simeon.[2] When this successful assault was made cannot be discovered, for in the list of cities which fell to the lot of Judah, as given in the fifteenth chapter of Joshua, the city of the Jebusites was the one exception to the universal conquest. It was strong enough to make terms of peace, and, as the writer of Joshua puts it, "The Jebusites dwell with the children of Judah at Jerusalem unto this day."[3] How long these terms of peace were satisfactory cannot be learned, for the next record[4] mentions that Judah had taken Jerusalem, "smitten it with the edge of the sword, and set the city on fire." From this conquest Judah's forces went to the south and east of their territory to overthrow the Canaanites, and seem to have left Jerusalem in the care of their brothers, the Benjamites, it being in reality one of the cities which had been assigned to them.[5] But Benjamin was not strong enough to keep the Jebusites in subjection. They made the mistake of permitting the conquered race to remain in their old habitation. Expulsion of the Jebusite was the only method which would have allowed Benjamin to enjoy the benefits of Judah's victory. This not having been employed, the Jebusite soon raised himself to a position of equality, and, though Benjamin wished to expel him, he could not. So the next record[6] informs us that the Jebusite and Benjamite are dwelling together in Jerusalem.

An effort has been made to reconcile these rather difficult passages, which appear to contradict each other, by assuming that at this early period the city was, what it certainly became at a later date, double in form, that is that there were two divisions of the city, an upper and a lower. In this case the children of Judah were able to dislodge the

[1] Judges i. 8.   [2] Judges i. 3.   [3] Joshua xv. 63.
[4] Judges i. 8.   [5] Joshua xviii. 28.   [6] Judges i. 21.

Jebusite from the lower city, which was less strongly fortified, and the Benjamites dwelt in this part, while the Jebusites from their stronghold on Zion repelled all assaults. The Hebrew dual form which the name sometimes has, *i. e.*, Jerushal*aim*, has been thought to support this hypothesis. But it gives weak support. On the two occasions[1] when the last half of the word is used for the whole it is written Shalem and not Shalaim. In five other places where the dual form is used, and which the Masoretic points indicate, no support is given this theory; for these are of a much later date when the double form of the city was well established and was so familiar as to be reflected in the name.

This difficulty will remain until further records, if any such exist, are discovered. For the present it can only be said that in the troublous times of the Israelitish conquest of the land there were periods when first one and then the other of the contending parties held the supremacy.

A period of moral and religious degeneracy succeeded the death of Joshua. The Israelites of the next generation forgot their divine commission and are found serving " the gods of the people that were round about them."[2] The martial spirit that made them conquerors had sunk so low that they could no longer maintain what they had won. They were even sold as slaves by the nations that had stood in fear of their fathers.[3] Occasionally a man of great personal power arose among them and revived their old spirit for a time. But with the decay of their sublime religion they degenerated as men, and for a time their national existence was threatened; they were sinking to the level of the Canaanite. During this period of disgrace the Jebusites were strong enough to expel them entirely, and for nearly three hundred years the city was regarded by the Israelites as " the city of a stranger " in which it was neither desirable nor safe for an Israelite to tarry.[4]

[1] Gen. xiv. 18; Psalm lxxvi. 2.　　[2] Judges ii. 12.
[3] Judges ii. 10-14.　　[4] Judges xix. 12.

The period of the judges, until the authority of Samuel, the greatest of the judges, was recognized, was a time of political and religious anarchy. "Every man did that which was right in his own eyes."[1] As a consequence the record of the period is a story of corruption involving, except in a few cases, even the priests and judges. Under such circumstances no advance could be made, and we may pass rapidly over an epoch the study of which tells us nothing of Jerusalem. Secure in their rock fortress on Zion the Jebusites remained, doubtless using past experience to make more safe against attack the city for which nature had done so much. And they would have remained in insolent possession, had not a great leader appeared.

In the midst of this national degeneracy Samuel, second only to Moses as a ruler and guide, came upon the stage of action. With the duties of a judge he combined those of a teacher and a prophet. In time he shamed the Israelites out of their idolatry and delivered them from the power of the Philistines. The spirit of Jehovah came upon them again and their departed glory returned. In the hands of Samuel the theocracy became a fact, for he was virtually a dictator. And yet, so long as the various tribes retained their individuality and the numerous princes and princelings and leaders were under no universally acknowledged head, there were petty jealousies and internal strifes which seriously weakened the nation. In fact up to this time, and after it, there was no Jewish nation. Each tribal leader was nothing more than a condottiere in Italy in mediæval times and maintained his position only by his ability to overpower his rivals and to gratify the propensity for spoils of his clansmen.

Amid such adverse conditions the task of Samuel was not an easy one; and it took him forty years to accomplish it. The details of his efforts to educate and elevate the lawless chieftains and dispirited people are unknown; history records only

[1] Judges xvii. 6.

the grand result. He aroused fresh courage and inspired new hope; he combined the factions into a harmonious whole; he laid upon them the responsibility of conquest and incited in them a belief in their own powers to accomplish the mission to which he as God's spokesman called them. He revolutionized the state by reviving the religion of the people and thereby prepared them for that advance in civilization,—a political revolution, and the founding of a monarchical government. This was not the result Samuel had desired. In fact he was opposed to the establishment of the monarchy, fearing lest the change in government should wean the people from their newly awakened devotion to their religion and draw them from that simplicity of life and manners which he, as a wise judge, felt to be their real security. He warned them of the loss of liberty that would follow the crowning of a king, but the popular voice assented to a curtailing of its liberties in the hope of having greater individual protection and of being able to take its place among nations. Despotism is preferable to anarchy.

Saul, the first king, was a man of royal bearing. The early years of his reign were marked by military successes; but tribal jealousies did not immediately disappear. It was not until David was made ruler that the tribes really united to form the Jewish nation. Hebron was the first capital, and here it was that the leaders came and offered their allegiance to the new monarch; but Hebron was too far to the south to remain the centre of government. The stronghold of the Jebusites would meet the local requirements for the new capital, and to expel these hated strangers from the midst of the land would be a signal victory with which to establish David's reign over united Israel and instill a wholesome respect for his arms among the surrounding nations. These nations on the other hand were already jealous of the advance Israel was making and, fearful of their own security, were ready to thwart her by every power at their command.

Everything being in preparation for the siege, David moved northward from Hebron in command of the very flower of the armies of united Israel, who had come to Hebron "to turn the Kingdom of Saul to him." It was an army of which any commander might well be proud. For that early period the numbers are startling. Two hundred and eighty thousand warriors,[1] skilled in the use of arms, seems an overwhelming number to send against one city. Doubt has been expressed of the accuracy of the figures given by the author of Chronicles. It is much easier, however, to raise a doubt than to prove an inaccuracy. The size of David's army gives us an idea of the strength of Jebus. During the centuries of their undisturbed occupation the Jebusites had doubtless grown in numbers and power, and, adding to their city's fortifications, would invite the greatest effort Israel could make to dislodge them. Even this tremendous force did not daunt the spirit of the Jebusites. They beheld it coming and expected a result similar to the outcome of past attempts.

David probably assailed the city from the south. The lower city was immediately taken, but the inhabitants, retiring to the stronghold in the upper city, heaped reproaches upon the king and showed their contempt for him and his by the manner of their defiance. They insulted him from the battlements, placed the city's lame[2] and blind upon the walls, and informed him in ridicule that these would have to be taken before he could enter. The insult was soon avenged, for the intrepid Israelites, with Joab at their head, soon scaled the walls, put the Jebusites to the sword, and were masters of both the lower and upper city, including the citadel of Zion. This capture was made about the year 1040 B. C., and from it dates the history of Jerusalem as the city of the Jews.

[1] 1 Chron. xii. 23–39.   [2] 2 Sam. v. 6; 1. Chron. xi. 5, 6.

THE CITY OF DAVID AND SOLOMON

Effect of David's Victory—Establishing the Kingdom—
War and Peace—"City of David"—Wealth—Arc—Tabernacle—King's Palace—David's Thought to Erect the Temple
—Temple Site—Threshing Floors—Collecting of Materials—
Closing Years of David's Reign—Solomon's Inheritance—
Temple Building—Hiram of Tyre—Number of Workmen—
Cost of Construction—Size of Temple—Origin of Design of
Temple—Location—Brief Description—Solomon's Other Labors—Colonnade on the East—Royal Palace—House of the
Forest of Lebanon—Mural Improvements—The "Ascent"—
Water Supply—Commerce—Ophir—Extent of the Kingdom—
Insufficiency of Revenue—Solomon's Apostasy—Internal
Weakness of the Nation—Solomon's Death.

II

THE CITY OF DAVID AND SOLOMON

THE effect of the fall of the Jebusite stronghold was felt throughout Israel and among the surrounding nations. By this victory the warrior king had established himself firmly on his throne and overcome any opposition that still lingered among those of his subjects who favored the succession of the house of Saul. Neighboring powers began to fear him and sought by allying themselves against him to check his progress. The Philistines led their forces against David,[1] but were not permitted to come to the walls of Jerusalem, the king meeting them in the valley of Rephaim and defeating them. Later a strong alliance was effected of "all Syria and Phœnicia, with many other nations besides them."[2] These were met in the same valley and effectually routed. These successes won for the new monarch the friendship of Hiram, king of Tyre, from whom an embassy soon appeared in Jerusalem offering David the usual gifts of one royal personage to another and promising materials and artificers to assist in the erection of a palace.

While these wars on the one hand and peace negotiations on the other proceeded, David was further occupied by the fortifying and embellishing of his capital. It was to be made a seat of government worthy of a strong and progressive nation. To make it more impregnable, the two cities—the upper and lower—were united and enclosed by a wall. This wall crossed the intervening valley on an artificial embankment to which some authorities have given the name Millo. On Mount Zion the royal palace was built, and this, the stronghold of the Jebusites, was afterward known as "the City of David."

[1] 2 Sam. v. 17–21; I Chron. xiv. 8–12. [2] Jos. Ant. vii. 4, § 1.

During the thirty-three years of David's reign there was little peace for the armies of Israel. But the result of the wars added to the glory of the nation and increased the territory over which the supremacy of the king was acknowledged. The city grew in numbers and in wealth. The trophies of victory and the tribute from vassal princes filled the royal treasuries. In the midst of this material prosperity and outward glory there was one thing lacking which was essential to the peace of the royal mind and to the religious ideas of the nation at large. Though a human king was on the throne, the theocratic idea was still strong. David was the nominal ruler, but only as the servant of Jehovah, Israel's real sovereign. The Ark of the Covenant still witnessed to the divine Presence though it had as yet been provided with no permanent resting place. Since it had crossed the Jordan after the desert wandering, it had had a varied experience, being carried from place to place as the movement of the tribes necessitated. Now the nomadic period was over. The tribes were a nation, settled in their own land, with a permanent seat of government at Jerusalem. A habitation suitable to its character must be provided for the ark—that most sacredly significant emblem.

The old "tabernacle of the congregation" was at this time with the altar of burnt-offering at Gibeon. It had been taken there after the destruction of the priestly city of Nob.[1] Since it could not be removed, a new tabernacle was prepared for the reception of the ark on Mount Zion. Since the return of the ark to the Israelites after its capture by the Philistines at the battle of Aphek it had been kept at Kirjath-jearim in the house of Abinadab. David resolved to bring it to its newly appointed place and, amid the rejoicings of the entire people the attempt was made. But their joy was checked and the removal of the ark to the city delayed for three months because of the irreverence of Uzzah.[2] During these three months it was deposited in the house of Obed-edom, the Gittite.[3] Re-

[1] 1 Sam. xxii. 19.   [2] 2 Sam. vi. 7.   [3] 2 Sam. vi. 11.

ports coming to David of the signal manner in which the Lord was blessing the house of Obed-edom, the king took it as an evidence that the divine displeasure was appeased. Accordingly "David and the elders of Israel and the captains over thousands went to bring up the Ark of the Covenant of the Lord out of the house of Obed-edom with joy." On this occasion the Levites, the appointed bearers of the ark, carried it. With sacrifice and song, with dancing and the music of many instruments,[1] "all Israel brought up the ark." With burnt-offerings and peace-offerings and gifts to the people the king placed the sacred relic in the tent in the city of David.

The tent for the ark on Mount Zion was a temporary structure, to be used only until such time as the plans which the king had for a more noble sanctuary could be carried into execution. The thought of his own palatial residence and the comparison that followed between it and the curtain-protected ark disturbed David's peace of mind.[2] On communicating his intention to erect a worthy edifice in which to place this emblem of the divine presence it appears that he received from the prophet Nathan a sanction.[3] However, on the night following David's avowal of his plans and Nathan's encouragement the "word of the Lord" altered the plans by informing the king that not during his own reign, but during that of his son should the actual construction be done. Not discouraged by this change David immediately began with royal generosity and sublime faith to prepare the material for a structure he was never to behold.

The place where the house of the Lord was to stand was chosen by divine direction in David's lifetime. At the threshing floor of Araunah the Jebusite, the angel of the pestilence that followed the sin of the numbering of the people put up his sword and there by command of the angel, David "set up an altar to the Lord" and offered "burnt-offerings and peace-offerings" which were acceptable unto the Lord. This thresh-

[1] 1 Chron. xv. 29.   [2] 2 Sam. vii. 2.   [3] 2 Sam. vii. 3

ing floor was purchased from the Jebusite for six hundred shekels weight of gold.[1]

The threshing floor of Araunah was doubtless similar to many that may be seen on the rocky hilltops of Palestine to-day. It was an exposed summit where, when the grain had been tramped out, the winnowing could be done easily by means of the unhindered breezes that would blow over it. But its level surface would not be at all sufficient for the needs of the temple. One of the works of preparation was to elevate the sloping sides of the hill and make a level platform. "The strangers that were in the land of Israel" which David commanded to gather together[2] may have been set to this work, though it was left to Solomon to complete this truly wonderful piece of engineering. David's real work, however, was in amassing gold and silver, iron and brass "in abundance without weight."[3] Cedar wood was brought from the Lebanon by the Zidonians and Tyrians. Precious stones for temple ornamentation were stored up. Special taxes were levied and masons were set to hewing wrought stones. So that when Solomon came to the actual work of construction he found at his hand a supply of materials that numbers could not indicate.[4]

Besides all this prepared material David handed over to his son and successor the plan of the entire structure that was to be "The pattern of all he had by the spirit,"[5] the temple with its porches, chambers and courts. No details were lack-

---

[1] I Chron. xxi. 25. About $5,250. This appears a large amount for a mere Oriental threshing floor, but in the purchase was doubtless included all that part of the hill of Moriah that was afterward enclosed by the temple precincts. This place, now occupied by the mosque of Omar and known as the Haram area, has the singular distinction of being the only sacred place within the walls of Jerusalem whose identity has not been seriously disputed in modern times.

[2] I Chron. xxii. 2. [3] Ibid. xxii. 3.
[4] Ibid. xxii. 14–16. [5] I Chron. xxviii. 12–21.

ing even to the prescribing of the orders of the priests and Levites and the porters at the gates.

Of the other public works of David only the names are known. Of his making probably were the "royal gardens," as Josephus calls them, which were located near Joab's well, at the junction of the valleys of Hinnom and Kedron, just south of the city. He also prepared in the fortress of Zion the sepulchre which in time received him and most of his successors.

The closing years of David's reign were free from foreign wars. There was indeed little to fear from the enmity of his neighbors: the power of Assyria was broken; Egypt, under the last kings of the twentieth dynasty, was in decay; Philistia had been humbled and was confined to a narrow section of her former territory; the friendship of Tyre was sincere. The kingdom Solomon inherited reached from the Maritime plain to the Euphrates, toward the north including Damascus, and as far south as the Red Sea.

David's death occurred about the year 1015 B. C. Under God he had been the founder of Israel's greatness and of the glory of Jerusalem. He was the very soul of Hebrew enterprise. He was great! If at times he forgot his honor as a man he repented in sincerity and with the humility of a great soul. He had that rare gift, knowing how to rule as an absolute king and be loved as a friend by those over whom he ruled. He had another faculty, still less common, being able to touch the heart-strings of humanity in all ages and make them throb in unison with his own Godward emotions. These inspired songs of David would have made his name great even though he had no other claims upon posterity.

Solomon succeeded to the throne of a nation united in itself and at peace with the world. With the exception of a few petty factions which were soon reconciled, his inheritance was all that could be desired. Soon after his accession he began the erection of the Temple. The plan which had been given him for the new structure was not original; the temple was to be little more than a large copy in stone of the ancient wilderness tabernacle, the pattern of which God showed to Moses at Sinai. The arrangement of parts in the tabernacle and temple were identical; they differed only in size; the measurements of the temple were just double those of the tabernacle. An examination of these measurements will reveal to us that the temple—wonderful in many respects—was of meagre dimensions. It was only ninety feet in length, thirty in width and forty-five in height; yet the finished work was deserving of all the praise that has been bestowed upon it. It was not size—though we shall see that some parts of the work connected with it were cyclopean—but exquisite workmanship and splendor of ornamentation that have made this temple world-famous for all time. To the Hebrews of that early day it was a most impressive structure, both for the splendor of its architectural appointments and for its religious significance. They were not then and never have been a nation of great builders, and without foreign assistance it is not likely that they could have brought their temple to completion. At Solomon's request[1] Hiram, King of Tyre, sent his master-workmen of every class to superintend the construction and perform much of the labor. Thirty centuries ago the Tyrian workmen were forgotten, but on the Temple Hill their work may still be seen with the unmistakable Phœnician marks upon it.

"Incredible" has been the exclamation of many who have considered the biblical account of the number of men employed and the wealth expended on the preparation for and construction of that temple. The spoils of thirty years of successful warfare, the revenues of the richest of kings, costly presents from neighboring monarchs, all these were consumed in that work. The treasures David had collected were so enormous in value that the brain is bewildered in an attempt to compute them. It has been estimated that Solomon in-

[1] 1 Kings v.

herited from his father thirteen millions of pounds (Troy) of gold and one hundred and twenty-seven millions of pounds of silver. No less amazing is the number of men employed. Ten thousand hewers of wood were in the forests of Lebanon, felling the cedars and working them into the desired shapes. This force worked for eleven years. There were seventy thousand common laborers whose duty was to bear burdens. Eighty thousand quarrymen and dressers of stone were kept busy, while over them were three thousand superintendents.[1] In all there were one hundred and eighty thousand men engaged. Some idea of the immensity of the work necessary to prepare Mount Moriah for the temple can be gained from these figures. The sides and summit of the mountain were completely altered. Therefore in expressing an opinion as to the reliability of the biblical figures, the greatness of the substructures—almost equal to mountain building—must be borne in mind; it must be remembered that it was, so far as we know, all hand labor, and that, though much of the work cannot now be traced, there is evidence that it was far greater than is usually supposed. The immensity of some of that masonry, still remaining where Solomon's builders placed it, causes more wonder in the fact that it was built at all than that it took so many thousands of men years to do it. Some of those stones were brought from the Lebanons and some from Bethlehem, though the greater part were quarried near the city, probably in what is now known as Solomon's Quarries. But whether brought from near or far the puzzling thing about them is *how* they were brought.

The actual work of temple construction began in the third month of the year 1012 B. C., the fourth year of Solomon's reign and the four hundred and eightieth after the Exodus. It was completed in eight years and five months.[2] Language has been exhausted in attempts adequately to describe it when it was completed and stood in its grandeur. In richness

[1] I Kings v. 13–18.   [2] I Kings vi. 38.

and exquisite finish, though not in size, it surpassed the great temples of Egypt and Babylon; it transcended all that the world had seen. In contributing artificers Hiram of Tyre thus introduced Phœnician ideas into the construction of this temple. It is true that but little is known of the architecture of this great commercial people, but wherever on coin or vase a design of one of their sacred edifices has been found, it is fronted with a pillar, or pillars, similar to those that graced the front of Solomon's temple. It has generally been conceded, also, that from Egypt the builders of Israel received suggestions. That there is a resemblance is true, but the effort to prove the entire indebtedness of the Jews to the temple-builders of the Nile valley has not found warrant in the facts. This resemblance is confined to the courts and cloisters, the porch and the dark adytum. In the mural decorations there is also a likeness, but the "figures of cherubim and palm-trees and open flowers" are a contrast to those figures of gods and goddesses and men which were the chief ornaments of the temple walls of Thebes and Karnak. Some see an Egyptian idea in the pyramidal form of the towers.[1] Admitting these apparent resemblances there is one respect in which the House of the Lord on Moriah differs from all the others. Its courts were "pleasant"; there was nothing defiling near them. In or near there was nothing suggestive of immorality or impurity. What little imagery there was, detracted in no way from the spiritual significance of the whole. It was a fit resting place for the ark and the tabernacle, and here they were fixed,[2] never to be separated until the temple was destroyed by Nebuchadnezzar, king of Babylon.

The temple proper stood on the highest part of Mount Moriah, a little to the west of the present Kubbet es-Sakhra, or Dome of the Rock. The rock at the surface had been cut away to make a level platform. On this platform none but

[1] Stanley's "Jewish Church," Vol. II., p. 174.
[2] 1 Kings viii. 4, etc.

The City of David and Solomon 37

the priesthood were ever admitted. Within the sacred walls of the temple there were but two small rooms, that to the east the Holy Place, that to the west the Holy of Holies. Plates of beaten gold hid every particle of woodwork. Into the carvings, representing the cherubim and the lily-work, gold was beaten. Darkness reigned in the Holy of Holies, no light entering it except through the portal from the Holy Place, over which a heavily wrought curtain hung. Within this most sacred place were two massive figures of solid gold whose wings reached from wall to wall and were emblems of protection to the Ark of the Covenant which found rest beneath them. Here was the earthly abode of Jehovah and it was accepted "amidst evident tokens of the Divine Presence." No eye was to peer into the sacred enclosure and no foot pollute it except those of the high-priest and that but once a year on the great day of Atonement.

A "wall of partition" stood between the Most Holy and the Holy Place. This latter was never to be entered except by priestly feet. It was but dimly lighted from without by small windows,[1] but this lack of natural light was made up for by an array of golden candlesticks. Ten seven branched golden candlesticks stood on as many golden tables. They gave all necessary light and must have made very effective in appearance the sculptured forms of winged creatures and palm-trees, which, carved in the cedar walls, were overlaid with beaten gold and garnished with precious stones.[2] In the "greater house," as the Holy Place was also called, stood the altar of incense and the table of shew-bread, from which ascended daily the cloud of incense and on which was presented the offering of consecrated loaves. The whole was a vision in pure gold.

Fronting the Holy Place was a porch, "the most startling novelty of the building."[3] It extended along the entire front

[1] 1 Kings vi. 4.   [2] 2 Chron. iii. 5–7.
[3] Stanley's "Jewish Church," Vol. II., p. 178.

of the temple, was elaborate and complicated in design and more than any other part of the structure reveals the ideas of foreign architects. It was more than a porch, as the term is now used, and was out of all proportion to the height of the building proper.[1] The most striking feature of this "startling novelty" were the two large pillars that stood one on either side of the entrance, known as Jachin and Boaz. These pillars were of finest brass, resting upon pedestals of gold and crowned with chapiters of brass, wrought with "network interwoven with small palms and covered with lily-work." Around the chapiters, festooned in double rows, were two hundred pomegranates. Jewish writers are unwearied in their praise of the grand effect of these pillars; but the object of this device and its symbolic significance are in doubt, though theories as to their significance are not lacking.

Another feature of the temple, having no counterpart in the tabernacle, were the rooms built around it abutting on the temple walls. These were thirty in number and in three stories.[2] One room opened into another and a winding staircase led from story to story. No communication was possible between these rooms and the temple itself. The rooms were necessary adjuncts to the temple, being used as storehouses for the utensils employed in the services[3] and for the depositing of sacred and historic trophies. There appear also to have been rooms above the Holy Place and Holy of Holies.

Such was the temple; on the outside a combination of stone and wood; on the inside a mass of gold and precious stones. It had been erected without the sound of the workmen's tools being heard within the sacred enclosure. The plan was so well understood by the architects that the various parts were made in different places, then brought to the sacred mount and fitted each to each in silence. The stones had been so accurately dressed that when laid one upon the other the line of meeting could hardly be traced. It was the per-

[1] 2 Chron. iii. 4.   [2] Jos. Ant. viii. 3, § 2.   [3] 2 Chron. v. 1.

fection of architecture as then understood, and the perfection of beauty. No structure ever made a greater and more lasting impression on the minds of any people than their first temple made upon the Jews; none has received such generous praise in all ages and from all people, or been regarded with such tearful reverence by the living representatives of the race whose fathers built it.

To speak in detail of all Solomon's work on the Temple Hill would carry us beyond the province of a work of this kind. The courts, the altars, the lavers, the rooms for the priests, the implements and vessels of gold, silver and brass, running into the thousands in number, all these are interesting as works of art and as expressive of the complexity of the temple service. In the native rock, or built in the substructures that brought the lower levels up to the desired height, were immense cisterns. Canals for the conveyance of water for the numerous ablutions connected with the service and drains for the carrying away of the refuse were constructed and undoubted remains of them may still be seen.

There are two features of the temple surroundings which must at least be named. These were the altar of burnt-offering and the colonnade on the eastern side of the enclosure. The former was on the highest part of the rock of Moriah and stood just a little in front of the temple. It contrasted strikingly with the splendor of the other appointments, being but an enlargement of the altar used during the wilderness wandering. It was thirty feet square and fifteen feet high. The exterior was of brass, while the altar itself was of earth and stones. The top was covered by a brass grating on which the fire was made and the victim for the sacrifice laid. This was "the Hearth of God," where was daily illustrated the expiatory idea of the Jewish religion.

The colonnade was on the east side of the enclosure facing the Mount of Olives. In later times succeeding kings added to this until it surrounded the entire temple area. Solomon's work was confined to the one side, and long centuries afterward, even when Herod's temple had taken the place of this first one, the name of Solomon was applied to this part. The colonnade consisted of three rows of marble columns protected by a roof, thus forming a cool retreat in summer and a protection from the storms in winter.

The temple, while by far the grandest of Solomon's building operations, was but one of many princely works. Every part of his capital felt the touch of his lavish hand. His own palace, erected in the City of David, was a royal residence indeed. The time used in the construction of this—thirteen years,—together with the number of apartments in connection with it, mark it as second only in grandeur to the House of the Lord. The main building was only one hundred and fifty feet long, seventy-five wide and forty-five high. It was in three stories and had a grand porch supported by lofty pillars. The adjacent buildings were those in which the king resided with his court and harem. To the main building was given the name of "the house of the forest of Lebanon"; this because of the material used in its construction.[1] Next to this was the judgment hall, built of cedar and squared stones. This was the "gate of judgment," where from a throne of ivory the wise king decreed righteousness and administered justice. This throne was unique. The ivory had been brought from Africa or India. On each side of the steps that led up to it were six golden lions. The throne itself was on the back of a golden bull.[2] The lions were emblematic of the lion of the tribe of Judah, the bull of Ephraim. This combination of ivory and gold into a seat of judgment made the famous throne of the House of David, "the theme of many an Arabian legend."[3] In the house which Solomon built for his Egyptian queen nothing was lacking that skill and wealth could supply.

[1] 1 Kings vii. 2.   [2] Jos. Ant. viii. 5, § 2.
[3] Stanley's "Jewish Church," Vol. II., p. 166.

Of all the apartments connected with the palace it is impossible for us to speak with any degree of accuracy. The Bible and Josephus are our only authorities and Josephus adds but little to the sacred record. A difficulty in the way of exactness is due to our ignorance of the precise meaning of Hebrew architectural terms. This makes all descriptions little better than theories. However, enough is known to assure us that in the city as Solomon left it nothing was lacking that could add to its grandeur. It was the capital of an Oriental monarch and despot whose will was law and whose every wish must be gratified no matter what the cost. His servants and retainers were numbered by thousands, his table was weighted with service of gold, and the world was levied upon for delicate viands. His household, with his guests, consumed daily thirty oxen and a hundred sheep, with game of all kinds. This extravagant use of unlimited wealth excited the wonder and aroused the envy of contemporary monarchs.

In the midst of his other labors Solomon saw the necessity of strengthening the defences of the city. Pride had a place in these improvements, for Josephus informs us that Solomon "thought the walls that encompassed Jerusalem ought to correspond to the dignity of the city." Accordingly the walls were made stronger and higher, and great towers were built upon them. At this time also the Temple Hill was brought within the city. Some of the remains of these walls still stand, revealing the character of the mural work of that day.

The ascent by which the king went up to the House of the Lord was a gigantic and splendid work. This was a bridge that crossed the valley that intervened between Mount Zion and the Mountain of the House, or Mount Moriah. This is the "ascent" that excited the admiration of the "Queen of Sheba."

Another of Solomon's great works was the procuring of an abundance of water for city and temple use. It has been a continual wonder how Jerusalem was supplied with this most

necessary commodity. The "Virgin's Fountain" is the only
living spring near, and unless its flow was considerably more
copious than at present it would not suffice for the needs of
very many of the residents of the city. It is a matter of history,
however, that Jerusalem never suffered from lack of water even
during periods of drought or long protracted sieges. Famine
has raged within the walls and slain its thousands, but only
once did the besieged want for water. This, as Josephus reports, was in the one hundred and sixty-second Olympiad,[1]
during the siege of Antiochus.

The sources of Jerusalem's water supply were the heavy
rains of winter, which were caught and preserved in cisterns,
and the springs in the valley of Urtas, about eight miles south
of the city, whose abundant flow was conducted by an aqueduct along the Judean hillsides and emptied into a reservoir
within the temple enclosure. The making of this aqueduct
was, for that day, a wonderful piece of engineering. The
three large pools in the valley of Urtas, which are still called
Solomon's Pools, give an idea of the immensity of this work.
In many places along the hillsides the aqueduct may still be
seen and to this day the Bethlehemites use it to bring water to
their city. This conduit, connected with the "Fountain
sealed," was the source of that continual supply which the
temple and city enjoyed, and its great resources gave to later
visitors the idea that there was a perennial spring bubbling up
within the temple area. Not knowing of the connection between the Urtas fountain and the cisterns, and hearing the
water running, or perhaps seeing it at some opening, it was
not unreasonable to infer that there was a natural spring near.
There are still people who are inclined to this belief, though
there is nothing whatever to support it. If there were such a
spring there would have been no need for the immense labor
and expense of making the pools and aqueduct.

The city was improved and beautified by these princely

[1] Jos. Ant. xiii. 8, § 2.

operations when "all that Solomon desired to build" was completed. But his works of construction were not confined to the city proper. Temples and fanes dedicated to the worship of the gods of his various wives, were the ornaments of the neighboring hills. Though considered as abominations by the more orthodox Jews of that time, they were allowed to remain to the latest times of the monarchy. On the southern spur of the Mount of Olives was the temple of the worship of his Egyptian queen, and because of this defilement that part of the mount is still called "the Hill of Offence."

Much labor was spent on the roads leading to the city. These were well made and paved with hard black stones, perhaps the basalt from east of the Jordan or from Galilee. Josephus speaks of these roads in the highest terms.[1] The building of them gave the king another opportunity for the display of his wisdom and his wealth.

During Solomon's occupancy of the throne Jerusalem became a commercial centre. On the great highway of trade between the East and the West, caravans were continually coming and going; the roads running in from every direction looked like the spokes of a great white wheel of which the city was the hub; commercial transactions were carried on with nations most remote; the royal vessels were seen on all seas; a fleet was constructed at Ezion-Geber, a city on the western arm of the Red Sea, which controlled the eastern trade; its vessels sailing as far as Ophir—the extreme East; Jewish merchantmen vied with those of the maritime city of Tyre for the trade of the West, and that Tyre lost by this rivalry is indicated by Ezekiel.[2]

How far eastward and westward the ships of Solomon sailed is not known. Ophir may have been in India, though some locate it in Africa, because of the latter's reputation as a gold-producing country. Tarshish was a city of Spain, though having journeyed thus far there is every reason to suppose that

[1] Jos. Ant. viii. 7, § 4.   [2] Ezek. xxvi. 2.

they went further, passing beyond the fabled Pillars of Hercules and reaching Britain. Centuries later, when Columbus sailed westward and discovered the islands lying east of North America, he believed he had found the lands whence the wealth of Solomon had come, and named the islands the West Indies. It has been suggested as an explanation of the length of time—three years [1]—that it took to make some of their voyages, that the Jewish vessels must have circumnavigated Africa. The nature of the cargoes brought back favors the suggestion, for they consisted of "gold and silver, ivory and apes and peacocks," aloes, almug wood and cassia. This commercial enterprise was one of the fertile sources of Israel's great wealth at this time; it may also have helped to hasten that degeneracy which before long was to result in the disruption of the nation.

The kingdom over which the word of Solomon was law, was greater in extent than that governed by any succeeding Jewish monarch. The promise of God to Abraham was fulfilled during the reign of this king or not at all. Scripture language is sufficiently exact on this point to warrant us in saying that the territory over which Solomon ruled did include "the Land of Promise." The covenant with Abraham reads, "Unto thy seed have I given this land, from the river of Egypt unto the great river, the river Euphrates." Of Solomon the record says, "He reigned over all kingdoms, from the river unto the land of the Philistines, and unto the borders of Egypt." In the thirty-fourth chapter of Numbers, Moses gives the boundaries of the land the Israelites were to possess. The southern border was the "wilderness of Zin"; the northern border was unto the "entrance of Hamath." Under Joshua this described territory was conquered by the soldiers of Israel. When the ark was to be brought from Kirjath-jearim, "David gathered all Israel together, from Shihor of Egypt even unto the entering of Hamath."[2] At the dedicatory services of the

[1] Kings x. 22.   [2] 1 Chron. xiii. 5.

temple, "Solomon held a feast and all Israel with him, a great congregation, from the entering in of Hamath unto the river of Egypt."[1] The language of prophecy and of fulfillment is strikingly similar, and whatever may be one's opinion as to the return and resettlement of the Jews, we certainly do not have to look to the future for a redemption of God's promises to Abraham.

All this extent of country was under the sceptre of the mighty and magnificent king. Every part of it contributed to the maintenance of the throne and the fulfillment of the royal ideas of grandeur. But the enormous revenue was not sufficient. To supply the want the taxes were increased and monopolies for the benefit of the royal treasuries were established. Compulsory labor, similar to the hated *corvée* of Egypt, was laid upon Solomon's subjects. With good cause the people complained, and thus were sown the seeds of revolt, which ripened during the reign of Solomon's son, and whose fruit was a disrupted nation. Added to his oppression of his people was his apostasy from his God. In their belief in the unity of God and their worship of Him alone lay the unity and strength of the Hebrew nation; to destroy that belief was to endanger the existence of the nation. In his later days Solomon departed from the purity of his early faith, and with a desire perhaps of conciliating neighboring princes, he turned from Jehovah to "Gods many and Lords many." Famed for his great wisdom, renowned for his magnificence, proverbial for his "glory," Solomon nevertheless bequeathed to his followers the destructive heritage of luxury, selfishness and oppression, of extravagance, sensuality and apostasy—a double trinity of sins any one of which was fatal. As one has said[2] "Not less truly than the son of Nebat might his name have been written in history as Solomon the son of David who 'made Israel to sin.'"

[1] 1 Kings viii. 65.
[2] Plumptre in Smith's Bib. Dict. article "Solomon."

Solomon made Jerusalem grand in external appearance, but its temple of "snow and gold," its palaces of surpassing splendor, its gardens of delight, its tower-embattled walls could not conceal its inherent weakness. He had sacrificed his nation for his personal glory. He came to the throne of a united people at peace with the world. He lived to see the forces at work that were to bring national dissolution and make his proud capital an easy prey to ambitious monarchs. His own magnificence was no compensation for such disaster. As he contemplated the coming wreck well might he say, "What profit hath a man of all his labor" and, "On all things is written vanity."

After ruling forty years " He died ingloriously," "and was buried in the city of David, his father."[1]

[1] 1 Kings xi. 43.

JERUSALEM AS CHRIST SAW IT

Changes in Topography—Rehoboam—Jehoram—Jehoash—Ahaz—Rezin and Pekah—Assyrians—Hezekiah—Manasseh—Jehoiachim—Zedekiah—Disastrous Siege—Cyrus the Persian—Return of the Jews—Temple and Walls Rebuilt—Alexander—Ptolemy Soter—Antiochus—Mattathias—Maccabees—Aristobulus and Hyrcanus—Antipater—Pompey—Antigonus—Herod the Great—Grandeur of Jerusalem—Comparison between Solomon and Herod—Grecian Influences—Herod's Temple—Its Arrangement—Appearance and Condition of the City—Tyropean Bridge—Porches of Temple—Cloisters—Temple Courts—Gentiles Forbidden—Beautiful Gate—Nicanor Gate—Altar of Sacrifice—Brazen Laver—Description of Temple Proper—Business District—Kinds of Business—Life—Laborers—Wages—Population—Pharisee—Sadducee—Language—Schools—Seeds of Decay.

III

JERUSALEM AS CHRIST SAW IT

DURING the thousand years that intervened between the reigns of Solomon and Herod the Great, Jerusalem had been the victim of many a siege by foreign conquerors, and many a disastrous internal strife. These had had their effect upon the appearance of the city; if the royal sleepers in the tombs in the City of David could have looked upon its streets and palaces and temple, they would not have recognized them as parts of the city they once knew. The very hills had been altered and the deep beds of the valleys raised by the debris of repeated wars. The same old walls were still standing, but they had been broken and repaired so often that the original builders would hardly have known their work. New walls had also been built.

It may be well to give a brief account of the causes of these changes before the changes themselves are noted.

In the fifth year of Rehoboam,[1] successor to his father, Solomon, on the throne of Israel, Shishak, king of Egypt advanced to Jerusalem, threw open the city gates apparently without resistance, appropriated the treasures Solomon had collected, and carried off the rich decorations of the temple. The son of the great Solomon became the vassal of Egypt for a time. This was the first and one of the least destructive of seventeen sieges before Herod was in possession of the kingdom.

The next was under the reign of Jehoram about 889 B. C.[2] A coalition of the Philistines and Arabians were the assailants. Again the temple with its accumulated riches was their prey. The king's house was also entered, "and all the substance

[1] 1 Kings xiv. 25; 2 Chron. xii. 9.   [2] 2 Chron. xxi. 16.

that was found " was carried away, together with the king's wives and sons, except the youngest of the latter.

These two entrances of foreign foes were simply for the purpose of plunder. At least there is no account of their having had any other object. The wealth of the city aroused their cupidity, and when they had secured all they could of this, they departed without doing injury to the city itself. But the next attack was more disastrous. It was made by Jehoash,[1] ruler of the Northern Kingdom, who broke down four hundred cubits of the north wall, plundered the temple of its gold and silver vessels, and also the treasures of the royal palace. Uzziah repaired this breach and further fortified the walls.[2] During his reign the city was visited by an earthquake, which shook it to its foundations, caused a breach in the temple and almost destroyed the king's gardens near En Rogel.

In the reign of the wicked Ahaz,[3] about 740 B. C., the next attack occurred. A coalition of the forces of Syria under Rezin and of the Northern Kingdom under Pekah was effected. The comparatively small realm of Judah and Benjamin was not able to withstand such a combination, and great numbers were slain. It does not appear that the city itself surrendered and was given over to the hand of the spoiler. Later Ahaz called upon Tiglath-pileser[4] to assist him against the Edomites and Philistines—a fatal invitation, for the Assyrian king as the author of Second Chronicles tersely puts it, "came unto him and distressed him, but strengthened him not." Ahaz then in a fruitless effort to buy his friendship, stripped the temple of its costly vessels, which were carried to Assyria.

Under Hezekiah (740-700 B. C.) the country was invaded by the Assyrians under Sennacherib,[5] though what damage, if any, was done to the city is not known.

[1] 2 Kings xiv. 13, 14.   [2] 2 Chron. xxvi. 9.   [3] 2 Chron. xxviii.
[4] 2 Chron. xxviii. 16, 20.   [5] 2 Chron. xxxii.

Jerusalem as Christ Saw It 51

About 667 B. C., Manasseh, king of Judah, was carried a prisoner to Babylon.[1] On his restoration to his kingdom he entered upon some great building projects. In the valley of Gihon and on Ophel the greater part of his work was done. Parts of the great wall on Ophel may still remain, though where his wall "without the City of David, on the west side of Gihon in the valley"[2] was is an unsettled question.

Under Jehoiachim and Jehoiachin, Nebuchadnezzar, king of Babylon, besieged and took Jerusalem, despoiled the temple of all its remaining treasures, which were replaced after each spoliation, and stripped the palaces of the king and nobles. The royal family and nobles were deported, along with ten thousand of the chief men, to pass the remaining years of their life in Babylon.

In the next reign, that of Zedekiah,[3] the siege by the "king of the Chaldees" was most disastrous. When this warrior had finished his work Jerusalem was depopulated and her temple and palaces were nothing but heaps of charred ruins. The walls were broken down and all the citizens who had escaped the sword were deported to the great capital of Assyria; only a few peasants were left to till the ground. This first great overthrow of their city has been considered so great a calamity by the Jews that on its anniversary it is commemorated by solemn fasts. This destruction occurred about the year 588 B. C.; for fifty years the city and temple remained in ruin and desolation, visited, perhaps, by pilgrims who came to weep over the departed glories and pray for their return, as they do now at the Wall of Wailing.

In the first year of the reign of Cyrus, king of Persia, a decree[4] was issued permitting the exiled Jews at Babylon to return and build again their temple and city. Not all of the expatriated chose to return, but 42,360 did. Nor did they come empty handed, for they were given "the vessels of the

---
[1] 2 Chron. xxxiii. 11. [2] Ibid. 14.
[3] 2 Kings xxv. 4. [4] Ezra i. 1. *et seq.*

house of the Lord, which Nebuchadnezzar had brought forth out of Jerusalem."[1] The work of reconstruction of the temple began immediately on their arrival. Hindrance from outsiders and lack of zeal on the part of the builders prevented its completion until twenty years had passed, when it was finished and dedicated in the year 516 B. C.

Fifty-eight years more passed away and no effort was made to protect the city itself. The walls lay in heaps as the Assyrians had left them. It was not until the time of Nehemiah that sufficient influence was secured at the Persian court to allow the Jews to rebuild the walls. In 445 B. C., one hundred and forty years after the destroyer had left, Nehemiah came to Jerusalem with the royal permission. Work was soon begun and in the incredibly short period of fifty-two days, in spite of much opposition, the walls were again in condition to furnish protection.[2] They were built on the old foundations with much of the old materials.

For a long time afterward there was comparative peace, during which the city grew and prospered. Then Alexander of Macedonia "rolled back the tide of war across the Hellespont" and humbled the pride of the Persian monarchs. Having defeated Darius at the battle of Issus, this conqueror reduced to submission all the cities and provinces whose importance attracted his attention. After the maritime cities of Tyre and Gaza had fallen, the Macedonian hero led his forces against Jerusalem. About three miles out of the city he was met by the people carrying garlands, by the priests dressed in the white linen indicating their sacred office, and preceded by the high-priest, resplendent in his robes of purple and scarlet and wearing his mitre, on which was a plate of gold inscribed with the not to be uttered name of the God of Israel. This peaceful reception secured the city from attack. Alexander is said by Josephus to have prostrated himself before the high-priest and then to have gone to the temple and offered

[1] Ezra i. 7.   [2] Neh. vi. 15.

sacrifices in the name of God: this is doubted, but at all events the city was especially favored by the conqueror.

At the death of Alexander and the disintegration of his kingdom Judea fell to Ptolemy Soter of Egypt. He succeeded in taking Jerusalem which he ruled with an iron hand. Many of its inhabitants and of the Samaritans were carried off to Egypt, where under this ruler and his successor they attained positions of influence and trust. Their number increased in the land of the Pharaohs till Alexandria became the capital of Western Judaism and no doubt exercised considerable influence over the eastern capital. By way of Alexandria Greece and her civilization were making inroads into the private and religious life of the Eastern Jews. Then in 203 B. C., Antiochus the Great took the city. Four years later it fell before the Alexandrian general Scopas who left a garrison to protect his interests. The very next year Antiochus again came and the Jews assisted him to expel the Egyptians. But as it turned out the Syrian monarch was no friend of the people or their religion. Taking advantage of a quarrel between rival claimants for the high-priesthood, he treated the city as seditious, and in the year 170 B. C., demolished the walls, burned the palaces and stripped the temple of all that was worth taking. A citadel was erected where it could command the temple enclosure and garrisoned with soldiers, among whom were many apostate Jews. Added to this sacrilege was an attempt on the part of Antiochus to exterminate the people and thus stamp out their religion. Ten thousand captives were deported and the sacred altar was daily defiled by the offering of swine upon it. Reading of the Law was forbidden and to practice its injunctions brought cruel tortures upon the faithful. Under this severe pressure the greater part of the inhabitants apostatized from the religion of their fathers.

When the city and nation had reached their lowest stage of degradation a deliverance was effected through the family of Mattathias, the great grandson of Asmoneus, from which ancestor they are called by Josephus, Asmoneaus. Mattathias was a priest whose home was at Modin, the present Midiyeh, an eminence about eighteen miles west of Jerusalem, near the union of the hill country with the Plain of Sharon.

Mattathias, with his five illustrious sons, belongs to the number of Israel's most justly celebrated heroes. He originated, and his sons sustained, a successful revolt against Greek oppression. The account of their campaigns forms one of the most picturesque chapters to be found in history. Under them the temple was repaired and reconsecrated, the Macedonian garrison dislodged from its fortress on Acra and the fortress destroyed, even to the cutting away of the hill on which it stood. Another stronghold was built to the north of this site and named Baris. The Asmonean family descended through John Hyrcanus, son of Simon Maccabeus. Simon was murdered at Jericho in 135 B. C. Shortly after John Hyrcanus was besieged in Jerusalem by Antiochus Sidetes, king of Syria. The valiant spirit of the Maccabees was diminishing, for this representative stooped to purchase peace from Antiochus with the proceeds of the desecration and robbery of the sepulchre of David.

The next few years are marked by internal troubles—civil and religious. The successor of John Hyrcanus was his son Aristobulus who was at the same time king and high-priest. After reigning a year this ruler died of remorse for his unnatural crimes. The reign of his brother Alexander Jannæus— the Jewish Nero—which occupied the next twenty-seven years, was marked by wars at home and abroad. Aristobulus and Hyrcanus, sons of Alexander, made a peaceful settlement of their disputes by dividing the offices held by their predecessors, Hyrcanus, the elder, retaining the high-priesthood and his brother the kingly crown. The peace did not last long however. A new power began to be felt in the state. Antipater, an Idumean, enterprising and unscrupulous, was high in the favor of the young Hyrcanus. He used this favor to plot against the interests of his benefactor. By continually working upon the mind of the gentle and unsuspecting high-priest, Antipater made him believe that his brother Aristobulus was seeking to destroy him so as to unite in his own person the priesthood as well as the kingship. Hyrcanus fled to Petra where he put himself under the protection of Aretes, king of Arabia. Antipater had already let this ruler into the plot. Judea was invaded and Aristobulus defeated. After his defeat he fled into the city and took refuge with his supporters in the temple. The party under Hyrcanus besieged the temple. At this juncture the Roman general Scaurus, acting under commands of the great Pompey, appeared and ordered that the siege be raised. This was in 65 B. C.

Both factions had requested the assistance of the Romans. The cause of Aristobulus was favored, but for some reason this prince was dissatisfied and took up arms against his protectors. Pompey himself on his advance to Arabia invaded Judea. Aristobulus promised submission, but soon violated his promise and caused Pompey to return and begin a siege of Jerusalem. The followers of Aristobulus took refuge in the temple again and offered stubborn resistance. They would not, however, defend themselves on the Sabbath and Pompey taking advantage of this moved his engines, made a breach in the north wall of the sacred enclosure and was master of the entire city. The slaughter of the inhabitants amounted to twelve thousand. Antigonus was established in the high-priesthood. This was in the year 63 B. C. For twenty-three years there was comparative rest. Antipater, father of Herod, assisted in ruling the city. In the year 40 B. C. Antigonus, son of Aristobulus, with the assistance of a Parthian army took Jerusalem and plundered it. The family of Antipater had by this time become well established in the governing office, but it was with the greatest difficulty that Herod escaped from the plots of his enemies. After much adversity and an appeal in person to Rome, Herod was made King of Judea. But he had to conquer his kingdom. With a large body of Roman soldiers he entered Jerusalem after a five months siege. Then began that reign conspicuous for two things—its great splendor and its awful crimes. The Idumean king was as he has been well termed by Williams[1] a "splendid monster."

Under this monarch—half barbarian, half Jew—Jerusalem rose again and attained a grandeur equal to if not surpassing the glory it had in the days of Solomon. But there was this difference, that under the latter it was a strictly Jewish metropolis, while under Herod it became in fact, though not in name, a second or eastern Rome. And yet there was much in the later city that resembled the earlier. Herod, as did Solomon, ruled over the entire land. Herod, as was Solomon, was given to extravagance and adorned the city with numerous monuments of splendid architecture. Each king was influenced by foreign ideas, Solomon by those of Egypt and Tyre, Herod by Greece and Rome. The early and later city were the resort of strangers from all lands and in their streets could be seen representatives from every known land. Each king fortified his capital and each adorned Moriah with a temple. Solomon's was the first, Herod's the last; but the former was built in honor of Jehovah and to win the divine favor, while the general belief is that the latter was designed to add to the glory of its builder and to win the favor of his suspicious subjects.

Great changes were to be seen in the buildings and the purposes to which they were devoted. In the Jerusalem of Solomon—at least in the city proper—there were no structures dedicated to the worship of the gods of the nations, or to the exhibition of heathen games. After the revival of pure religion under the Maccabees the office of the high-priest was filled by several unprincipled men who used their high position to corrupt the people. Joshua, one of them, dissatisfied in the possession of a Jewish name, changed it to Jason, and still un-

[1] Holy City, Vol. I., p. 116.

satisfied sought by every means in his power to supplant Judaism by Hellenizing his countrymen. He went so far as to build a hippodrome and circus in the valley just west of the temple, near enough so that the voices of the priest chanting the service, could be drowned by the tumultuous shout of the rabble cheering the victors in the games. What a contrast and in Jerusalem!

On Herod's accession these foreign notions of religious and social life obtained among a considerable portion of his subjects. His own inclinations favored them and for his gratification, as well as to win the approbation of this class of people, he spared no expense in adorning the places of amusement with gold and silver and the trophies of victories. He added an immense amphitheatre outside of the second wall to the northwest, where were witnessed chariot races, gladiatorial combats and entertainment of all sorts appealing to the senses. Side by side with this element, representative as it was of a lack of religion and a laxity of morals, was an intensely Jewish element seeking in the midst of surrounding heathenism to guard the sanctity of religion, and, by obedience to the Mosaic institutions, preserve from heathen contamination the Hebrew life and character. This element was at enmity with Herod, whose Idumean blood was reason sufficient. But no matter what his origin, he was king of the Jews. He would not allow them to forget this nor give them cause for complaint that he was wholly unmindful of them and their religion. If he had any religion it was the same as theirs. In honor of it, but more to reconcile the Jews to himself he built that wonderful temple on Moriah. It was a worthy successor to that of Solomon, and of it Jewish tradition records, "He who has not seen the temple of Herod has never known what beauty is."

This temple was a larger structure than the first one that graced Mount Moriah's rocky summit. The enclosure in which it stood was also larger. From investigations made on the spot by Captain Warren it is reasonably assured that the temple area as enlarged by Herod was a square of nearly a thousand feet, nearly a half greater than that of Saint Peter's in Rome. This enlargement was made at an immense cost of labor and money. But the motives for it were many. The king had a passion for building. In this great work it was gratified. He had a desire to surpass the greatest triumph of Solomon and be known as "the great builder." The rabbis of his time said that he was doing this to atone for the slaughter of so many of their number. But no doubt one of the reasons, if not the chief, is that already given, that he might win a place in the affections of his Jewish subjects. In this latter he was unsuccessful; they despised him to the end.

The temple did not stand in the centre of the square. It was somewhat to the north and west of the centre. In general arrangements its courts were as those that surrounded the first "house of the Lord." They were not on a level, but rose in a series of terraces, on the highest of which, facing the east, was the "golden fane" itself. To collect the material for it Herod employed ten thousand men under the direction of a thousand priests for two years. A thousand vehicles were needed to convey the stone. And yet he did not live to see it finished in all its parts.[1]

It was not in size that this temple was conspicuous though its dimensions were somewhat greater than that of the first Holy House. It was ten cubits longer. The general arrangements were the same. There was the Holy of Holies and the Holy Place; the candlestick, table of shew-bread and altar of incense. The finest of needlework was to be seen in the rich texture of the veil that divided the Holy of Holies from the Holy Place. In the former apartment there was nothing. It was a simple room, ten cubits in each measurement, but void of ornament or vessel of use since the ark and its contents had been lost in the Babylonish wars. In the erection of the

[1] John ii. 20.

temple proper only priests labored. It was considered too sacred a place for the feet of the Ionian artificers to touch. These skilled "barbarians" could be employed at any other part of the work, but not here. The priests completed their part in eighteen months. The work on the courts and porticoes employed Herod eight years; and the colonnades, entrances, halls, offices and other subsidiary structures required thirty-eight years longer.

A better idea of the arrangement of all its parts might be obtained if in imagination one entered the sacred area at one of the principal entrances. Of these there were four all leading in from the west. By far the most imposing was the one crossing the Tyropean on the arches of a colossal bridge and entering at the southwest angle. It joined the ancient city of David with the "Royal Porch of the Temple." This bridge was a wonder in its day, and probably survived all the vicissitudes of the city through the decade of centuries extending from Solomon to the siege of Titus. Its ruins are a wonder in this present day. The spring-stones in the arch in the temple wall are twenty-four feet in length and six in thickness. Forty-two feet from the wall Captain Warren discovered a pier on which one of these arches rested. The present remains of this pier are forty-two feet below the surface.[1] The stones in the pier are of the same quality, of the same height and have the same mason marks as those found in the southwest angle of the temple wall.

From this bridge a splendid view of the city could be obtained. Looking toward the south one could see on the left Ophel, the priest's quarter with its high walls and towers, the wall running southward, crossing the Tyropean near the pool of Siloam and circling the southern brow of Zion. Turning westward the observer would see the Upper City, or the "City of David." Then it was a city of palaces, rising terrace on terrace, till in the northwest corner stood the citadel-

[1] Recovery of Jerusalem, p. 100.

palace which Herod had erected for his own safety and comfort. It stood in the midst of gardens and was protected by three imposing towers. Other residences of dignitaries were here, as the palace of the Maccabees and that of Annas the high-priest. To the north was the Xystus, a large enclosure with many colonnades, where important public assemblies were held; while further on stretched the new city, or Bezetha, which was yet unenclosed by walls. Beautiful villas embowered in luxuriant gardens, graced the view in this direction. The street which led to the important northern gate was lined with columns and could be traced to the point where it merged into the great north road, along which caravans and pilgrims were continually coming and going. But the most imposing and most suggestive sight of all was that on the east. This swept the temple enclosure with the Mount of Olives for a background. Of this let me quote the words of the learned Alfred Edersheim,[1] "The temple—oh, how wondrously beautified and enlarged, and rising terrace upon terrace, surrounded by massive walls: a palace, a fortress, a sanctuary of shining marble and glittering gold. And beyond it frowns the old fortress of Baris, rebuilt by Herod, and named after his patron, Antonia."

This bridge of the Tyropean, connecting Zion with Moriah was three hundred and fifty-four feet long and fifty feet broad. It was probably "the ascent . . . into the house of the Lord" which aroused the wonder of the Queen of Sheba.[2] The roadway crossing it joined with the avenue of the Royal Temple Porch. The "porches" were not what is now meant when that term is used. They were rather cloisters, and extended all round the inside of the wall facing the court of the Gentiles. No part of the temple was, from an architectural point of view, finer than these. They were composed of double rows of Corinthian pillars, monoliths thirty-seven-and-a-half feet high. The roofs were richly ornamented. The

[1] Jesus, the Messiah, Vol. I., p. 112.   [2] 1 Kings x. 5.

Photograph by Rev. P. Cady.
ROBINSON'S ARCH.

Royal porch had a treble colonnade made up of four rows of columns forty in each row. But as there were in all a hundred and sixty-two it is supposed that the two odd ones served "as a kind of screen where the 'porch' opened upon the bridge." This was by far the highest of the porches. Its central pillars are said to have been a hundred feet in height. These formed a nave, forty-five feet in width. The two aisles were each thirty feet wide with pillars fifty feet high.[1] From the top of this one looked down into the bed of the Kedron four hundred and forty feet below.

The cloisters afforded a cool retreat in summer and in winter were a protection against the heavy rains and occasional snows. Teachers and pupils took advantage of them and those interested in public religions or civil questions here discussed them. Audiences were gathered and orators here addressed them. It was here that the earthly parents of the Christ-child found Him disputing with the doctors; and in the years of His public ministry the common people heard Him gladly in these precincts as He taught them the "spirit" of the law. Solomon's porch—the only remnant of the great work of this king—was on the eastern side of the temple enclosure. In this particular place "Jesus walked" and taught His unity with the Father.[2] Here were the first assemblies of the early Christians, when they continued "daily with one accord in the temple."

The largest of the temple courts was that enclosed by these porches and on the same level with them. To this court is given in Jewish writings the name "mountain of the house."[3] It was the outer precinct of the holy enclosure and was paved with marble. It was public to the extent that any one of any or no religious belief might enter it so long as he conformed to certain prescribed rules. It served the purposes of a market and about the time of the great feasts must have presented

[1] Smith's "Dictionary of the Bible," Vol. iii., p. 1462.
[2] John x. 30.
[3] Relandus Ant., p. 78; Edersheim's "Temple and its Services," p. 22.

scenes having little resemblance to, and perhaps little sympathy with, the sacred observances so near. There were stalls for oxen and sheep, cotes for pigeons and doves, and tables where the crafty money-changers gave temple coins for the current money of foreign lands, charging exorbitant rates of exchange. At intervals in this court were notices in Greek and Latin warning Gentiles that they were not to approach nearer to the sanctuary itself—an offence punishable by death.

M. Clermont Ganneau had the good fortune to discover one of the very signs of warning. On a stone set in the wall of a little Moslem cemetery, just across the Via Dolorosa from the Bab el-Aksa, Ganneau was able to read in Greek letters the following inscription :

"No stranger is to enter within the balustrade round the temple and enclosure. Whoever is caught will be responsible to himself for his death, which will ensue."

This inscription, the oldest and perhaps most satisfactory yet discovered amid the ruins of the city, can be seen in the museum at Constantinople ; no treasure of this nature that the Sultan or his agents can control is ever taken out of his dominions.

Beyond these posts or "screens" of warning was a flight of fourteen steps which led to a terrace fifteen feet in width. Then came the inner wall that surrounded the temple, and beyond this the sanctuary itself with its three courts, each higher than the former. Nine gates covered with plates of gold and silver gave entrance to the sanctuary. Of these six led into the court of the priests and three into the court of the women. Four were on the south and four on the north ; the ninth was on the east and was the principal entrance as well as the richest in ornamentation and most imposing in size. The gate itself was of finely wrought Corinthian brass. So heavy were its double folds on their hinges that twenty porters were necessary to open and close them. It was known also as "the Beautiful

Gate" and is associated in the minds of Christians with the
"notable miracle" of the healing of the cripple by Peter and
John. The court of the women, into which it opened, was so
called because no women were allowed, except for sacrificial
purposes, to pass beyond this. In it both men and women
were free to worship.

Directly opposite the Beautiful Gate, in the western colonnade, was the Nicanor Gate. Fifteen steps led through this
gate up to the Court of Israel. These steps are generally
thought to have given the name to the "Psalms of Degrees,"
fifteen in number,[1] which the Levites chanted at the Feast of
Tabernacles. As they ascended each step they stopped long
enough to sing the psalm that corresponded to it in number.
At the gate Nicanor, the worshippers came to perform that
which was ordered to be done "before the Lord."[2] The
priests here received all who had come for purification. Passing through this gate the Court of Israel was reached, a very
narrow section, separated from the Court of the priests by a
low railing, or balustrade. Two steps led up to the latter. To
the right and left were chambers used for the vestments of the
priest. Directly in front and but a few feet distant was the
great altar of sacrifice—the exponent of Israel's religious life.
It was a square of nearly fifty feet and elevated fifteen feet
above the level of the court. Constructed of unhewn stones it
was void of ornamentation. By an inclined plane the officiating priests reached the platform which extended around the
altar at a height of ten-and-a-half feet from the ground. "A
red line all around the middle of the altar marked that above it
the blood of sacrifices intended to be eaten, below it that of
sacrifices wholly consumed, was to be sprinkled."[3]

Beyond the altar, and somewhat to the left as one approached the temple, was the immense laver of brass resting
upon the backs of twelve lions. Its water was used by the

[1] Psalms cxx.–cxxxiv.   [2] "Temple and its Services," p. 28.
[3] Edersheim's, "Temple and its Services," p. 38.

priests to keep themselves ceremonially clean. It was filled every morning by machinery, having been drained the evening before. The rabbis report that so immense was this machinery and so great the noise made when it was being operated that it could be heard even to Jericho. The water was abundant; brought from the hills near Hebron, from Etham and the Pools of Solomon, by an aqueduct nearly forty miles long, it was stored in the immense subterranean cisterns which had capacity for ten million gallons.

The Holy House itself is now before the beholder—a gem of the highest art known at that time. With its porch it was one hundred and fifty feet long by as many broad. Without including this porch, which extended thirty feet beyond each side of the building proper, the length was one hundred and twenty feet and the breadth ninety. As the Holy Place was sixty feet long and thirty broad and the Most Holy thirty long by thirty broad it will be seen that there was around the sides and rear of the sacred edifice a space thirty feet in width which has not been accounted for. It was occupied by rooms devoted to sacred uses. Though the rooms were in three stories they did not reach to the height of the main structure. Rooms were also built over the Holy and Most Holy Places. The entire building was then covered by a gabled roof of cedar, each piece of which had been nailed into position by a golden spike.

There it stood on the summit of Moriah in all its marvellous beauty of "gold and snow," facing Olivet and the sunrising; the pride of every Jewish heart, the centre of the nation's thought, the earthly dwelling-place of their God. In conception and execution Herod's artificers had surpassed those of Solomon. He to whom the credit for this restoration is due and who fondly hoped that it would give him a place in the affections of his subjects and in the memories of men was to be disappointed. His people hated him and not once do the rabbis mention his name in connection with the temple.

They praise without measure the completed work, but for the one whose genius and ambition made it possible they have no reward but silence.

To this temple the child Jesus was taken to be presented to the Lord. Here His parents brought Him, that He might become a "son of the law," on the first Passover after He had reached His twelfth year. Here He came and taught the people; here He proclaimed His Messiahship, and here He was rejected by "His own." Of this temple, with its massive masonry, built as if for eternity, He, in answer to the admiring remark of His disciples, "What manner of stones and what buildings are here," foretold a speedy and complete destruction. It has been fulfilled. Of the buildings as they then were, there is "not left one stone upon another that has not been thrown down."

After passing out of the temple enclosure by the northwestern gate the observer was soon in the centre of the business district of the city. Here the streets were narrow and crowded just as they were when Solomon made Jerusalem a centre of traffic, and just as they are now though the present is but the past in miniature. There was a noticeable difference in this part of the city. During the reign of the first great king the business and residence portions were separated. In the city as Christ saw it the residences of merchant princes, and of the princes of the ruling family rose above, but side by side, with the bazaars and shops. On the street, as to-day, the members of the various trades can be seen plying their craft: the shoemaker preparing his leather; the cotton worker using his odd shaped tool which resembles a harp with one string; the iron and brass workers hammering their wares into the required shape, the scribe sitting on his mat ready to write the letters of his patrons. On the more important streets were the larger shops whose proprietors dealt in goods and fabrics of foreign production and manufacture. Anything in the way of necessity or luxury that was known at that time could be purchased in Jerusalem. Jewels and precious metals of rarest design and perfectly wrought; glassware, rich in color and of attractive shapes; silks, fine linens and woollen stuffs in costliest colors; essences and perfumes of almost fabulous values,— in fact everything to grace the person and please the palate, brought from the remotest lands of the Gentiles and from the distant "isles of the sea," were for sale and found purchasers.

Luxuries commanded enormous prices, but the necessities of living were very cheap, or seem so to us at this age. And yet necessities must be procured at low figures where labor brings but fifteen cents a day. Skilled labor was paid something more. This is but little less than the amount received by the unskilled laborer of Jerusalem to-day. It enables him to live much as the laborer of Christ's time must have lived. Lodging was almost free and bread and vegetables sufficient for the day could be purchased for a few cents. Thus the two extremes of society met in the city and were increased by travellers who had come to see the glory of the place or to worship at its world-famed temple, and by laborers who hoped to find employment in the public works. The resident population has been variously estimated at from 200,000 to 250,000, which was increased to more than five times that number during the great annual feasts. At such times the city must have been densely crowded, even assuming that it covered twice the area of the modern city, or four hundred and twenty acres.

In the city as Christ saw it there were two extremes of religion. The long-robed Pharisee represented orthodox Judaism, the haughty Sadducee liberal Judaism; but both were Jews and were jealous of their beliefs. Jehovah was supreme and His law was obeyed by each as it was interpreted for him by his religious leaders. There was another party conspicuous for its lack of religion, at least certainly opposed to Judaism, made up of renegade Israelites and Gentiles from many lands. Its members were the patrons of theatres and amphitheatres, favorers of the ideas of Greece or of any country or people that con-

Jerusalem as Christ Saw It 67

tributed to the pleasures of the senses. The former found its chief exponent in the august Sanhedrin, the latter in the king and his court. The former was pious, the latter frivolous. Likewise there were two distinct languages in common use. The Semitic in the form of the Palestinian Aramaic was the language of the common people, and was undoubtedly that used by Christ and the disciples; while the pure Hebrew was employed by the rabbis and priests in the temple service. Along with this was the polite Greek, the language of the court and camp.

There were also to be seen side by side in the street and in market and temple the ignorant, unlettered peasant from the villages and the polished product of the Great College of the Temple. The former looked with a feeling of reverence upon the latter and received in return such consideration as is accorded brutes. He who did not know "the Law" had no soul, so thought and acted the leaders of Jewish thought. The study of the Law then, as now in the Jewish schools of Jerusalem, was the chief pursuit. The schools were numerous in the city of Christ's time, and though Herod had placed them under state control, were free to any who paid the fees charged by the official porters. The Great College of the Temple inspired and guided Jewish thought and no doubt acted as a strong bulwark against the growing skepticism and the learning of the Greeks.

Such was the city as Christ saw it, with its heterogeneous population ruled over at the time of His first visit by a king half Jew, half Idumean, on His last by a procurator of Rome. Already it had in it the seeds of decay that were rapidly germinating and would soon produce a harvest of destruction to the city and of death to its inhabitants. Still it was the city of David and Solomon, of the prophets and inspired seers of the past—the City of God.

THE CITY AS IT IS TO-DAY

How many times described!—A Mountain City—Position—Disadvantages—First Impressions—Geological Facts—Extent—Character of Buildings—Streets—Cleanliness—Habits of the Natives—Residences—Number of Inhabitants—Stores and Shops—Turkish Bazaars—Methods in Business—"The Custom of the Country"—Religious Appearance of the City—Synagogues—Churches—Mosques—Religious Indifference of the Moslems—Street Scenes—Venders—Market Day—Moslem Rule—Consulates—Justice—American Privileges—Treaty of 1830—Amusements—Contrast between Day and Night in the City—Modern Progress—Jaffa Jerusalem Railway—Hindrances to Improvements—Telephones—No Census—Sources of Information as to Population—Number of Jews—Number of Christians—Number of Moslems—Jerusalem Unique.

IV

THE CITY AS IT IS TO-DAY

HOW many times has it been described! How many volumes of travel, by the amateur and professional tourists, make a specialty of the Jerusalem chapter! How many letters to religious and other papers, in every Christian land, tell the story of the city as it now is! The number of such publications proves that the reading public has been interested in the subject. In the belief that this wide-spread interest still continues this chapter on the general condition and appearance of the city is here introduced.

Jerusalem is a mountain city. Its position is on one of the high points of that broad ridge which runs north and south through the Holy Land from fertile Jezreel to barren Idumea. Of this range which abounds in peculiar hill and valley formations Jerusalem occupies two hills, or one hill partly divided, and the valley of division. The higher of the two, Mount Zion, is 2,593 feet above the level of the Mediterranean and nearly 4,000 feet above the level of the Dead Sea, which lies but eighteen miles to the east. The lower hill, Mount Moriah, has an altitude of 2,440 feet above sea-level. The city stands just east of the water-shed, and is in latitude 31° 47′ N. and longitude 35° 14′ E. In a direct line it is thirty-two miles from the Mediterranean and twenty-two from the river Jordan. At the first glance one wonders why this site was selected for an important capital; and the only reason that can be given is that the choice was made because of its great natural advantages for defence. However, the city has always suffered great inconvenience because of its limited water supply. In earlier days this was overcome by immense labors in cisterns to preserve the rains of winter, and in aqueducts to bring water from distant springs. The latter are now broken and useless, though a little labor and money would make them serviceable. Cisterns are still almost numerous as residences. Every house, or group of two or three houses, has one in which is stored the supply for the year.

On coming to the city the visitor is struck by the rocky character of its surroundings. In many places on the plateau on which it stands the outcropping of the limestone is a common sight. The character of this formation varies in the different strata. In the bottom of the Kedron valley, half a mile south of the city is found a very hard pink-and-white stratum of uncertain depth, called "Santa Croce" marble. Just above it is a stratum of soft white limestone called "Malaki" having a thickness of about forty feet. Just above this is a hard silicious chalk, called "Missae," having a thickness of seventy feet; while above this again, and forming the summits of the hills is nummulitic limestone 291 feet in thickness. This is descriptive of the strata of the Mount of Olives and Mount of Evil Council.[1]

The barren condition of the neighboring hills and valleys, and in fact of the two hills on which Jerusalem is built, detracts much from the beauty of the place. These hills and valleys were once carefully cultivated and doubtless over them trees and vines grew luxuriantly. Centuries of neglect have caused the soil to be washed down into the valleys and the hills are little more than bare rocks. Debris from the many destructions Jerusalem has suffered has also helped to fill up the two surrounding and one intersecting valley. This process of denudation of the hills and filling of the valleys has toned down the scenery and made it less abrupt and striking. The modern visitor views a very different topography from that which the visitors in the days of Solomon or of Herod beheld. The surface is altered almost as much as the city itself. Still

[1] See "Our Work in Palestine," p. 22.

The City as it is To-day 73

Mounts Zion and Moriah are quite prominent, the Tyropean can be traced without difficulty and the Kedron and Hinnom valleys are very decided depressions.

The location of the city has been changed, or rather it occupies but a part of the ground covered by the Jerusalem of Herod and his immediate successors. The old city, including the Mosque area, covers only 209½ acres. At the time of its greatest importance it must have embraced within its walls nearly three times as much territory, and, judging from the estimates of its population at that time, the houses must have been even more closely built than now. That they are close enough at present no one who has examined them will question, and yet there are several quite good sized pieces of vacant land. The houses are generally poor and patched, and have a mottled and ancient appearance. The mottled aspect is due to the fact that the stones composing the walls have done previous duty in buildings or walls that have fallen before the besieger. The ancient look is genuine; they are old; some of them were quarried thousands of years ago. Many of the interior walls are supported by props stretching overhead across the narrow streets and braced against some stronger wall. They have an ominous "bulge," which means that some of these days they are going to spill out over the street in spite of their supports. The wonder is how some of them resist the law of gravitation even now. There are old arches in every part of the city which have some mysterious way of keeping up, when from all appearances they ought to fall immediately. The crowds pass and repass however unconscious of their danger. Some day the keystone having crumbled to powder will let the whole structure tumble, upon some devoted heads, whereupon the owner will say "It is the will of God," and the bereaved will console themselves with the same pious ejaculation.

The streets are in no way attractive; they are narrow, tortuous and bewildering, running here and there with as little order and regularity as is manifested by the average mortal who passes along them. The only thoroughfares whose situation and direction are capable of explanation, are David street, which runs east from the Jaffa Gate and makes connections which lead out at St. Stephen's Gate on the opposite side of the city; Christian street, which is the thoroughfare from David street to the church of the Holy Sepulchre; and the through street leading from the Damascus Gate on the north to Zion's Gate on the south. These are streets; the rest that bear the name are in fact something less than alleys and something more than paths. As to cleanliness, all that can be said is that it is noticeable for its continued absence. The people who live along the streets use them as receptacles for the refuse of their living, and when the street cleaning brigade—consisting of two men and four donkeys—gets ready to carry it away, it does so. Sometimes it remains for a month and, being added to continually, makes a very uninviting passage for pedestrians—only for some pedestrians, however, for the native Jerusalemite minds it not. Long residence has accustomed him to such visions and odors, and when he cannot pass by it he passes through without a murmur. In other respects the habits of the Arab and Jew residents are most abominable and actions violating common decency are tolerated—actions which in any city whose authorities had any regard for the appearance or health of the community, would land their perpetrators in jail. Here such punishment would be considered a blow at personal freedom and therefore resented with great positiveness. But until some such richly deserved treatment is meted out, the modern city within the walls will be considered by intelligent and reasonably cleanly foreigners as a very good place to keep out of. There is a sewer system, but so crude and badly managed that it is a misnomer to call it a "system."

The residences are small, ill-ventilated and poorly lighted. In the poorer Jewish quarters humanity has not breathing-

The City as it is To-day

room, and apparently does not desire it. I have found ten persons sleeping in one small room with every door and window tightly closed; it was a room to be looked into for curiosity, but not to be entered voluntarily. Even among the better class of Hebrews, living in the less crowded quarters, there is this same objection to fresh air and neat surroundings. It has been remarked that an Ashkenaz Jew can thrive in an atmosphere which would be deadly to an ordinary mortal. There is similar crowding, though less filth in the Mohammedan quarter. These people live more in the open air. This does not mean that there is no room for improvement. There are spots in Moslem Jerusalem too awful to be described. One excuse for the Jew, which may also be offered for some of the Christians who are none too clean, is the lack of water. The Moslem need not suffer this lack, for there is at his disposal the almost inexhaustible supply in the immense cisterns of the Mosque area. It requires some labor to transport it to his house, labor which many of them consider too great a price to pay for comfort and cleanliness. The Christian quarter is likewise sufficiently filled with inhabitants and sufficiently neglected. This overcrowding seems to be necessary, but no apology can be offered for the wretched condition of many of the houses and yards and most or all of the streets. Nor does it help matters to remark that the same filthiness is characteristic of all Oriental cities, and that Jerusalem is not worse than the majority.

In spite of these unfavorable conditions there are some houses of very commodious and respectable appearance in each of the three quarters, and, on entering them, it will be seen that those who reside there have some ideas as to the comforts of life and also the ability to illustrate them. In the various convents, schools and buildings, used as residences for the orders of the clergy of the various churches, there is also comfort and plenty. Some of these, together with the churches in connection, are very handsome pieces of architecture and would be ornaments to any city of the western world. They stand out in striking contrast to the low, rough, irregular houses and shops of the native population.

It will thus easily be inferred that there cannot be much waste space in the old city. Altogether it covers only 209½ acres of ground and out of this must be taken thirty-five acres, which are enclosed within the walls of the great Mosque. At least as much more is occupied by military barracks and fully as much is the private and unoccupied land of the various religious orders. Subtracting from what remains that on which stand the churches and other buildings not used as homes, and it leaves something less than 100 acres of ground to furnish the homes and the places of business for a population approximating thirty thousand. There may be more people than this number within the walls; there are no means of knowing the exact population, as no census is ever taken. A conservative estimate, based on as complete a count as can be secured, gives the entire city a resident population of 55,000 and divides it almost equally between the Old and the New Jerusalem outside the walls.

The stores and shops are very primitive, but the methods of doing business are something to be wondered at. Along Jew street, which is in the centre of the city and runs south from David street, can be seen on any day but Saturday a sight which for variety of dress, language, features and goods, cannot be paralleled. This is the main Jewish business street, and you can buy here anything in the way of raiment or food that a Jew of the Holy City is likely to want. The stores are minute, some of them having only a few feet each way; the largest not more than ten feet wide by fourteen long. The way the goods are packed in, however, and the amount that can be exhibited to a probable purchaser, is wonderful to the uninitiated. Every type of Jew from the lithe, dark-skinned and rather attractive Yemenite, to the heavy, fair-skinned and generally very unattractive Russian, is here. Between these are the German, Spanish, Morocco, Persian and native Jew. Each can speak the language of the land from which he has come, and within the space of a few yards one may hear them all, with the addition of Hebrew and English. It is a Jewish cosmopolitan trading place.

North of David street and continuous with Jew street are the Turkish bazaars, where can be found anything that the Turk or Arab is likely to want. These are even more curious to the western visitor than are the shops of the sons of Jacob. Every large city has its Jew quarter where a pretty good idea of the methods of that "peculiar people" can be got; but the Turk and Arab are not so easily met. In these bazaars there are always to be seen a profusion of richly colored stuffs. The Turk is fond of gay apparel and brightly ornamented articles. The dress of his wife or wives, the trappings of his horse, his narghili, or smoking apparatus, must lack nothing in the way of decoration that his purse can afford.

But the great thing in the bazaars is to see the buyer and seller proceed to business. The former comes along as unconcernedly as possible, as though the intention to purchase anything was farthest from his thoughts. Coming to the bazaar he patronizes, the greeting is passed and some general conversation indulged in. Seeing what he wants he may pick it up, examine it indifferently and lay it down carelessly, all the time talking about something else. Finally he ventures to ask, as though the notion had just struck him, how much the desired article is worth. The dealer is just as sly and asks about three times what he is willing to take and expects to get, but he does it in such a way as to convey his belief that the one about to purchase has no intention of doing so. With the same indifference the purchaser replies offering about a third the amount mentioned. Then comes the battle, first quietly, then more emphatically, until finally their voices are being used under full pressure. You would imagine a real fight was imminent, but there is little danger. The bargain-driving may last half an hour or half a day. The buyer may go away without the article, but he is likely to return on the same or some succeeding day and renew the business. When he does secure his purchase it is at a price from a third to a half the amount first asked. I once purchased some rugs from one of these Turkish merchants. He came with his wares at a time when I was busy with other matters. He had three rugs of good quality which I wanted. I told him I had no time to bargain with him and therefore he must name me his last price. After pondering a moment he named it very solemnly, as though it were wrenching his soul to let them go so cheaply. I pursued the same tactics, thought a moment, then took another small rug and added it to the three already selected and offered him for the four just half the amount he had said was the last price for the three. He was shocked and insulted, to judge from the expression on his face, and said it was impossible to think of selling them at the price I had mentioned. I started to go and when he saw I meant it called me back and gave me the rugs at my price and was glad to do it. I have no doubt he made a fair profit on the sale.

This is the way of doing business at every place in the city except in one or two European stores. It is annoying and unsatisfactory, but objecting to it does no good. You are met with the assertion, "It is the custom of the country"; and that is final. He who attempts to reform the customs of the Oriental gets little sympathy and less success. He has always done a certain thing a certain way and will continue to do it just that way "even unto the end."

Another characteristic, and perhaps the most striking one, is the religious appearance the city has. It holds easily the title of the Holy City for this reason if for no other. Look in any direction you may and you will see the roof of mosque, steeple of church or dome of synagogue, and here and there the tall minaret overlooking all. Largest of the churches is that of the Holy Sepulchre, but there are at least twenty-five others.

Photograph by the Author.
NATIVE WATER CARRIERS.

Photograph by T. J. Alley.
STREET MARKET SCENE.

Largest of the synagogues is that known as Khal Stamboul, or Congregation of Constantinople, but there are two hundred others scattered throughout the town. Largest of the mosques is the El Aksa on Mount Moriah, but there are inferior ones to the number of thirty-seven. Added to these are the religious and eleemosynary institutions of priests and monks and nuns. At nearly every hour some of the numerous bells are ringing the call to service. At stated intervals, namely at dawn, noon, middle of the afternoon, sunset, and at one-and-a-half hours after sunset, the muezzin call is given "from the tapering summit of tall minaret," and the faithful Moslem obeys. But I am told the response to the calls is not nearly so general as in former years, that among the younger generation of Mohammedans there is noticeable a great lack of religious spirit and a lamentable neglect of the outward forms. Nevertheless, when the muezzin sounds, one can see in the public squares, in front of their shops, by the roadside or in the field the faithful going through their prostrations and genuflexions.

As in all other Oriental cities, there are venders of goods along all the principal streets. In some quarters they are so numerous as to occupy all of the narrow pavement and where there is no pavement a large part of the street. This hinders passenger traffic and forces man and beast to use the same way. With water-skins or jugs of various shape strapped to them, with a wide board carried on the head, or a basket in the hand, the walking merchant transports his wares along the street crying their peculiar excellence and marvellous cheapness.

"Oh, ye thirsty ones, come and drink," calls the seller of lemonade or other refreshment.

"Eggs and cakes for ten paras (about a cent). Here they are, oh, for nothing."

"He who wants a good clean meal come buy of me. My bread is fresh and made of whitest flour."

"Let him who is thirsty partake of my lemonade. It is cold and refreshes the heart."

"Buy of none but me. I sell for nothing and if you want a special bargain be sure and let me know."

Such invitations never cease from early morning till darkness.

Camel and donkey drivers hold sway on the streets. Laden with various goods from every quarter the camel comes stalking through the city gates with that look mildly disdainful of the opinions of human bipeds, whom his obstinacy invites to move out of the way or be trampled on. Take him all in all, the camel is the homeliest of God's creatures. Neither in face nor form is there anything to commend him to the lover of the beautiful. An American lady, celebrated as a writer of delightful and helpful fiction, was in Jerusalem in the winter of 1893 and 1894. One of her remarks about the ungainliness of this plain, but profitable animal, as a long caravan of them went by, was, "Well, I do not like to criticise the Creator, but it does seem to me that I could have attached the hind legs of those animals to their bodies so as to make just as useful and a much more graceful creature."

In spite of the fact that the railway from Jaffa to Jerusalem is prepared to bring freight from the only Palestine seaport, the conservatism of many of the people is so intense that they preserve the old method of transportation. Accordingly camel and donkey trains make the journey laden with every variety of goods. Overland from Damascus, they come along the great north road, bringing to Jerusalem and Egypt the products of the Oasis City. From the country of Moab and Ammon, east of the Jordan, they bring the "finest of the wheat" for sale in the Jerusalem market or for shipment to some far country, the name of which the raisers of the wheat have never heard. One may ridicule the camel for his exceeding ungainliness, and in sarcastic tones, because of the unpleasantness of his voice, term the donkey "the Jerusalem canary," nevertheless, these two animals are deserving of the highest consideration from the dwellers in this land. They make living here reasonably endurable, and the wretch who treats them harshly is a "marble-hearted fiend," guilty of the basest ingratitude, and deserving only of the contempt of men.

Friday is the big market day of the week. Both the wholesale and retail dealers make the most of it. Whatever product of the season is due will be found in abundance at every prominent street corner and in every vegetable bazaar. Just outside the Jaffa Gate to the northwest is the wholesale vegetable stand. The producer who can bring in several camel or donkey loads disposes of them here. But to do so takes as much energy in bartering—voice at highest pitch and arms flying—as would sell a trans-continental railroad on the New York Stock Exchange. In the basin of the lower pool of Gihon the cattle market is now held every Friday. Here any one wishing to sell or buy camels, cattle, sheep or donkeys, may be accommodated. It is true that Friday is the Moslem Sabbath. It is also true that a great deal of the business is carried on by believers in this religion; but to do so on their holy day is not sacrilegious, provided the business may be completed before, or dispensed with, during the noonday hour of prayer. This they all manage to do.

For centuries the city and land have been under Moslem rule. The nominal head of the local government is a pasha, or mutaserif, who is appointed by the sultan. It depends altogether upon the character of the pasha whether he shall be anything more than a nominal head. A man of weak or vacillating will is sure to be made the dupe of his underlings, the majority of whom have received by inheritance and acquired by years of constant practice capacities for deception and sharp dealing that are truly wonderful. The pasha who is pasha indeed, must be shrewd to see, and quick to execute. The inferior officials can have only as much power as the pasha allows them. They constitute a sort of municipal council, and consist of nine Moslems, one Jew and one Christian. This is an exceedingly unfair division, seeing that the Moslem body is the smallest.

The great foreign powers all have consulates in the city, and the citizens of each power are responsible in all civil and criminal actions to their respective consuls. This guarantees them some certain protection. In all actions between parties all of whom are foreigners the case must be tried before the consulate of that power to which the defendant owes allegiance. In a case in which a Turkish subject is the plaintiff against a subject of a foreign state or in which a Turkish subject is in any way involved either as plaintiff or defendant the case must go before the local Serai, or court, for trial. There is an exception to this rule only when an American citizen is the defendant. By treaty entered into between the United States and Turkey in 1830, and which has never been altered, the right is reserved of having such a case tried before the American consulate.

It is true that Turkey makes objection to the right of Americans to exercise this special privilege asserting that we base our claim to it on a mistranslation of Article IV. of the treaty of May 7, 1830, referring to it. But it is just as true that competent Turkish scholars assert that the disputed clause does grant to Americans this right. It is a question that was not raised till after the treaty had been accepted by both powers. American ministers and consuls go on exercising the privilege as though there were no dispute. The local authorities in Jerusalem make objection in nearly every case, but reference to the treaty and suggestion of an appeal to Constantinople if they are not satisfied cause them to acquiesce.

Were they some day to insist upon the carrying out of this stipulation of the treaty, as they interpret it, a delicate question of international importance would be raised. And if a commission of other powers were appointed to settle the difficulty it would decide, without doubt, in favor of the Turk. Although each of the great nations of Europe should enjoy, according to its treaty with the Sublime Porte, the privilege granted to "the most favored nation," the United States is alone in possession of those privileges. Americans residing in Turkish dominions care not how soon the representatives of other countries are put on an equality with them, but they hope that the day will never come when their own government shall submit to a Turkish mistranslation of the treaty and surrender privileges that are necessities if Americans are to secure what they consider their rights.

This is one of the very few advantages accruing to an American citizen resident in the Holy City. Unless such an one is here engaged heart and soul in missionary work time will hang heavily. In the way of amusement there is nothing: not a place where an exhibition of any kind can be given, were there anything worth exhibiting; not an opera nor a play; not even a concert from one year's end to the other. During my residence of four years there were four concerts given by amateurs. Lectures are occasionally given in the tourist season under the auspices of the local branch of the Palestine Exploration Society. For the rest of the year the town closes at sundown. The only places that keep open after this hour are a couple of German beer-halls and some Arab coffee-shops. The streets are deserted by humanity and all is quiet until daybreak, except the canine part of the population.

Wonderful is the transformation that comes over the city when night falls. The streets that were a few hours ago crowded and noisy are deserted and quiet. I have walked through the city and round the walls between the night hours of ten and twelve and not met a single person, except the silent watchman in his little garden. The effect of the times when the city gates were shut at sundown and it was unsafe to be out at night, is still felt. The people have nothing to stay up for, so they retire early. The natives are early risers; they may have nothing to do, but no matter; they are up before the sun.

The spirit of modern progress has not touched the city yet. It has come from the west, swept across the Mediterranean, left its impress on Alexandria and Cairo, but has passed through the Suez Canal and on to the Far East. Jerusalem has been passed by and, were it not for its popularity as a stopping-place for tourists from Europe and America, would be as Oriental as any one could wish. These visitors are leaving some of their customs and costumes. Some of the rising generation of natives affect the European dress. The combination of the man and the habit is not a success; each detracts from the other.

When the railway from Jaffa to Jerusalem was completed in 1893 it was the wonder of the year, not only of the day. The great majority of the people had never seen such a thing as a locomotive. It frightened them so that when some of them saw it coming they could not get out of the way. It might reasonably have been expected that other improvements would follow rapidly. There has not been a single one.

Some of the letters of inquiry from our enterprising American firms which are sent to the consulate are laughable in the light of present conditions. Electric engineers and manufacturers of electric goods want to know all about the system of street railway now employed and what is the likelihood of introducing their special improved appliances for rapid transit. If they could only see what system is in use! To go from one part of the city within the walls to another, one must walk or mount a donkey. A line of carriages runs from the Jaffa Gate a mile west along the road. But such carriages! He who enters some of them does so at the expense of comfort and safety.

Street illumination is still in its infancy. In the entire city there are twenty-eight small oil lamps stuck up here and there on the sides of the houses. They are uncared for and on a dark night do nothing more than indicate that they are lighted. To believe that they do anything in the way of lessening the gloom is a freak of imagination. American companies wish to put in electric lights if the way is clear. But it is not; several insurmountable barriers intervene. In the first place the Turkish authorities do not desire so much light; it would reveal too much. They would not permit the introduction of electricity for illuminating purposes if some company should agree to furnish it gratis. Another reason is it would never pay. With the great scarcity of fuel the expense of operating the electric plant would be enormous. Another reason is that the Turk fears electricity in any form. He only admits the telegraph because he is compelled to. In Bergheim's flouring mill, however, and in the French Pilgrim's Building, both in the New City, there are some incandescent lights.

There are no telephones and not likely soon to be any. An American missionary who had charge of some schools several miles away and with which it was necessary for him to have frequent converse had a telephone sent to him. When he proceeded to put it in condition for service a Turkish officer was sent to make inquiries. The affair and the benefit of it was explained to him and he went away and reported it to his superiors. Word soon came to the progressive missionary that he must desist in its operations. Such an innovation could not be allowed unless he had an order from the sultan. He had no such order and was in no mood to pay the sum necessary to obtain it. The telephone has been lying unused for several years.

This is the kind of people who have control of the city. As long as they retain it Jerusalem will be mediæval in appearance. The native and Jewish inhabitants do not care; the visitor prefers to see a city untouched by the hand of modern improvement. The former are indifferent in the matter; the latter have a sentiment. The one will not be roused from their indifference so long as the Turk is governor; the other is in no danger of having his sentiment destroyed.

The population numbers fifty-five thousand. This is a conservative estimate and yet only an estimate; nothing more satisfactory can be had under present conditions. The Turks never take a census. Certain individuals or societies have attempted a systematic canvass, but have had too many difficulties to meet in the way of overcoming fears and prejudices. The people look with suspicion upon any one who comes to their houses and asks questions about the inmates. They fear some new tax list is about to be prepared, and if they must answer are sure to minimize their numbers. With these difficulties to contend against it is not to be wondered that estimators differ somewhat in their calculations and their differences must not be charged to intentional error.

The estimate here given includes the permanent residents of both the old and the new city, and is based upon careful observation after a continuous residence of nearly five years and upon the opinions of the various civil and religious authorities. It was taken for granted in making the estimate that the patriarchs and bishops of the various Christian bodies would be in positions to know the exact number of their adherents and would be honest in stating that number. On the other hand great dissatisfaction resulted from efforts to learn the real number of the Jewish population. The leading rabbis know, but soon convince an inquirer that they wish to preserve their knowledge. The inference from this desire to conceal the number is that there are many more than the Jews wish the Turkish authorities to believe. They have an object in decreasing the number, or the report of the number of their people, and I have no doubt that they do so, by from ten to fifteen thousand.

The most careful estimate yet made was in 1892, by the missionary workers of the London Jews' Society. The result was as nearly exact as has yet been made and may safely be depended upon. According to this there are just about forty-two thousand Jews in the city and contiguous colonies, whose in-

The City as it is To-day

habitants are justly classed among Jerusalem residents. Since that partial census there has been little variation in the number, for it was made just about the time restrictions were placed upon Jewish immigration. Some have come since, but about an equal number have left. Should the restrictions against the immigration of the Jew be removed they would come in ever increasing numbers, until the Christian and Moslem dwellers in the Holy City would be so few as to be conspicuous. As it is, nearly three-fourths of the entire population are descendants of Jacob.

Next in numerical strength are the Christians, including all sects who so call themselves. Of this part of the population nearly a half are adherents of the Greek orthodox body. In wealth as well as in numbers this is the leading sect. The entire number of Christians is about 8,630, divided as follows:

Greek Orthodox	4,000
Roman Catholic	3,200
Armenian	600
Protestant (all branches)	500
Coptic	120
Greek Catholic	100
Abyssinian	60
Syriac	50
Total	8,630

The Moslems number about 6,500, and though the smallest numerically, are the strongest officially. They look with a measure of scorn upon Jews and Christians, and, were it not for the financial benefit to them resulting from the presence of these representatives of despised religions, would gladly be rid of them.

There is less friction between members of these three great religions than is generally supposed. In fact there is very little. The worst exhibitions of intolerance are between certain of the Christian sects. Each devotee of religion enjoys full freedom to worship God as he wishes so long as he respects the rights of the others. There are in the city Jews, orthodox and reformed—though the latter are few. There are Ashkenazim, or Jargon-speaking, Sephardim, or Spanish, and Caraites, or repudiators of the Talmud. There are Christians of every shade of faith, orthodox, unorthodox and peculiar. There are representatives of the various sects of Islam. So in every respect, civil and religious, physical and political, Jerusalem is unique among the cities of the world.

THE NEW JERUSALEM

The Term—Its Application—Appearance and Age—Ancient Architecture in the Old City—Modern in the New—Old City Streets—New City Streets—Dust—Street Sprinkling—Growth of the New City—Jewish Immigration—Condition of the People—Their Character and Nationality—Estimates of Robinson and Williams—New Jerusalem Residences—Jewish Colonies—Names of Colonies—Jeremiah's Prophecy—Zechariah—Conclusions.

V

THE NEW JERUSALEM

THE term is old; the application of it here made is new. When the Seer of Patmos was "in the spirit on the Lord's Day" he beheld a city where all was perfect; he called it the New Jerusalem. To his mind Jerusalem was the queen of cities, and when there arose before his vision the indescribable city of God no name was better suited to it. That name brought to his mind a suggestion of all that was beautiful and all that was sacred. The contrast between his home on the sea-washed rock of Patmos and "the holy city, New Jerusalem, coming down from God out of heaven" was far more decided than that between the Old and the New that stand side by side on the hills of Judea to-day, but the latter contrast is striking enough to warrant the application of the term "old" to that city within the walls, and "new" to that which has grown up during the last few years outside the walls toward the west and north.

The contrast is one of appearance as well as age. In the old city the buildings have an ancient look. And their looks do not deceive, for some of them have seen twenty generations of frail humanity appear and disappear; indeed, some of these walls, I am sure, were standing in the time of Constantine. Some of these houses may go back to the time of Christ, if we are to believe some observers, who see in the claim no violation of the Saviour's prophecy, "They shall not leave in thee one stone upon another."[1] The architecture is ancient, even in the buildings which have been erected in recent years. The scarcity of timber and the expensiveness of iron have forced

[1] Luke xix. 44.

builders to resort to the arch, and with very few exceptions the houses in the city proper have vaulted ceilings and dome roofs. As one looks over the city from the terrace of the Grand New Hotel the entire place seems to be made up of little mounds, very quaint and very picturesque. In the new city new ideas in building are illustrated. The houses are modern. Iron rafters take the place of the arch, and flat, or slanting roofs with the ordinary red tile so common in German villages, are the order. This does away in many cases with the amazing thickness of walls, but in some the old method of a wall so thick that it will keep out heat in summer and dampness in winter prevails, even in the newer quarters. A wall four feet in thickness has a substantial appearance and great powers of resistance to the elements.

Within the walls the streets are narrow, devious, and, for two or three reasons, very uncertain. A stranger on entering one of them never knows just where he will find himself after a few minutes' walk. The street may make several turns in as many minutes. Another uncertainty is that one never knows on entering a street just how long he can continue on it. A camel loaded with boxes or large sacks comes swinging along and demands, and generally gets, the full right of way. He who wishes to contest the ungainly creature's progress may do so, but one experience of the kind is usually satisfactory and on the next occasion the quiet demands of the brute are quietly granted. There is only one piece of a street in the whole city where carriages can pass. The place was laid out as it now is before there was a carriage in the country.

The New Jerusalem differs in this respect. North of the old city the streets are wide and reasonably well cared for—I mean reasonably well for Jerusalem, for they are not paved, and many loose stones make carriage riding somewhat more violent exercise than most people care to indulge in. The exception to this is the Jaffa road which is lined with houses on both sides for nearly a mile beyond the gate of the same

The New Jerusalem 93

name. This road is well ballasted and comfortably smooth. Its great drawback is the choking dust which covers it all through the long rainless summer. A light yellow cloud hangs over it all the time, sustained by the continual passing and repassing of carriages, camels and donkeys. A little public spirit in the way of street sprinkling would remedy this, but public spirit requires the expenditure of a little money and a little time. There are plenty of people who will furnish the time if paid for it, but too few who will contribute the money. There is a little sprinkling done, but so little that it is ridiculous. A couple of water carriers each evening go along with water skins on their backs and scatter a little dirty water here and there. You can see in the dust the mark of their passing, but there is no diminution in the amount of dirt in the air.

All this new city has grown up within the last twenty-five years. This is not a very rapid growth if it be compared with some of our western cities, but it is rapid for this part of the world, especially that on which the throttling Turk has his grip. In a country whose government discourages all progress by taxing every improvement beyond the benefit it can bring to the one making it, that discriminates against certain classes of its population and prohibits the entrance of many new settlers the rapid advance of a city is a cause for wonder. Visitors to Jerusalem now who have seen the city twenty or even ten years ago, are amazed at the advance that has been made. The improvement appears mostly in the new city. Here many Jewish colonies have grown up and seem to be thriving. They are continually being added to and yet the Jewish authorities persist in saying that their numbers are not increasing by immigration. But as the authorities have very good reasons for wanting it to be believed that they are not increasing in numbers their persistence in assertion has no effect upon the opinions of persons who wish to see. The new houses are occupied just as soon as they are ready for occupation and the old houses are not vacated. The Porte has issued an order forbidding the settlement of Jews in Palestine. But the Jews are coming just the same. Not as rapidly nor in such numbers, it is true, as before the order was issued, but still rapidly enough to keep adding to their strength in and about their ancestral city. An examination into the methods of the customs officials at Jaffa would no doubt disclose how this is done in spite of the law.

As in the old city so in the new the great majority are Israelites. Take these away and neither city would be much more than a village. In 1838 Doctor Robinson, whose statements can usually be relied upon, estimated that there were eleven thousand inhabitants in Jerusalem of whom three thousand were Jews. In 1845 Doctor Shultz claimed that there were seven thousand one hundred and twenty Jews. In the second edition of his work, entitled "The Holy City," which appeared in 1849, George Williams approves[1] Doctor Robinson's computation. Accepting the estimate of Robinson and Williams, we must account for a tenfold increase in forty-five years, and this is a very conservative ratio. Any fair-minded person will be convinced of its accuracy by a walk through the twenty separate colonies of the New Jerusalem.

Here, too, are the finest residences. Many of the Turkish officials and families of high social and financial standing among the Moslems consider this a desirable location. The European population generally has followed them, and on the north ridge are the homes of the English and German, and the few American missionaries, the hospitals and schools, and the consulates of the various powers. On the highest part of the ridge stands the consulate of our own great nation, and when the "Stars and Stripes" are floating they can be seen from nearly every part of the city. That flag of a nation undreamed of two hundred years ago, waves over this city that counts its age by decades of centuries, yet represents a civilization as far in

[1] Holy City, Vol. II., p. 614.

Photograph by T. J. Alley.
UNITED STATES CONSULATE.

Photograph by the Author.
CONSULAR GUARDS.

The New Jerusalem

advance of what it sees as the parlor car is in advance of the camel as a method of travel.

In this New Jerusalem the air is always pure. This is a matter about which tourists can afford to be unconcerned for a time, but which residents must consider. Because of its compact nature, the narrowness of its streets and its lack of proper drainage, the old city has at times a woeful lack of fresh air. But on the high land on the north there is never any want of this preventive of fever and other diseases. It comes up moist from the Mediterranean and fragrant with the odors of the hills, or down from the high Lebanon country bearing refreshment and invigoration. Nearly every house has its garden or small vineyard about it where the air can have full play. Yet this is not true of all the Jewish colonies; strange as it may appear, some of these people certainly prefer villainous surroundings. With every chance of having their precincts clean and comfortable and wholesome, they manage to keep them in the very opposite condition. They are satisfied to crowd together in small ill-lighted houses, all of which front on a court that too often is made the dumping place for the refuse of the colony. But in spite of themselves they thrive.

Others of these colonies in the new city are about as attractive and well cared for as they can be. Their founders and residents have a pardonable pride in their settlement in the Holy City. Notable among these is that one just west of the Pool of the Sultan facing the Bethlehem road. This was started by a fund raised in London in honor of the great Jewish philanthropist, Sir Moses Montefiore. A committee in Jerusalem, working with a similar one in London, builds the houses and sells them on easy terms to worthy families. The number of houses is to be limited to one hundred and thirty, and the limit is almost reached. This colony has a very pleasant location along the eastern slopes of the hill and has about it an air of thrift. During the lifetime of Sir Moses the ground was purchased and thirty-two cottages erected. These are given free of rent to those Jews fortunate enough to secure them, and a family once located remains without fear of being removed. The entire population of this settlement amounts to six hundred, and when all the residences are completed will be a very comfortable little village of eight hundred souls.

Beyond the high wall which the Russians have built around their property north of the city and along the Jaffa road the houses are with few exceptions occupied by Jews. The names they have given to their colonies are in many instances suggestive of a degree of prosperity and glory that appearances will hardly sanction. "The House of Jacob," "The Hundred Gates," "The Glory of Israel," "The Right Hand of Moses" are fair samples of these names. One called "The Corner Gate" is regarded by many good people as a prophetic indication, or rather as indication of the near fulfillment of prophecy. The coincidence is at least striking. In the thirty-first chapter of Jeremiah, thirty-eighth to fortieth verses, the prophet exclaims, "Behold, the days come, saith the Lord, that the city shall be built to the Lord from the tower of Hananeel to the gate of the corner. And the measuring line shall yet go forth over against it upon the hill Gareb and shall compass about to Goath. And the whole valley of the dead bodies, and of the ashes, and all the fields, unto the brook of Kidron, unto the corner of the horse gate toward the east, shall be holy unto the Lord; it shall not be plucked up nor thrown down any more forever."

Now there may be some way to adopt the statements of this prophecy to present conditions and those who say that it plainly foretells the modern growth of the city toward the north may be correct. The great difficulty is in identifying the places to which Jeremiah gives these names. It is not known just where the tower of Hananeel was; the hill Gareb and the place called Goath are uncertain in their location. If we had any grounds for believing that the tower of Hananeel stood near the northwest corner of the present city, and that the hill to the northwest is Gareb we might assert quite positively that the growth of the past few years has followed the line marked out by Jeremiah. Gareb is the name usually given to this long, sloping hill on which most of the new city is built, and only by placing Hananeel where we have, can any possible application of the above passage be made. But in matters of this nature it is not wise to be too positive. In any case the city is growing toward the north, including and crossing "the valley of the dead bodies, and of the ashes," which are known places, and moving as if the intention were to occupy "all the fields unto the brook of Kiedron."

Another prophecy[1] foretells the growth of the city in this direction, but in it we meet the same difficulty encountered in the former. The gates of the old city have been the sport of theorizers, and, though the prophets knew their exact location and spoke intelligently about them we cannot. So when Zechariah describes the coming city as extending "from Benjamin's Gate unto the place of the first gate unto the corner gate and from the tower of Hananeel unto the king's wine-presses," we may only know the general directions. The gate of Benjamin was on the north side of the city in the time of Jeremiah.[2] To Anathoth, the city of this prophet, northeast of Jerusalem, he was going when "the captain of the ward" arrested him on suspicion as a deserter to the Chaldeans. So the gate of Benjamin may have been on the east of the north wall. If so, and we identify as "the king's wine-presses" those ancient rock cuttings about a mile straight north of the present Damascus Gate to which the name is now given, we have the exact direction in which the new city is growing. There are a good many "ifs" to be accepted, but it is a reasonable method to permit the facts to interpret the prophecy, and if we do so all the "ifs" may be omitted. Certainly no one can read the many prophetic utterances about Jerusalem in a rational way and hold that they all refer to a "spiritual

[1] Zech. xiv. 10, 11.   [2] Jer. xxxvii. 13.

city," unless he accept a method of interpretation, which robs the Bible of the greater part of its value as "the book" for men.

He who sees in the growth of the New Jerusalem the fulfillment of some of the visions of the inspired seers has plain scripture with him and the stubborn facts of this new city as it is and is fast becoming. Out in the direction of the so-called king's wine-presses, it is moving slowly, but irresistibly. Many fields between the last colony and the "presses" are still in the hands of the husbandman, but ten years more of progress, such as has been witnessed during the last decade will see Zechariah's prediction realized. Once the Turk gets over his animosity toward his elder brother, the Jew, there will be nothing in the way of the increase of the new city. The Jew wants to come. He is anxious to buy a plot of ground and build him a home in or near the city of his fathers. He simply asks to be let alone, freed from oppression and permitted to enjoy his religion. The land of the new city is ready for him. In all other directions growth is prevented by deep valleys. Thus topography assists in the development of prophecy.

The colony of Jews from Bokhara is the latest addition to the new city, and, taking everything into consideration, the most attractive and promising. These are a superior looking people, being of much finer physique than their brethren from the west. The men are tall and vigorous and the women attractive in face and form. They are also people of means and on the large tract of land they have purchased, almost a mile north of the New Gate, are erecting some residences that would be an ornament to any city. Only within a few years have any of them been seen within the limits of their ancient city. They are no doubt the descendants of those exiles who preferred to remain in the land of the strangers after the seventy years of captivity had expired. After twenty-five hundred years something moves them to return to the homes of their fathers. Is not that "something" the hand of Providence?

Thus the new Jerusalem grows by accessions from every part of the globe. On its streets "all sorts and conditions" of Jews and Gentiles meet and pass one another. They may be strangers to each other and ignorant of the part they are playing, but I cannot resist the belief that each is doing his part in God's plan for the rebuilding of the city and its enlargement far beyond the borders it has occupied in the past.

THE WALLS AND GATES

Circumventing the Walls—48th Psalm—Walls of Jebus—Solomonic Additions—Nehemiah's Account—Restorations—Walls in Time of Christ—First Wall—Second Wall—Gate Gennath—Third Wall—Josephus' Account—Modern Wall—Sulieman—Jaffa Gate—Needle's Eye—Bethlehem Road—Southwest Corner—Zion Gate—Inscription—Angles of Wall—Double Gate—Triple Gate—Single Gate—Southeast Angle—Excavations—Mason Marks—Ancient Arch—Golden Gate—Ancient Masonry—St. Stephen's Gate—Northeast Corner—Herod Gate—Bezetha—Damascus Gate—New Gate—Length of Entire Wall.

VI

THE WALLS AND GATES

WHEN visitors to the "City of the Great King," as is their custom, take a walk around the walls, they should bear in mind that they are accepting a very ancient invitation. The patriotic author of the forty-eighth Psalm, glorying in the safety of his capital, was anxious that the "generations following" should hear about her towers and bulwarks.[1] Perhaps he felt that the day was coming when these mighty defences would be unable to withstand the assaults of mightier forces. Then they would have to depend upon the memory of men for the honor that was their due. If so, he was not mistaken. The walls of his day were battered down by the enemy; the towers and bulwarks and magnificent palaces were levelled to the earth. It matters not at what period of the city's history the writer of this psalm lived; the statement is correct. Repeatedly were the fortifications rebuilt by the lovers of Jerusalem, and just as often were they overthrown by her enemies.

All that can be said of the walls of the original Jebus must be largely hypothetical, and yet, if the opinion advocated in the chapter on the "City of David and Solomon" be correct, conjecture may here reach reasonable accuracy. Mount Zion was a well defined elevation surrounded on all sides by valleys. A people depending for safety upon the strength of city walls, would place those walls where they would present the most effective resistance to attack. This would be on the very brow of the hill where the depression of the valleys would be most precipitous. Accordingly we can hardly be far wrong in asserting that the walls of Jebus skirted the brow of Mount

Psalm xlviii. 12, 13.

Zion, so that one standing on them could look from any quarter and see below him the steep hillside terminating in the bed of the valley. Josephus' declaration, when speaking of the place at the time of its capture by David, bears out this conjecture. He says that "The upper city (Jebus) was not to be taken without great difficulty, on account of the strength of its walls and the nature of the place."[1] As the valley on the north was not so precipitous as the hillsides on all other quarters, the fortifications would here be made doubly strong. Support is given to this opinion by the fact that the attack was made and the entrance effected on the eastern side, where the hill was especially steep. Nature having here done so much, the Jebusite trusted most in it; herein lay his fatal mistake.

When Jebus became Jerusalem and Solomon reigned over united Israel, the weak parts of the old walls were strengthened and additions made. The language used in describing these improvements is not definite enough to warrant positive statements as to their nature or location. Solomon added much, if we suppose his moral operations confined to that wonderful masonry that surrounded the temple area. But he accomplished more than this, for "he built Millo and repaired the breaches of the City of David,"[2] and added "the wall round about."[3] Notices of repairs and improvements to the walls are scattered and fragmentary, and no satisfactory conclusions can be drawn from them. After the return from the Babylonish captivity, the ruined walls were reconstructed; as we read in the third chapter of Nehemiah, the most important document we have for the study of the city at that time. Those who wish to investigate more thoroughly the varying interpretations of this chapter, are referred to Thrupp's "Ancient Jerusalem," Barclay's "City of the Great King," and Williams' "Holy City."

Nehemiah's rebuilding of the walls was begun about 450 B. C. Sixty-five years previous to this the temple had been re-

[1] Jos. Ant., v. 2, § 2.   [2] 1 Kings xi. 27.   [3] 1 Kings iii. 1.

built. Owing to the diminished population and wealth, these walls were probably not so imposing as those whose place they took. They were, however, the work of a zealous and patriotic people, seeking the return of their departed glory. As they were constructed then, so probably they appeared in the time of the Master's visits to the city. During this period— 450 years—Jerusalem passed through many fiery trials. One destroyer followed closely upon the heels of another. Persian, Egyptian, Syrian, Roman, each took possession, held it for a time and was expelled. The walls fell, but in each case were rebuilt, and probably without change of location.

In the time of Christ there were two walls on the north. The most southern of these, now called the old or first wall, began at the tower of Hippicus, near the present Jaffa Gate, followed the northern brow of the hill, crossed the Tyropean on the earthworks of Millo and joined the west wall of the temple near the Council House, or quarters of the Sanhedrin. According to Josephus this wall "was almost impregnable, both on account of the valleys that surrounded it and because of the hill above them, on which it was erected." In addition to the advantages of its position, it had been strongly built; David and Solomon, and the kings that followed them, having been very zealous about the work.[1] Of this wall nothing that can be positively identified remains, though were excavations permitted in the heart of the present city, there is no doubt that the exact course of the wall could be traced and one or two of its important gates located. This permission will not be granted, and, should it be, so much expense would be involved that no exploration society would undertake it.

The direction and location of the second wall are questions that have been warmly discussed, but not yet conclusively settled. Of this Josephus says: "The second wall had its beginning at the gate they called Gennath, one of the gates of the first wall, and encircling only the northern part of the

[1] Josephus' Wars, v. 4, § 2.

town, reached as far as Antonia." Where was the gate Gennath? It has been located on paper at various points between the tower of Hippicus and the "middle of the northern wall of the upper city." It has not been located on ground by modern explorers, but there was found a few years ago some very heavy masonry under the New Hotel that strongly inclines one to the belief that Doctor Robinson was correct when, more than thirty years ago, he located the Gennath Gate near the Hippicus tower, at the northwestern corner of the upper city. There is no doubt that these remains are part of an ancient city wall, they tend in a northerly direction, and are in line with some magnificent mural ruins now forming the foundation of the Freré's College. These two fragments are identical in the style of their stonework and in size with that at the present Damascus Gate, which is acknowledged by all to be part of the second wall. The only reason why all these are not so acknowledged, is because of the result that would follow in connection with some sacred sites. This wall included a considerable space north of the first wall. Its western extremity was at the present Damascus Gate, from which point it proceeded southward and united with the fortress of Antonia. Josephus assigns no date to the building of this wall. It was probably the work of the two kings, Hezekiah and Manasseh, who added in this way much to the city's strength. A very considerable part of this second wall stood just where the north wall of the modern city stands, at least from the Freré's College to the Damascus Gate, thus leaving out the northeast corner of the present city.

 The third wall was begun twelve years after the crucifixion of our Lord. Herod Agrippa undertook this immense work intending to surround certain parts of the city that had grown up on the north and which were without any protection in case of an attack. This included a great part of what is now known as New Jerusalem. Beginning at the tower Hippicus it proceeded "as far as the north quarter of the city and the

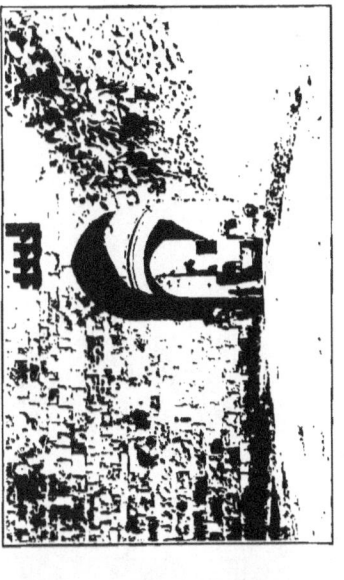
Photograph by T. J. Alley. GATE OF ST. STEPHEN.

Photograph by T. J. Alley. INTERIOR OF DAMASCUS GATE.

Photograph by T. J. Alley. THE GOLDEN GATE.

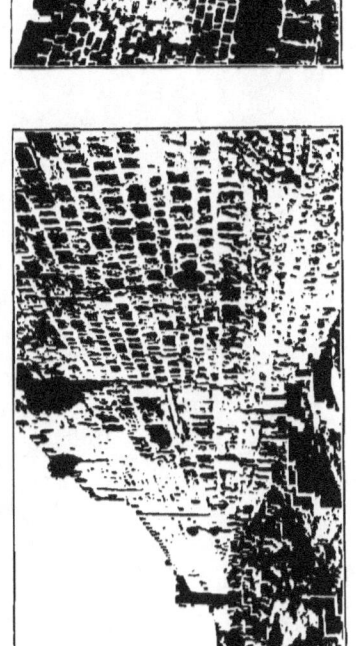
Photograph by T. J. Alley. EAST WALL AND MOSLEM CEMETERY.

tower Psephinos, and then was extended till it came over against the monuments of Helena, which Helena was queen of Adiabene, the daughter of Izates; it then extended further to a great length and passed by the sepulchral caverns of the kings and bent again at the tower of the corner, at the monument which is called 'the Monument of the Fuller,' and joined to the old wall at the valley called the Valley of Kedron."[1]

This description of the Jewish historian was no doubt well understood in his day. We of to-day know the starting point, but are in doubt as to the whereabouts of the tower of Psephinos. That tower was octagonal in shape; hence the ruins under the Freré's College are not, as some have claimed, the remnants of it. The probability is that this tower was much further north. But wherever it was, from it the wall of Agrippa turned to the east, crossed the upper Tyropean valley and went by the tomb of Queen Helena, of Adiabene. A remnant of this wall is still to be seen in this neighborhood, just near the residence of the Anglican Bishop, the masonry of whose house is largely composed of stones derived from it. Reaching the brow of the hill above the valley of Jehosephat the wall turned toward the south and joined the temple wall at the northeast corner.

The character of Agrippa's work was such as to excite the suspicions of Marsus, Roman procurator of Syria, who feared that the Jews were thus preparing for an insurrection against the domination of the foreigner. Accordingly Marsus wrote to Claudius Cæsar expressing his fears as to the result if the work was allowed to be carried on to completion. In reply Claudius commanded Agrippa to discontinue his labors in this direction. Agrippa had to obey the imperial mandate. Had he been permitted to complete the undertaking there was no enginery of war in those days that could have successfully besieged it. The Jews afterward were granted permission to carry out, at least partially, the plan of Agrippa. According

[1] Josephus' Wars v. 4, §2.

to Tacitus [1] the Jews were able to buy this privilege of fortifying their city from corrupt Roman officials. Josephus is loud in his praise of this wall. "Its parts were connected together by stones twenty cubits long and ten cubits broad, which could never have been either easily undermined by any iron tools or shaken by any engines." [2] "Now the third wall was all of it wonderful."

Hardly a particle of this great work now remains *in situ*. The succeeding wall and church and house builders used its good material in their inferior structures. The disastrous experiences through which the city passed shortly afterward levelled all its pride of walls with the earth. Succeeding rulers—Roman, Greek, Christian and Moslem—sought to give the city some of its former glory of mural strength and decoration; they were not successful. Since the destruction by Titus the recovery has only been partial and although the walls of the modern Jerusalem are as substantial as were any of their recent predecessors, they are altogether inferior to the works of the early kings and of the Herods. The latter are built of immense stones—many of them twenty feet long by two feet thick and four feet wide—carefully and accurately laid; the former are composed of material but a foot or two in each dimension.

But he who would seek to cast reproach upon the present wall for the smallness of its stones and its inferior workmanship has a serious fact to contend against. Three centuries and a half have tested it, and work that even in times of peace will endure through so many years is in no danger of losing by comparison with similar work done to-day. Sulieman, the Magnificent, was the builder of this wall and that he was not ashamed of his achievement is attested by the inscriptions found on several of the city gates. The date of their erection was 1536 to 1542. There is a local tradition which narrates that the construction was effected by two brothers who began

[1] Tacitus Hist. v. 12.   [2] Josephus' Wars, v. 4, § 2.

The Walls and Gates 109

work at the Jaffa Gate and did not see each other until seven years later, as they worked in opposite directions, and at the end of this time met on the eastern side of the city where the St. Stephen Gate now is. The four lions on this gate are the brothers' marks. These lions are not the work of the iconoclastic Moslems, but rather of some previous Christian occupants of the city.

The Jaffa Gate is the most convenient starting place for making a tour of the walls. This gate is called by the natives Bab el-Khaleel—the Gate of the Friend, because from it travellers from the city go to Hebron, the place of Abraham the Friend of God. The road from Jaffa meets the Hebron road here, making this the most important entrance to the city. A crowd of carriages, donkeys and shouting men are always near, and a constant stream of varied and variegated humanity is passing in and out. An important gate has always been in this vicinity, and writers generally locate here the site of the Valley Gate of Nehemiah.[1] From this point Nehemiah made a circuit of the ruined walls. There is no question that a valley did commence here and, tending to the east through this part of the city, merged into the Tyropean valley.

Turning to the left after leaving the gate one passes a little "receipt of custom" where a lynx-eyed Turk is supposed to watch every camel, donkey, wagon or man bringing any article of merchandise into the city. The contraband goods are wine, salt and tobacco and it goes hard with the individual who tries to smuggle any in, if he is detected. Until within a few years this and all the city gates were closed at nightfall and any one unfortunate enough to be overtaken by night on the road was obliged to do the best he could on the outside and in those dangerous times the best he could do was sometimes very bad. Later a small door was cut through the large gate, and a belated traveller who could give a satisfactory account of himself and a satisfactory "bucksheesh" to the

[1] Neh. ii. 13.

sentry in charge could be admitted. This small door has been used to illustrate the Saviour's saying of the camel going through the needle's eye. There are two things against the application, first that there were no such doors in the large gates of the city in our Lord's time, and secondly, that no camels would ever have been admitted if there had been such doors; they could not have been. Now the large gates are never closed. At any hour of the day or night one can come and go as he will, provided only that at night he must carry a lantern or explain its absence to the police.

For two hundred yards we follow the Bethlehem road having on our left the citadel and barracks. A fine escarpment of smooth-faced masonry, which descends at an angle of forty-five degrees to the ditch, is visible. A steep road leads off to the left and brings us up to the wall near the southwest corner. All along here the wall is admirably located and sufficiently strong to resist the ordnance used when it was built. The height here will average about forty feet, but is irregular owing to the immense amounts of debris that have been allowed to accumulate. In fact this is the average height of the entire wall, though in some places it is twice this. At this southwest corner we turn to the east and see just before us the Mount of Olives. The wall along this south side bears strong evidence of several ages and builders. Here and there is a large bevelled stone, while near it will be a smaller smooth-faced one, and perhaps one bearing signs of ornamentation showing that its original place was in some palace or temple. Just south of the wall here the various Christian churches have their burial grounds each surrounded with walls almost as imposing as those of the city.

About two hundred yards from the southwest corner is the Zion Gate—called by the Moslems the Bab en-Nebi Daud because it is near their tomb of David. Behind one of its doors was discovered in January, 1895, an inscription dating from Roman times. The walls had been carefully inspected for inscriptions but this one was hidden behind a solid gate, until a winter storm, overturning the gate, gave us this interesting proof that the Third Legion was at one time stationed in Jerusalem.

The architecture of this gate corresponds with that of the Jaffa Gate. The descent of Mount Zion into the Tyropean valley commences just a little east of here; the wall makes a right angle to the north for a short distance then turns again to the east. In the middle of the valley is the Dung Gate, much smaller and less interesting than any of the others. Eight minutes' walk brings us to another angle which is made to the north where the city wall joins that of the temple enclosure. The wall just here is in very bad condition and looks as if it might topple over on slight provocation. The union is made just at the Mosque el-Aksa, near the ancient Double Gate, where can be seen some fine Jewish stonework, though the exterior has unmistakable Roman additions. The Triple Gate is soon reached and a walk of ninety-three yards brings us past the Single Gate to the southeast angle, the most interesting because the least modern, part of the modern walls. The immense stones I do not hesitate to date from the time of Solomon. They are beginning to crumble in certain places, though the great thickness of the wall they compose guarantees that they can bear the burden resting upon them for a few centuries longer.

At this southeast angle Captains Warren and Wilson carried on some interesting explorations in 1868. They were hampered a great deal by the Moslem officials, who were jealous lest they should penetrate the walls of the Noble Sanctuary. The character of the earth through which they had to drive their tunnels also retarded them, but in the main they were successful.[1] The earth was composed largely of debris, " principally of stone chippings, alternating with layers of fat earth, and in some places rough stones about a foot cube."[2] The most

[1] See " Recovery of Jerusalem," p. 135, *et seq.*   [2] Ibid. p. 137.

satisfactory discovery was the marking of the stones in the lower layers, some eighty feet below the present surface. Some of these markings were made with red paint, others by the tools of the workmen and were pronounced by Mr. Emanuel Deutsch, an authority on such matters, to be undoubtedly characters representing Phœnician numerals; pieces of pottery were also found at this depth bearing legible inscriptions in the same characters; so that the evidence that these were the very stones put in place by the masons of Hiram, king of Tyre, is, if not conclusive, very strong. One of the stones found in this angle is estimated by Captain Warren to weigh one hundred tons. A short distance from this angle can be seen the spring of an immense arch. It is not quite so evident as that known as Robinson's arch, which corresponds almost exactly with it on the west wall of the temple enclosure, but is just as certainly the remains of an arch. Standing near it and looking across the Kedron valley one can see that a bridge at this point was not impossible to those builders and not much more of a feat than the one that crossed the Tyropean from the temple enclosure to Mount Zion at Robinson's Arch. The Rabbins speak of such a bridge.

Coming north from this point we pass some of the ancient, but very much more of the modern wall; there is nothing of note till we reach the exterior of the Golden Gate; the interior has already been spoken of. Just before we reach this, however, the filled-in masonry indicates that a small door once opened into the temple enclosure. The history of this is obscure, but it is supposed to have been made by the Crusaders, and to have conducted by a flight of steps to the Kedron valley. The Golden Gate projects six feet from the wall. The double entrance and richness of ornamentation are noticeable from this side. In the hope of securing some valuable information Captain Warren sought to excavate here, but owing to the nature of the ground and the proximity of Moslem tombs the results were not satisfactory. North of the gate for about 373 feet can be traced the magnificent and massive masonry of the ancient builders. One stone measures five feet in height and twenty-seven in length. At the northeast angle of the temple the ancient stones are seen to the very top of the wall. These are many of them not *in situ*, but have been replaced by later restorers. Here once stood an important tower, supposed by some to be the Tower of Hananeel. About 200 feet north of this is the Gate of St. Stephen, known to the natives as Bab Sitti Miriam, or Gate of the Lady Mary, so called because it leads to the supposed tomb of the Mother of Christ which is near it in the valley.

Its name, St. Stephen, was given to it in the fourteenth century when it was somehow considered that a mistake had been made in giving that name to the Damascus Gate. Accordingly, on the belief that near this eastern entrance the proto-martyr was stoned the name was transferred from the north gate. Just a short distance outside the east gate on the Bethany road the spot where Stephen met his death by being stoned is pointed out; the place on the rock is worn smooth by the lips of the devout. There is nothing of note about the gate itself except the four crude lions cut in the stones let in the wall, two on each side.

A ten minutes' walk northward brings one to the northeast corner of the present wall. It is all modern along here and is built on the face of the cliff, which has been cut away to form a ditch which did the double service of furnishing material to build the wall and assisting in the protection of it. The same is true of the eastern part of the north wall, which, from this corner west as far as the Damascus Gate, is nearly all modern.

Between the northeast angle and the Damascus Gate is the unimportant Herod Gate called by the natives Bab ez Zahiré— Gate of splendor. Its splendor is confined to its name, for there is nothing in itself or about its surroundings to warrant the appellation. Until recently it was continually closed.

Between this and the great north gate is the deep cut

through Bezetha. This cut is nearly a hundred yards wide and at some points must have been a hundred feet deep. The ditch has been much filled in. Here is the entrance to the royal caverns. A little further west is the Damascus Gate, built on an old foundation out of all kinds of material. The natives call this Bad el 'Amud—Gate of the column. Some old masonry is to be seen here. There are two angles in the gate. Coming out of the city and just before turning the first angle one can see, nearly on a level with the present surface, the top of the arch of the ancient gate. This gives some idea of the filling in process that has gone on during the centuries.

The wall now turns slightly toward the south and proceeds to the northwest angle. The only break is at the New Gate which is a modern improvement. This angle at which are the ruins of the Kala't al Jolûd, castle of Goliath, is the highest point in the city, and from it a good view can be obtained. It is now Latin property.

The wall then turns straight south until the Jaffa Gate is reached. Between the corner and this gate it is almost hidden from view by buildings, which are about the best in the city, and are occupied by European shopkeepers, bankers and the like.

The measurement of the entire city wall is two and a half miles. To walk the distance gives one a very good idea of the general topography of the place, and of the neighboring hills and valleys and villages. The walls are no longer useful for protection; they can hardly be called ornamental; they add to the city's quaintness and picturesqueness, and for this reason only it is to be hoped they will remain.

THE HILLS ROUND ABOUT

Mounts Zion and Moriah—Their Prominence—Mount of Olives—Roads to and Over—View From—Judean Wilderness—Ancient Churches On—Felix Fabri—Excavations—Greek Possessions—Russian Tower—Associations of Olivet—Ascension—Chapel of Pater Noster—Hebrew Cemetery—Jerusalem and Olivet—Christ and Olivet—Mount of Offence—Hill of Evil Council—Aceldama—Nikophoria—Monument of Herod—Mt. Scopas—Psalmist's Accuracy.

VII

THE HILLS ROUND ABOUT

THE hills upon which the city is built have already been sufficiently described in this book; their importance is due to their selection as the site for the "City of the Great King." Mount Moriah and Mount Zion—they are Jerusalem—as well known to the world at large as any two mountains that may be named. It is perhaps an exaggeration to call them mountains: Mount Zion is less than 2,600 feet above the Mediterranean, while the summit of Moriah is a little more than 100 feet lower than its western neighbor. They are hills, rising out of the long range that runs north from the desert to Esdraelon. Their prominence is historic and religious rather than physical. The hills about Hebron are 400 feet higher, and had King David been seeking for altitude he might better have continued to make Hebron his capital. The Mount of Olives and Mount Scopas are both higher than either of the hills in the city by more than a hundred feet. It was what Nature had done in the immediate vicinity of Zion and Moriah that made them "admirable for defence," and defence was the great requisite in the troublous times when the city was founded, and later when the Jews were conquering the land. Had it not been so, the plains of Rephaim a mile to the southwest, or the broad plateau just north of Jerusalem, would have furnished a much better site for city construction.

In the estimation of Christians, the Mount of Olives will rank as an equal in importance to the two already mentioned. It lies directly east of the city and, unless one is on an elevation, shuts off the view in this direction. Passing out of the city at the St. Stephen's Gate the Bethany road is followed till it leads down to and across the Kedron valley and as far as the northeast corner of the Garden of Gethsemane. Here one of three roads may be taken. The easternmost is the old Bethany road—the only one until within a few years, the one along which the Christ often came with His disciples as He walked from the city of Mary and Martha to the City of the Great King—a distance of two miles. If for the sake of sentiment we follow this old road we pass around the southeastern spur of Olivet, descend into a deep wady, climb the steep side of the eastern spur and gain a view of the town of Bethany. A closer inspection will not increase our attachment or respect for the modern town. From this point one can get a very comprehensive view of the wilderness of Judea that lies between the valley of the Jordan and the central mountain range; for the desert reaches almost to the city.

It is a view at once curious and suggestive. Its conformations, due to the character of the soil composing it, are unlike anything I have seen and are only approached by the Bad Lands of western North Dakota. Except for two months in the year, every part of this wilderness is devoid of vegetation, except where an occasional spring in the mountains sends its little stream through the wadies. Along this stream a few shrubs find life, but are so hidden in the gorge-like valleys as to be beyond vision, and thus have no effect upon general appearances. Occasionally in the landscape can be seen a conical hill, looking very much like a Montana butte. The limestone mountains have taken during the ages many strange forms, and are honeycombed with caves in which the jackal, hyena and other animals find protection from the hot rays of the summer sun and the cold rains of winter. And beyond the Ghor—the name the natives give to the Jordan valley—rise the purple hills of Moab looking like a wall against the sky.

From this Bethany spur one can ascend gradually to the summit of the mount itself, going in a northerly direction and passing on the way one of the traditional sites of the village of

Photograph by E. Warren Clark. MOUNT OF OLIVES AND GARDEN OF GETHSEMANE.

The Hills Round About

Bethphage. Two buildings mark the place. From here the road is quite steep. On either side are terraces well cared for and yielding profitable returns, as would most of these barren-looking hillsides of Judea if they had proper attention. Soon the place where recent excavations have been made is reached. The Christian world had forgotten that the early defenders of its religion had built imposing edifices upon Olivet. There are scattered allusions to such churches in the writings of some of the Fathers, but since the Moslem possession of the land all traces of the buildings themselves had disappeared. A native Christian, sinking for a foundation for a house he proposed to erect came upon some well preserved pillars *in situ*. The report soon spread and the excavator of the Palestine Exploration Society, who was then operating on Mount Zion, unearthed a number of columns and three small rooms with well preserved mosaic floors.

Felix Fabri, the great traveller, who describes in detail all he saw in Palestine, passed right by the place of these discoveries over 400 years ago. As he mentions nothing about them it is altogether probable that they were then buried beneath the surface.

Besides the rooms, or perhaps chapels, above mentioned, cisterns, a pool and drains were unearthed. In one of the pavements was found a very interesting well-executed mosaic inscription in Greek letters.

The summit of the mount is soon reached or rather one of the summits, for there are really three. The principal one, however, is meant and this is the one that has been selected by Latins and Greeks as a suitable place to locate some of their religious buildings. The Greeks—as usual—own most of the desirable property here and have spoiled it with their structures; not that these are not fine and costly buildings, but because Olivet is one of the places one would prefer to see free from any effort at human ornamentation. But here they have their church, and tower and shrines and residences of ecclesiastical functionaries. The Latins are vying with the Greeks and have their chapel of Paternoster, and have lately purchased quite a tract of land and are preparing to build something. It will probably mark some traditional site— whether authentic or not matters little.

The Russian tower is a very imposing edifice, and from its lofty summit can be had a most excellent view. It is said, and correctly, that the Russians have so located towers on certain high points throughout the land that each can be plainly seen from the others that are near it on either side. It is also said, though I cannot vouch for the correctness of this, that they have a well-established and well-understood code of signals, and that while these towers were ostensibly built for religious purposes they were really intended as a preliminary to Russian occupation of the country. It is no secret that the great Muscovite power would willingly add this bit of Turkey to her present immense territory. The other European powers know this, and it is whispered that if Turkey is ever dismembered one or two of them may put in a claim for Palestine. There is also a desire on the part of Christendom outside the Czar's dominions that when a change comes it may be a beneficial one to the long oppressed Holy Land, and with this there is a deep-seated and almost universal conviction that Muscovite civilization is but little in advance of that illustrated by the Turk.

It was somewhere near this summit of Olivet that Christ viewed the city and wept over it; somewhere near that He gathered the Twelve at various times and taught them what it was necessary for them as first ministers of a new Gospel to know; somewhere near that "a cloud received Him out of their sight." At the same time there is no evidence whatever that any of the memorials of these events, which various branches of the church have built, are located on the places where these events took place. For most of them even the tradition is comparatively recent. The place of the Ascension

The Hills Round About

cannot be where the church of that name now stands in which is shown on a limestone rock a marking somewhat resembling a footprint which is reputed to be the spot of earth last touched by the pierced foot of the Christ.

On Ascension day an immense crowd of native Christians, and whatever pilgrims are in the city, resort to this place. Various services commemorative of the day are held. A circular wall, which, judging from the broken pedestals of columns built in it, follows the line of an ancient wall, surrounds the small chapel of the Ascension. On this day the ground which it encloses is occupied by tents of the various churches. Each must be careful not to encroach upon territory allotted to another. A Moslem minaret overlooks all, and, as at the Holy Sepulchre, the followers of the Arab Prophet hold in check the followers of the Prince of Peace.

The chapel of the Paternoster is near the top of the mount on the southwestern slope, and is a very pretty little building. Upon the walls of an arcade built around a small garden is inscribed the Lord's Prayer in thirty-two different languages. The Princess Latour d'Auvergne built and endowed this chapel, and at her death her body was brought here and interred. The Carmelite Sisters reside in a near-by convent and care for this chapel. Prayer is made by them continually in this place, and no matter what hour of the day or night one were to enter he may see the sweet, holy face of one of these sisters as she kneels.

Coming down the western slope by one of the old roads, the one nearest the chapel of the Lord's Prayer, we are soon in an ancient Hebrew cemetery. The whole side of the mount along here is covered with the rude slabs lying flat upon the graves, some of them with the inscriptions clear and legible, others so worn by time that not a vestige of the epitaph can be made out. For centuries this has been a burial place of the Jews, and though there have been periods when they sought sepulture in other quarters they have come back to this. From the bed of the Kedron very nearly to the summit of Olivet the stones seem almost as close together as they can be laid. But the graves are used again. The dust of forgotten millions laid here in the time of the city's prosperity and later in her adversity awaits the awakening trump. For the Jews believe that those of their people who are buried here will have precedence in the resurrection, and many of the sons of Israel, whose whitening heads and tottering steps indicate that their earthly pilgrimage is nearly ended, come to spend their last days in their ancestral city that they may "be gathered unto their fathers" on the slope of Olivet.

Thus far the origin of the name Olivet has not been mentioned. It dates from the time of the Vulgate translation of the Bible, in which translation the Greek name of the mountain in Acts i. 12 is given as Olivetum. Of course the original name was given because of the abundance of olive trees growing on its sides and summit. The name is hardly applicable now, for the mountain, except here and there, has been stripped of its olive groves. In one of the depressions on the northwest side is a good-sized orchard yet remaining and, because of some ancient rock cuttings, here some have located Gethsemane, taking these cuttings as the remains of oil presses. The fig-tree still may be seen, though the pine, myrtle and palm that flourished in our Lord's time have entirely disappeared.

Jerusalem and Olivet are often mentioned together in Bible history, so often that they are "inseparably united." Dean Stanley[1] says that Olivet was, "The Park, the Ceramicus, the Campus Martius of Jerusalem." Before Jerusalem had become a Jewish possession the northern summit of this mountain had been selected as the site for one of the Hebrew holy cities. The tabernacle was set up here in the priestly city of Nob after the loss of the Ark in the Philistine wars. Here the worship of Jehovah was carried on before the temple was built on the

[1] Sinai and Palestine, p. 187.

lower Mount Moriah. When David fled from Absalom he escaped to Mahanaim, east of the Jordan, going "by the ascent of Mount Olivet." Because the sacrifice of the "red heifer" could not be offered in the temple the animal was brought to the top of this mountain and slain. But Olivet is chiefly associated with the life of Christ on earth—an association too well known to be given in detail here.

"By one of those strange coincidences, whether accidental or borrowed, which occasionally appear in the Rabbinical writings, it is said in the Mishna, that the Shekinah, or Presence of God, after having finally retired from Jerusalem, "dwelt" three years and a half on the Mount of Olives to see whether the Jewish people would or would not repent, calling "Return to me, O my sons, and I will return to you"; "Seek ye the Lord while He may be found, call upon Him while He is near"; and then when all was in vain returned to its own place. "Whether or not this story has a direct allusion to the ministrations of Christ it is a true expression of His relation respectively to Jerusalem and to Olivet. It is useless to seek for traces of His presence in the streets of the since ten times captured city. It is impossible not to find them in the free space of the Mount of Olives." [1]

The Mount of Offence lies to the southeast of the modern Jerusalem, and is usually called a part of the Mount of Olives. That this is the correct location of that elevation on which Solomon " built an high place for Chemosh, the abomination of Moab and for Moloch, the abomination of the children of Ammon," the fact that it is described as "the hill which is before Jerusalem" [2] indicates. The city at that time lay considerably further south than the modern one, and the Hill of Offence, on the side of which the village of Siloam is built, would be directly east of the southern part. It rises abruptly from the Kedron and presents on its face toward the city a very rough, rocky appearance. On these ledges of rock

[1] Stanley's "Sinai and Palestine," p. 189. [2] 1 Kings xi. 7.

Siloam is built—a quaint village, picturesque enough at a distance, but so disgustingly filthy are its inhabitants that one might well imagine that the "abominations" had never been removed.

There are some very fine sepulchral cuttings in the sides of this hill and the village is built in and over them. Otherwise there is nothing distinctive about it. It is much like hundreds of other hills along this central range. Its ancient history is not calculated to inspire respect and its modern Moslem "cliff-dwellers" are anything but attractive.

Southwest is the Hill of Evil Council, separated from Mount Zion by the deep valley of Hinnom. Its name is derived from the tradition that here was the residence of Caiaphas with whom Judas made his wretched bargain to betray his Master. Aceldama the Field of Blood is still pointed out and in Crusader times was used "to bury strangers in." Here also is the Judas tree, a desolate looking fig tree, gazed upon with awe by ignorant pilgrims, who are informed that it was the very tree on which "the traitor" hanged himself. There is that about it which warrants Barclay's characterization [1] that it is "evidently cultured and trained very carefully in due gibbet form by pio-tradition hands—well meant pious frauds of calculating monks."

This hill is honeycombed on its eastern side by ancient rock-cut tombs. The arrangement of the natural rock terraces caused it to be chosen as a necropolis when such tombs were used. They date from ancient Jewish times, were occupied in the Middle Ages as places of residence for religious recluses, then later for sepulture and now again have been—some of the better preserved—converted into human habitations and places of stabling. As usual the Greek church has secured possession of the best of them, and has made half-holy shrines of them. In one large excavation having several connected tomb chambers may be seen the skulls of hundreds of monks and

[1] "City of the Great King," p. 75.

The Hills Round About

pilgrims, thus supporting the belief that at a time not very remote it was a general burial place. The chambers here are in two stories; in the lower are these remnants of the forgotten dead; in the upper the guardian of the place dwells with his family. It is claimed for this place that it was the retreat where the apostles hid themselves during the time between the crucifixion and resurrection of their Lord. The words "The Holy Zion" in Greek characters may still be read over the entrance to this retreat. On the basis of these three words the great traveller, Clark, advocated the theory that this "Hill of Evil Council" was the real Zion. It was a foolish hypothesis, and is mentioned here only to show how small a foundation is large enough to support a theory as to the topography of Jerusalem.

It is argued by Dr. Schultz[1] that a large vaulted rock chamber, the ruins of which are to be seen in the Aceldama, was the sepulchre of Annas, father-in-law to Caiaphas, the high priest at the time of the crucifixion. Williams, in his "Holy City,"[2] supports this identification. If they are correct however, the tradition that locates here "The Field of Blood" must fall, for certainly no family of such distinction as that of Caiaphas would sell any part of their property as "a place to bury strangers in." It is not improbable that both tradition and theory are in error.

The modern city is growing in this direction as well as to the north, and, while for good reasons the intervening valley is still devoid of residences originally intended for the living, the sides and summit of the hill are having some very respectable houses built upon them. Let Jerusalem once throw off its present incubus of Turkish misrule and secure a safe and beneficent government, and this hill, and the others as well, will be built over as they were in the city's palmy days. And there are signs that these conditions are soon to be brought

[1] Shultz's "Jerusalem," p. 39.
[2] "Holy City," Vol. I., p. 62 of Supplement.

about—signs so minutely answering to the prophecies that it is only by repudiating the prophetic utterances that we can fail to read them. Surely the days that are to see Turkey in position to be classed among the powers of the earth are numbered; Reason and Revelation agree in this.

On the hill just west of the Jaffa Gate, the Nikophoria, an elevation but little higher than the plain to the south and east of it, the Greeks unearthed a very interesting tomb several years ago. The tomb is large, the work upon it well done, and one of the two marble sarcophagi found in it is as beautifully and delicately ornamented as anything of the kind that has been found near the city. The rolling stone that closed the entrance is the best preserved of its kind though it cannot be so readily examined as the one at the door of the "Tombs of the Kings." On the discovery of this tomb archæologists immediately sought an explanation for it. From accounts found in Josephus which point to this locality, it has been generally concluded that this is one of the monuments of Herod the Great and that the carved sarcophagus was the resting place of the beautiful Miriamne, the Asmonean princess whom Herod had married, and who, though reputed to be the only person this tyrant ever loved, was slain by him in a fit of mad jealousy.

The hills north of the city, with the exception of Mount Scopas, have been treated in the chapters on the "New City" and the "New Calvary." The former is really an extension of Olivet, being separated from it by a very slight depression. Titus here encamped with his legions—the Twelfth and Fifteenth—just before his destruction of the city. Josephus says of this: it is "very properly called Scopas, the prospect," "from whence the city began to be seen and a plain view might be taken of the great temple."[1] The view of the city from this point is grand. Where the Nabulus road crosses the ridge the natives have placed numerous little piles of stones, a custom

[1] Josephus' "Wars of the Jews," v. 2, § 3.

they have when coming to a place whence they get the first view of some holy site. It is a remnant of the practice followed in Old Testament times of setting up a stone of memorial.

From this account of the high places around Jerusalem the accuracy of the Psalmist's figure will be noted. These neighboring hills and those further removed, extending for miles in every direction, were the city's security, and from the contemplation of them and their protection the inspired poet drew the beautiful and expressive simile, that, " As the mountains are round about Jerusalem, so the Lord is round about his people from henceforth even forever." [1]

[1] Psalm cxxv. 2.

THE VALLEYS

Mosaic Description of Palestine—Application to the Site of Jerusalem—Effect of the Valleys—Similarity of Valleys of Palestine—Valley of Hinnom—Its Name—Character—Description—Rock-cut Tombs—Zion Slopes—Tophet—Gehenna—Jeremiah's Predictions—Junction of Kedron and Hinnom—Job's Well—Kedron Valley—Character—Description—Large Tombs—Simon the Just—Most Interesting Part of the Valley—Church of Mary—Grotto of the Agony—Gethsemane—Sentiment—Pillar of Absalom—Of Zechariah—Excavations in Kedron—Virgin's Fountain—Siloam Aqueduct—Ancient Walls at Siloam—The Tyropean Valley—View from Damascus Gate—Pools of Siloam.

CHAPTER VIII

THE VALLEYS—HINNOM, KEDRON AND TYROPEAN

IN an address issued by Moses to the children of Israel, an account of which is given in the Book of Deuteronomy, there is one sentence as accurately descriptive of the country which these wanderers were to possess as any one sentence can be made. "The land whither thou goest in to possess it, is not as the land of Egypt from whence ye came out, where thou sowedst thy seed, and wateredst it with thy foot, as a garden of herbs: But the land whither ye go to possess it, *is a land of hills and valleys*, and drinketh water of the rain of heaven" (Deut. xi. 10, 11). The italicized words briefly but accurately describe the land at large. "Hills and valleys" from one end to the other, not gradually verging the one into the other, but hills whose sides are rugged and precipitous, and valleys, which, with a very few exceptions, are but gorges torn out by winter torrents, having little arable soil in their narrow beds, but that little wonderfully fertile.

To the site and surroundings of Jerusalem the great Lawgiver's description applies; the city is built on hills and in valleys. In the day of its founding it was undoubtedly considered to be admirably located, and in later years, when its prosperity had made it the envy of ambitious kings, the wisdom of its founders was demonstrated. The deep valleys surrounding it on three sides enabled it to grow into a great city. The valleys of Hinnom and the Kedron made Jerusalem. Had they not been deep and their sides precipitous, had their courses been in any other direction, the city of Jebus and its illustrious successor would never have been here; Zion and Moriah, without Hinnom and Kedron and the valley between the two hills, would be no more conspicuous than a hundred other hills that push their heads up along that elevated ridge which extends from the Desert of the Wandering to fertile Esdraelon. They would have given no names to become so sacred to the Jewish, Christian and Mohammedan world as to be employed in description of the eternal city of God. A thousand valleys starting near the summit of this ridge cut their way through the hills till they are lost in the great valley of the Jordan or merge into the plain that borders the Great Sea; these two only—Hinnom and the Kedron—are known to all the world through the world's Book, which tells about it and the people who have dwelt there.

The valley of Hinnom takes its name from its first known possessor, or as Stanley[1] says, because in it "some ancient hero had encamped—'the son of Hinnom.'" By a combination of this proper name with the word "Ge," meaning "ravine," the word Gehenna was formed, and thus this "pleasant valley" supplies the name for the place of future punishment. The valley begins with a slight depression about half a mile north of the northwest corner of the present wall. It tends first in a southwesterly direction, then due south, where it widens considerably into a comparatively level space in which is situated the largest Moslem cemetery near the city. In the centre of this burial-place, which is a scene of desolation and neglect, is the [2] Upper Pool of Gihon, now called Birket-Mamilla. A little south of this pool the descent becomes more rapid, the limestone cliffs begin to appear on either side where they are not covered by the debris of which for ages this valley has been the receptacle. The new city is building out this way and on the east side of the valley residences and shops are being erected. A quarter of a mile lower down the Low Level aqueduct crosses the valley on nine arches. This aqueduct formerly brought the water from Solomon's Pools to the temple. The arches are now crumbling to decay

[1] "Sinai and Palestine," 172.   [2] 2 Chron. xxxii. 30; Is. vii. 3.

The Valleys

and, as they are no longer useful, no effort is made to preserve them. Just below this is a large pool, formed by throwing an embankment across the valley, formerly known as the Lower Pool of Gihon,[1] but now called Birket-es-Sultan. Over this embankment passes the carriage road leading to Bethlehem and Hebron. Beyond this there is a sudden narrowing and deepening, and as one looks to the left he can see the southwest corner of the present city wall, seemingly right above him. When the walls of the Solomonic city stood on the scarp of Zion (now occupied by Bishop Gobat's school) and swept round the southern brow of the Mount, the view must have been a very gratifying one to the lover of the city and a disheartening one to the enemy who had come against it.

On the right of the valley here the cliffs are high and present a smooth, perpendicular face. Rock-cut tombs are frequent, some of which are now used for residences by Fellahin. Above this the rock rises in terraces and forms the Hill of Evil Council. The slopes of Zion on the left are not so rugged or rocky, but are steep, and, being made up of earth and stones broken in small pieces, are very difficult of ascent. Along the narrow bed of this part of the valley are some of the finest olive trees in the neighborhood of the city. Then the valley makes an abrupt turn toward the east and widens out, forming an oblong space formerly called Tophet. This identification is in a measure conjectural, but it was certainly in this immediate vicinity that Solomon had one of his "Gardens of Delight." In order to reach Tophet from the city Jeremiah went out by the "Sun," or "East Gate." Whatever be the meaning of the word "Tophet," whether "garden," "place of burning," or "abomination," the locality so named was originally in good repute. Afterward the idols of false gods were here set up and the horrid orgies attendant upon their worship permitted. Sacrifices were offered to Baal and human victims were made to pass through the fires of Moloch—the tutelary

[1] Is. xxii. 9.

deity of the Ammonites. Ahaz and Manasseh, kings of Judah, were guilty not only of admitting, but actually practicing these abominations. The pious Josiah put a stop to such iniquities and to prevent their recurrence defiled the place by spreading human bones over it and making it the common dumping-ground for the refuse of the city. In Christ's time it was known as Gehenna, and, because of its continual fires for the burning of garbage, or from the fact that dead bodies were consumed here, it was commonly used as prefigurative of Hell. The Jewish rabbis say that "In Tophet is fixed the door of Hell." In spite of its past evil associations it is now a pleasant part of the valley, and on a hot day the shade of its olive-trees and the cool of its cliffs are very welcome.

Jeremiah twice predicted[1] that there should come a time when this valley "shall no more be called Tophet, nor the valley of the son of Hinnom, but the valley of slaughter." That the name given to it by modern Arabs is derived from a word meaning "slaughter" is somewhat conjectural; that it will sooner or later receive this name is a legitimate inference from the plain statements of prophecy. That it has earned this gruesome appellation already no one acquainted with the scenes that have here been enacted can question. Time after time it has been deluged with the blood of the slain; dead bodies have been thrown into it in such numbers that there was not earth enough to cover them, and underneath the present surface lies commingled the dust of Canaanite, Jew and Persian, Syrian, Greek, Roman, Frank and Arab.

This deep gorge of Hinnom was the great protector of the city on its western and southern sides. No foe could ever successfully scale those slopes of Zion, which in early days were even more abrupt than now. Where at present there is a loose composition of earth and small fragments of stone there was in early times the bare rock, scarped to make it even more difficult of ascent; and upon the platform made by the scraping

[1] Jer. vii. 32, and xix. 6.

stood the city walls, beyond the reach of any enginery of war then known.

Year after year for centuries the refuse of the city has been thrown over this side of Zion until now the rock is hidden from view under a depth of composite soil and stones of from one to thirty feet. On this "made" earth the Fellah lays out his garden and grows vegetables of surprising size and excellent quality.

Passing on down the valley for a short distance, seeing numerous tombs upon our right, we come to a level place of about thirty acres or so at the junction of the Hinnom and Kedron valleys. At this point we are nearly 350 feet below the level of the Mosque area on Mount Moriah. Near the south end of this level tract is the so-called Bir Eyyub (Job's Well), a well of mystery in many respects. The source of its water supply and the identification of the well with some ancient landmarks have given rise to many theories, with which we have not to do. No one can show whether this "well of blessing" is ancient or modern; it has existed since the Mohammedan occupation and by the followers of the Prophet it was first called Job's Well. The Crusaders named it after Nehemiah because the holy fire, which was hidden here during the captivity, was recovered by him.

During the summer especially the well is the centre of great activity. Women come with their water-skins slung on their backs, or drive a couple of diminutive donkeys who are able each to carry three skins full of the water. Men are continually engaged in drawing up the water. Those acquainted with life here wonder at seeing the men do this work, for whenever there is real labor to be performed the women are usually the ones who do it. As the water is over a hundred feet below the well curb the "draw" is somewhat of an effort. In the large stone troughs about the well water is always in readiness for horses, donkeys, cattle and sheep, and when a number of half-famished creatures happen to come at once the scene is exceedingly lively. They fairly scramble over each other to get at the cooling fountain.

The valley formed by the union of Hinnom and the Kedron is called by the natives Wady en Nar—Valley of Fire—a not inappropriate name as one learns by following it down through the wilderness past curious and desolate Mar Saba, till it loses itself in the desert of the Dead Sea.

The distinguishing topographical feature on the east of the city is the valley of the Kedron. It has been Jerusalem's natural protector on this quarter as Hinnom has been on the west. The name Kedron is used in preference to Jehoshaphat because more exact, though the latter is more common. Kedron is the Biblical term, the other not appearing.[1] Josephus never calls this valley Jehoshaphat; when the name began to be applied is not known. In the middle of the fourth century Jerome and Eusebius employed it and from that time until the present it has been in use. Many of the natives, both Christian and Moslem, speak of the vale as Wady Sitti Miriam,— valley of Our Lady Mary.

The name "Kedron" is, like the names of most places in this land, of doubtful origin and signification. Gesenius derives it from a Hebrew word meaning "to be black," descriptive of the dark color of the water when the brook is flowing or to the depth and obscurity of the valley itself. This is a very unsatisfactory reason to any one well acquainted with the place, for the brook never flows more than two days during the year, and there is nothing about the valley to suggest darkness.

The first depression is about a mile north of the present

---

[1] The prophet Joel surely could not have had this valley in mind (iii. 2). He must have idealized as the scene of the great conflict and judgment that valley in the wilderness of Tekoah in which Jehoshaphat gained his great victory over the allied enemies. That victory was "Jehovah's judgment." So when all nations are gathered together there also shall be Jehoshaphat—"Jehovah's judgment" upon them.

The Valleys

north wall of the city and is verdant with vineyards and olive groves. The valley tends in a southerly direction for half a mile and all along is well cultivated. Soon the rock cliffs begin and on them can be plainly seen the marks of the tools of ancient quarrymen. No doubt many of these stones found their way into the city's walls and residences. Rock-cut tombs are very abundant near the head of the valley and every few steps one may see the place where a former dweller of the city was laid away from mortal view until the hand of the enemy or vandal desecrated his resting place. The peasant farmer now plows among the tombs, goading his team of lean oxen or donkeys and shouting his abundant profanity.

This valley really deserves the name "Valley of Dead Bodies," for from earliest times all along its sides and in its bed the dead have been interred.

After its southerly course it makes a bend and runs in an easterly direction for about a quarter of a mile, then turns again to the south and continues this general direction until it is lost in the Dead Sea Valley. Just at this last mentioned turn are some exceptionally large tombs excavated in the face of the cliff. Among these is the traditional sepulchre of Simon the Just. On the anniversary of this worthy the Jews gather in multitudes at this tomb, and while the old men pray before the door the younger people seem to be holding a sort of picnic under the olive trees near at hand. This is by far the largest gathering of the "Sons and Daughters of Israel" during the year in Jerusalem. To witness it gives one an idea of the number of this part of the city's population. There are Jews of every condition from every civilized country, from the stylishly dressed representative from America or England to the degraded, unkempt specimens from Russia and Central Europe.

The most interesting part of this Kedron valley, judging it by natural scenery and hallowed associations, is that overlooked by the east wall of the city. The carriage road to

Bethany and Jericho descends the western slope at a heavy grade and just where it crosses the Kedron a most comprehensive view may be had. As one faces the south he has on his right, towering high, the Golden Gate, the interesting old "southeast corner," the Moslem tombs nestling close to the walls, and on the steep hillside the gardens and olive orchards of the Fellahin. In front of the observer is the bed of the stream, empty except for a day or two each winter, the pillar of Absalom and tombs of St. James and Zechariah with the countless grave-stones of the humble Jewish dead that are buried near. Just to the left, and very near, is the Garden of Gethsemane, lying at the roots of Olivet. On the left hand a little to the rear stands the ancient, gloomy church of St. Mary, in which are the traditional tombs of the Virgin and Joseph her husband, also those of Joachim and Anna, the father and mother of Mary.

This Church of the Virgin is undoubtedly an ancient structure, and rests its claims to cover the tomb of the mother of our Lord upon grounds similar to those used in the case of the Church of the Holy Sepulchre. The Empress Helena located the tomb and erected the first structure over it. The Church now belongs to the Greeks who tolerate the presence of other sects; but hardly with Christian toleration, if one may judge by appearances. A peculiarity of this Christian Church is that among its several altars is a praying place for Moslems. The latter religionists join with the former in venerating the memory of the mother of Christ. The example may have been given the followers of the Prophet by Omar when, as conqueror, he entered Jerusalem in 637 A. D. It is narrated by an Arab historian,[1] that as this warrior passed by the Church of Mary, then called the Church of Gethsemane, he offered two prayers. When the Crusaders arrived nothing remained of it but ruins. Mellicent, the wife of Fulke, fourth Christian

[1] Kadi Mejir-ed-Din.

OLD OLIVE TREE IN THE GARDEN OF GETHSEMANE.
Photograph by E. Warren Clark.

king of Jerusalem, in the middle of the twelfth century, erected, substantially, the structure that stands to-day.

An utterly baseless tradition fixes the place of our Lord's agony in a grotto just a little to the east of the Church of Mary. This is Latin property and is made much of because they have no proprietary right in the Church. No doubt it has been used as a sacred place for some centuries, but its form and the hole in the ceiling would lead to the belief that it was originally a cistern, or from its nearness to Gethsemane, perhaps a place for storing olive oil.

A few rods to the south is Gethsemane. There is no reason for disputing the genuineness of this site, for the tradition dating from the fourth century corresponds with the Gospel statements about the place. In Christ's time two roads left the city from the east and crossed the brook near this point. It would be a secluded spot, for those in the city would not often make the steep descent into the valley. But Christ, seeking retirement "went forth with His disciples over the brook Kedron where was a garden, into which He entered, and His disciples." The one beauty about the little, high-walled enclosure is that it is still a garden. Venerable looking olive trees, centuries old, are carefully preserved by the gardeners. They still, seven in number, yield their fruit, the oil of which commands a high price as well as the stones of the olives which are used for making rosaries. The garden is a quadrangle each side being about 200 feet long. A walk leads all round inside the wall to which visitors are admitted, but a high iron fence protected by a heavy wire netting prevents any pulling of flowers.

Most people, no matter whence they come, when Gethsemane is reached are overcome by a desire to possess some memento of the place. Had not the Franciscan monks in charge taken precautions to protect their floral treasures, the garden would soon be barren of vegetation. Though it lacks many of the natural charms possessed by it when Christ communed there with the Twelve, Gethsemane is still a pleasant, peaceful spot, where one may rest and indulge, without the distractions of superstition, the thoughts the name and place suggest.

About two hundred yards below the Garden of Gethsemane are the four sepulchral monuments whose origin and history are alike obscure. Two of these, those of Absalom and Zechariah, are monoliths, separated from the surrounding rock by the tools of the quarrymen. The other two, those of Jehoshaphat and St. James, are excavations. The first mention of these monuments is by the Bourdeaux Pilgrim (A. D. 333), who gives to the monoliths the names of Isaiah and Hezekiah. Arculfus, writing near the close of the seventh century, mentions the two excavations as the sepulchres of Simon the Just and Joseph, the husband of Mary. He also calls the tomb of Absalom that of Jehoshaphat, and this name it bore among Christians for many ages. At least since the time of Benjamin of Tudela (1170 A. D.) the Jews have regarded it as connected with Absalom and to this day treat it with the disrespect they still cherish toward the memory of that ungrateful son of David. It is beginning to show the wear of the numerous stones thrown against it.

These monoliths of Absalom and Zechariah exhibit a variety of architecture, Doric, Ionian and Egyptian. This has added to the confusion in attempts to assign dates to them. The Pillar of Absalom is generally assigned to the Græco-Roman Period. The masonry of the upper part is strongly suggestive of Egyptian influences and because of this the natives call it Pharaoh's Head-Dress. This masonry of large blocks rests upon the monolith and was necessary because the depth of rock at this point did not admit of a repetition of such work as that of Zechariah's tomb. The top of this latter tomb is pyramidal in form; but otherwise is very similar in general design to the former. The tomb of Absalom is broken in several places, and permits free entrance into its interior;

that of Zechariah is entire and has no entrance; unless there be one hidden by the accumulated earth of centuries. Unlike the tomb, or pillar, of Absalom, this of Zechariah is a very sacred place to the Jew. Their graves are close up to it and the tomb itself is covered with names written and carved in Hebrew characters. Prayers offered here are considered "specially efficacious."

Just near these tombs a second bridge on stone arches crosses the gully of the Kedron. Here the valley is narrowest and shows the marks where "the winter brook" flows. But there is no appropriateness in the phrase "the sweet-gliding Kedron"; it must have been written by one who never saw the place. A short distance south of the bridge the hills—Olivet on the east and Moriah on the west—rise abruptly; the "southeast angle" seems directly above the observer standing in the ravine; the top of the wall is 170 feet above. Captain Warren's excavations have revealed that the earth lying between the bed of the brook and this corner of the city wall is largely debris. The original east side of Moriah, or as it was when the first wall stood unhidden by the accumulations of the ages, was steeper than at present and now it is so precipitous that to ascend in a straight course is almost impossible. Warren's excavations also demonstrate that the bed of the stream has been moved at least thirty feet to the east by the debris and that it is now thirty-eight feet above its former level. When these excavations were begun, it was supposed that an underground stream would be found, as several professed to be able to detect the sound of running water. No such stream was discovered, but the soil lying near the bottom of the ancient bed was soft and muddy in places, and it is not at all improbable that in the rainy season such an underground brook does work its way through the loose earth and issue at some point further down the valley.

Five hundred yards south of this bridge is the interesting and mysterious "Fountain of the Virgin"; interesting because of its historical and topographical importance; and also because it is the only living spring near the city, unless we include the one under the school of the Sisters of Zion; mysterious, because of the intermittent flow of its waters and their peculiar brackish taste. The spring is in a cavern and the water is at least twenty feet below the level of the valley. Thirty rude steps lead down to it and up and down these steps the maids and matrons of Silwan (Siloam) go with their full and empty water pots. Because of these steps the natives often call it "Ain ed-Derej," "Fountain of Steps." In the rainy season the water flows four or five times a day, in the dry season but once or at most twice each day. This irregularity of flow can be accounted for naturally. "In the interior of the rock there is a deep natural reservoir, which is fed by numerous streamlets and has a single narrow outlet only. This outlet begins a little above the bottom of the basin, rises to a point higher than the top of the basin and then descends. As soon as the water of the basin has risen to the height of the bend in the outlet, it begins to flow through it and continues to flow on the syphon principle until it has sunk in the basin to the point where the outlet begins."[1]

An aqueduct, usually regarded as the work of Hezekiah, leads from this fountain through the rocky foundations of Ophel to the Upper Pool of Siloam. The engineering was not of the best, for the course of the aqueduct varies considerably and while the distance in a straight line from the Fountain to Siloam is only a thousand feet, the length of the channel is seventeen hundred. From a celebrated inscription found here in 1880, the oldest Hebrew inscription so far discovered, we learn that work was begun at each end; and the point where the workmen met has also been located. One wonders how such a work was planned and executed in those early times.

The valley widens a short distance below the Virgin's

[1] Baedaker "Palestine and Syria," p. 99.

The Valleys

Fountain and is soon joined by the Tyropean. These two valleys do not meet each other on a level, the Tyropean being at least thirty feet above the Kedron. Terraces lead from the one to the other. Just here is the richest garden land to be found near the city. It is watered by the Lower Siloam Pool and cultivated by the Fellahin of Silwan village. Modern excavations are demonstrating that the peasant gardeners have been growing their vegetables upon earth that covers the walls of the ancient city. Well preserved masonry of undoubted antiquity, and henceforth to be reckoned in all accounts, was uncovered in August, 1895, just where the two valleys meet and at a depth of thirty feet below the present surface. This discovery proves two things; first, how deep the soil is in these valleys of Palestine, and, secondly, how many theories on Jerusalem topography a little excavating may explode.

A hundred yards further south brings us to the junction of the Kedron and Hinnom valleys. In following these two from their starting points on the north we have surrounded the city almost entirely and described the most interesting points in each of them. There is one great event to take place in the future in the valley of the Kedron, but as it belongs to prophecy it is hardly in place in a descriptive work. Jews, Mohammedans and some Christians believe that in this valley the final judgment will be held, hence its name Jehoshaphat—Jehovah's Judgment. Whether the belief be well founded or not is a minor question to those who are prepared for that great day.

In an account of the valleys of Jerusalem that which divides the city must not be passed without remark. Josephus calls this the Tyropean, or valley of the cheese-mongers. It was a striking feature of the ancient city and is so now when viewed from certain directions. The first depression begins a short distance north of the Damascus Gate. At the north wall the valley features are hidden by immense accumulations of debris, but within the city the descent is rapid for a short distance. The observer who stands on the wall at the Damascus Gate and looks toward the south gains the very best view of the topography of the city. Right in front of him stretches the valley, the four hills—Gareb and Zion on the west, Bezetha and Moriah on the east—are plainly seen. But the modern view is quite inferior to that of the ancient city's glory, when the palaces of the wealthy crowned the two northern hills as well as the southwestern eminence, and the temple, glistening in the brilliant light, graced the summit of the southwestern hill. Bridges on immense arches spanned the Tyropean and a street adorned with columns proceeded from the main gate in the northern wall to a similar gate in the southern. Ruined foundations many feet under the surface are all that remain of the bridges, while not a vestige of the ornamental columns can be found.

Formerly a valley proceeding from near the present Jaffa Gate in an easterly direction joined the Tyropean at a point near where the modern Via Dolorosa crosses it. Some authorities have regarded this valley as a branch of the real Tyropean.

The street, now in the bed of the valley, is narrow, tortuous and generally dirty. The buildings cross it on arches; shops and residences, occupied generally by the air-despising classes of Jews and Mohammedans, line it.

A very large part of the valley included within the walls of the city is unoccupied by any buildings. Gardens and orchards of the prickly pear have taken possession of ground on which once stood the stately structures of Solomon and Herod. All along the bed of the valley is raised by the refuse and ruins thrown into it from city and temple, and the engineers of the Palestine Exploration Society had to sink their shafts from thirty to eighty feet through the debris before reaching the rock.

Passing through the south wall by the little "Dung Gate"

The Valleys

the course of the valley can be plainly seen, and, though the descent is steep, easily followed to the Pools of Siloam. It is not an attractive walk at any time; the city's sewage finds egress in this direction and charges the air with noisome odors. As the Pools of Siloam, lying in the mouth of the valley are the receptacles of this their usual condition can well be imagined. Nothing in its present degradation is so destructive to our ideas of Jerusalem's beauty and grandeur as a visit to Siloam, particularly in the rainy season when most strangers arrive. All our preconceived opinions of Siloam are of a pool of pure water surrounded by pleasant scenes; and that it was such in the Saviour's day there can be no doubt. Desolation and decay mark this part of the valley now, though the gardens are much benefited by the waters that gather in the Lower Pool.

The Upper Pool is now nearly filled with stones and earth, so that the measurements of Barclay and Robinson will not apply. The shape of it is oblong, the length being fifty, the breadth ten and depth about twelve feet. The rock-cut conduit from the Virgin's Fountain enters the pool at the northwest corner, but it brings no water now. The present stonework, is the work of the Crusaders, or perhaps of Saladin, who was very careful of the water supply of the city. Originally the water from the Virgin's Fountain filled this Upper Pool and passing out was conducted to the Lower Pool, which is only a few yards distant. Here it was preserved for use in the King's Gardens. Then as now the water could be drawn off when needed and because of its gentle flow may have given the phrase to Isaiah, "the waters of Shiloah that go softly."

Of the Lower Pool in its present condition but little can be said. It is formed by a dam thrown across the valley, and even when full of water, as it often is in winter, is insignificant in size and most unattractive. When the water gets low in early summer the place is a perfect fever hole. Of these pools it can be said that they are not in dispute; all authorities agree that they are the Siloam of Old and New Testament history, and when authorities agree, it is well to rest and be content. Would that the poet's lines were true and that we could rest

"By cool Siloam's shady rill" and see
"How fair the lily grows." [1]

[1] Heber.

THE TEMPLE HILL

Importance of—Genuineness—Theories of Topography—Temple Sites—Christian Association—Moslem Associations—Surrounded by Valleys—Ophel—Approach to Temple Hill—Visitor's Escort—Barclay—"Holy Ground"—Mosque Enclosure—Walls—"Mastaba"—Military Barracks—Acra—Simon Maccabee—Baris—Traditional Bethesda—Throne of Solomon—Golden Gate—Shushan Gate—Moslem Tradition—Flowers—View from East Wall—Bridge of Kedron—Southeast Corner—Immense Masonry—Solomon's Stables—Mosque el Aksa—Moslem Worship—"Narrow Way"—Knights Templar's Abode—Subterranean Passage to Double Gate—Well of the Leaf—Cisterns—The Holy Rock—Mosque of Omar—Kubbet es Sakrah—Architectural Beauty—Crusader Work—Sulieman—Interior Arrangement—Windows—Furnishings—The Dome—The Sacred Rock—Traditions—Size—A Moslem Legend—Cave beneath the Rock—"Well of Souls"—Judgment Seat of David.

IX

THE TEMPLE HILL

IN our accounts of Jerusalem in the time of David and Solomon and in the time of Christ the eastern hill has enjoyed a large share of attention. And if there be any part of the Holy City that can justly claim a place in history it is this —the Religious Mountain—venerated alike by the entire Jewish, Christian and Mohammedan worlds. Besides this, there is a satisfaction in speaking about it and the events that have taken place there and the world famous structures that have graced it, because it is an assured site. Among all the wild theories that have been advanced I know of none that doubts the genuineness of Mount Moriah. Accounts differ when it comes to assigning the locality to the event or to the building, but not as to the identity of the Mount itself.

One has to linger in the Holy City but a short time before becoming possessed by the "Devil of Doubt" about many things he sees and hears. There is just one thing certain about the many more or less "holy places" and that is their uncertainty. One authority asserts positively that Zion was on the southwestern hill, another just as positively informs us that to locate Zion anywhere but on the southeastern hill is an evidence of your ignorance. The present Church of the Holy Sepulchre is proved by one "beyond a doubt" to be on the place where our Lord was crucified and buried; by others it is demonstrated "beyond a doubt" that the crucifixion and sepulture could by no means have taken place here. Back numbers of the Report of the Palestine Exploration Fund— that record of the actual discoveries and fanciful opinions of many learned men—could not have been made more bewildering if mystification had been the only object of their editors. Practically every foot of underground and aboveground Jerusalem has been fought over.

There is no cessation of hostilities. Occasionally a truce is declared, but it is only for a breathing spell. The combatants get a little new information, or in their fertile brains imagine some, and the pens fly again. Some other champion of some other theory of location reads this real or supposed addition to our knowledge of Jerusalem and has an immediate call to protect the world against such vagaries. The results of the present exploration south of the city are sure to evoke a horde of opinions, each one backed by a self-appointed champion. Nor do we have to wait till results are announced. The gentleman in charge has but to express an opinion concerning some discovery he has made. Then he and those who are interested "discover" that he knows nothing about it.

In the midst of these diverse opinions it is refreshing to climb Mount Moriah and gaze upon the absolutely assured. Here some things can be seen that are not questioned, and for a time the Devil of Doubt is cast out. In this enclosure, belonging to the Dome of the Rock, stood the small, but exquisitely beautiful, Temple of Solomon; and later, the larger, and perhaps more imposing, Temple of Herod. Let us not ask just where they stood or we shall hear jangling voices. Enough, here! This fact concerning this enclosure on the levelled top of Moriah attaches to it an importance which gives it an unique position in the religious history of the world. Add to this that here were witnessed some of the great works, and were heard some of the great words of the Founder of the Christian faith; add to this that in the estimation of the Moslem the Rock is second only to the sacred Káaba at Mecca and we have a place that is without a competitor for the favor and veneration of the religious world. And this apart from any fables or traditions or fancies, many of which have come down to our time and are piously believed.

Like its loftier neighbor to the west Mount Moriah is surrounded on three sides by valleys; the Tyropean on the west and the Kedron on the east join each other on the south about half a mile from the south wall of the city. The part now outside of the wall was once a very important section of the city itself. Here was the original Salem of Melchizedek and later the lower city of the Jebusite. It seems to be pretty generally believed, and recent excavations are favoring the belief, that the walls of the Solomonic city extended clear down to a point very near the junction of the valley of the Tyropean with that of the Kedron. The part of the Mount now on the outside of the south wall was formerly called Ophel and is often so named now. The word means "a mound" or "tower." It is first used in connection with the improvements in fortification made in the reign of Jotham[1] about 775 B. C.

Ophel may once have been crowned with towers that were the pride and security of those who dwelt under their protection, but no sign of them now remains above ground. It is all given over to the peasant gardener, and the only buildings on it are the wretched little stone and mud huts of the Fellahin, who must live right in the gardens if they want to benefit by anything that grows in them. They must keep a strict and continual watch, or some near, or remote, neighbor will take advantage of their absence and the darkness, and in one night appropriate the product of an entire season. Thieving is a fine art among the Fellahin of Palestine. They prefer to rob a Frank, as all foreigners are called, but in the absence of Franks will not hesitate to prey upon each other.

However interesting the southern slope of Mount Moriah is, the important part has always been that now included within the Haram Es-Shareef, or temple enclosure; and to this section our discussion will be confined. Coming from any of the hotels in the city one passes down the western slope of Zion by the appropriately named David's street, turns a few steps to

[1] 2 Chron. xxvii. 3.

the right when in the heart of the city and in the midst of the intensely foreign-looking Turkish bazaars, and is on Temple street, which in my opinion runs along the crest of Millo, one of David's fortifications. This takes us across the Tyropean valley, which, however, is here so filled with the debris of ruined cities as to be almost imperceptible. The visitor may enter the sacred ground of the noble Sanctuary by any one of eleven gates. There are eight of these on the west side and three on the north. The east and south are closed though there are gates on both sides now filled with masonry which show that entrance on these sides was once possible.

No Christian or Jew can ever enter unless properly escorted —and "properly" according to Turkish idea of propriety. Those visiting the city now may congratulate themselves, however ludicrous or annoying Turkish restrictions may be, that they are permitted to see this enclosure and its attractions, certainly the great sights of Jerusalem to-day, at all. Dr. Barclay,[1] writing in the fifties, speaks of the impossibility then of securing entrance; he says: "So great is the fear inspired by the clubs and cimeters of the blood-thirsty savages, the Mauritanian Africans, to whose jealous custody the entire Haram is committed, that few indeed have been found of sufficient temerity to hazard even the most furtive and cursory reconnoissance of this tabooed spot." Then the best a Christian "dog" could do was to get an order to view the grounds from the top of the Serai; and as this was troublesome and expensive and after all very unsatisfactory it was seldom done. All a party has to do now is to send word to their consul specifying the time they wish to visit the Haram. The consul by a letter to the Governor of Jerusalem requests permission, which is refused only during some of the great Moslem feasts when ignorant fanaticism runs dangerously high. Then under the escort of a Consular Cawass, or guard, whose clothes are brilliant and who carries a wicked-looking cimeter at his side,

[1] "City of the Great King," p. 470.

The Temple Hill

aided by a Turkish soldier, less gaily caparisoned, but feeling his importance none the less, the visitor is "properly escorted." He is now free from all annoyances, except the wearisome monotony of that word—omnipresent in the Orient—"bucksheesh." A smile is not out of place on the face of an American as he sees his military escort conducting him through the streets of the Holy City, and imagines what a sensation he would create were he to pass along any street of any city in his own land similarly conducted. But he is now in Turkey, where nothing is done as other people do it.

Once inside you are on "holy ground," if there is any such thing; and if there is not you are on what Jew and Moslem consider "holy ground"—the holiest part of the Holy City. Jewish, Christian and Moslem tradition clusters about every spot here, but tradition may be dismissed where there is so much history. The entire enclosure is thirty-six acres in extent. There is thus included within the temple walls about one-sixth of the entire space bounded by the walls of the city. The walls of the Mosque area are of unequal length and face the cardinal points. Nor is it to be wondered at, considering the different masons who at different ages centuries apart worked on them, that they are not uniform in design or material. Beyond a doubt some of the work of the masons of Solomon can yet be seen; also that of Herod's artificers. As the Crusaders, than whom there have been no more industrious builders in the Christian era, once held this Mount, we can depend upon it that they laid their hands to this work. Added to all this is the inferior work of Sulieman I., the second of the Ottoman sultans who ruled over Jerusalem. The last is inferior to the others in the size of the stones and the manner in which they are dressed. But, as it has stood the ravages of time for nearly four and a half centuries, and is yet in a good state of preservation, it is not unworthy of at least a passing remark. The stones were not quarried by the Moslem builders, because so much labor was unnecessary as there was abundance of good wall-making material, the remains of houses and Christian Churches, at hand. For the time they were constructed they were admirable for defence. To-day they are toy fortifications: a modern gun would batter them to powder in a few minutes.

On the west and north side of the Mosque area are Moslem residences overlooking the enclosure. Most of the people dwelling here are in some way connected with the care of the holy place. As a rule they are not a pleasant looking set, and inspire a Christian "infidel" with a belief that they would do him bodily injury if they dared. They certainly consider that such unbelievers have no right to enter their Noble Sanctuary, no matter if their own governor did grant the permission. While the adults never annoy visitors except by sinister looks, the children sometimes make the intruder uncomfortable by volleys of dirt and small stones.

Passing in at the Gate of the Cotton merchants, we turn to the left to make an interior circuit of the walls, thus gradually approaching the Dome of the Rock—the chief glory of the place. A number of small raised places will be seen all over the area. These are called by the Arabs "mastaba" and are places of prayer. Several fountains are visible whose water is used for religious ablutions. They are blessings for other occasions than the strictly religious, for Moslems living near are permitted to take all the water they need for home use.

In the northwest corner it is to be noticed that the level is higher than at any other part of this particular platform. This is a very picturesque spot just now with the row of arcades on the west, the high military barracks on the north, and just in the corner a tall and graceful minaret, from which is heard at regular intervals the muezzin call to prayer. Besides its picturesqueness this corner has great historical interest. It was the site of the ancient Acra which was a fortress and which gave the name to the hill on which it stood. In the days of Jewish degeneracy, just before the revolt of the Maccabees

The Temple Hill

against the power of Syria, the fort was in the possession of the enemy. What had doubtless been intended by its original builders, namely a protection for the temple, was instead a protection to the enemy who from its walls could see all that went on in the sacred area. Simon, the Maccabee, having aroused the patriotism of his fellow Jews, drove out the hated foreign power and entered the citadel in triumph. The opinion is held generally that under the Maccabees the rock on which Acra stood was cut away, and that particular fort destroyed. The evidence on the scarped rock is conclusive that at some time it was so dealt with. But the Asmonean princes erected another fortress-palace a little to the north of Acra and gave it the name Baris; this was increased in size and strength by Herod, who, in honor of his great Roman patron, named it Antonia. The severest contests in Jewish history were fought around this northwest corner. The Apostle Paul was rescued from the infuriated Jews in the temple by soldiers from this citadel.[1]

It is still a military barracks and the soldiers of the Sultan look out over the same enclosure where formerly the Syrians, the Jews and the Romans watched the worshippers in the temple of their time. Here, as everywhere throughout the city where it was possible, the later builders have used the foundations laid by their predecessors. Above the rock scarp made by the Maccabees are some of the huge stones dating from Roman times. The smaller Saracenic masonry rests upon these. It is altogether probable that, in the days of Jerusalem's glory as a city, this stronghold was much larger, extending further toward the east, perhaps as far as the western end of the Pool of Bethesda. If so it has been destroyed and never rebuilt, for now from the barracks to this point there is nothing but some Moslem residences. Going under the arcade on this northern side one can look down into the immense hollow wherein the time of our Lord was one of the great

[1] Acts xxi. 27.

reservoirs of the city. It is now dry and is gradually being filled with debris. At present the bottom of the pool is about sixty-five feet below the level of the arcade. Formerly a valley ran from northwest to southeast, and its depression was utilized to make Antonia more difficult of attack and to afford room for the pool. Captain Warren was permitted to excavate in this vicinity, and among other interesting discoveries unearthed an opening in the north wall of the Haram through which he supposes the superfluous water of the pool found an exit. The natives now call this the "Pool of Israel."

Omitting the northeast corner, where is nothing of particular interest, we walk across to the east wall, meeting it at a small mosque called the "Throne of Solomon." This is the product of Moslem fables about the Wise King; their credulity enables them to believe that here Solomon was found dead upon his seat of judgment. There is one thing repeated here a thousand times, that is convincing as to the sacredness of the site. The place where a saint has been in life or where his body rests in death is regarded by the faithful as specially suitable for prayer. At such a spot a continual prayer can be offered without the presence of the suppliant. A piece of cloth from his garment will be a perpetual reminder to the saint, so he takes it and ties it on the tomb or house that has been erected in memory of the revered one. So all over the screened windows of this modern Mosque that commemorates the death of Solomon, are the many colored rags which have been torn from the garments of the devout, hardly an addition to the beauty of the Mosque.

A few steps further to the south and still along the east wall, bring one to the Bab el-Daheriyeh, or Golden Gate. This considerable structure can only be entered from the west. The custodians of the Mosque usually object to exhibiting it; but a little extra persuasion of the financial kind, in this, as in most other particulars, succeeds in smoothing the way. The "holy men" of this holy place are weak in the presence of this kind of temptation, and after an intimate acquaintance with them, I am convinced that they never grieve over their frequent falls and never pray to be delivered from the temptation.

The Golden Gate bears evidence of antiquity, though in its present form it dates from about the fifth century of our era. It was near here, perhaps on the very same site, that the ancient Shushan gate stood. A mistake is often made by confounding the Golden Gate with the Beautiful Gate of the temple.[1] The latter, which was in the inner court, was entirely destroyed when the Romans under Titus entered the city, and was never rebuilt. The date of this Golden Gate has been a fruitful source of discussion; the opinion advanced above is that generally accepted. The gate on the interior presents a double arch resting on large monolithic posts. The arches are ornately carved, and before they were defaced by time and neglect, must have been very beautiful. It is certainly one of the mural attractions of the interior of the Haram. Being now properly cleared out and cared for, it is worth visiting and going to the little necessary annoyance and expense of securing entrance. A flight of stone stairs leads down to the gate proper, which is fully twenty-five feet below the surface of the surrounding ground. It is, however, much more of a gate than were the other gates of the city. The one who enters sees a large room, in the middle of which stand two large pillars supporting the domes of the roof. There are several features about the interior decoration which authorities on architecture regard as proof of the Byzantine origin of this part of the structure.

The Golden Gate has been closed for many years. Soon after the conquering of the Christian forces by Saladin, this double entrance at the east was walled up. In Crusading times on the anniversary of Christ's triumphal entry into the city, the Latins made a great procession and came down from

[1] Acts iii. 2.

the Mount of Olives carrying palm branches and shouting "Hosanna," and entered by this gate. The Moslem custodian and others of the Faithful, have informed me that they walled up the entrance so as to keep the Christians out. There is a tradition among the present proprietors that on some Friday Jerusalem will fall into the possession of the Christians and that the conqueror will enter by this gate. This most reasonable of their local traditions is also sure of verification in the near future, except as to the use of this gate for entrance.

Keeping the course southward along the wall or on the grassy space near it, the visitor in February or March is struck by the profusion of wild flowers which display the most brilliant and most delicate hues. Conspicuous among them for abundance and rare coloring is the "lily of the field," which one has but to see to understand the force of the Master's assertion that "Solomon in all his glory was not arrayed like one of these." All along here for perhaps eight hundred feet the wall above the surface is modern, but is built upon very ancient foundations. On the battlement of the wall, as one approaches the southeast corner, is one of the best view-points in Jerusalem. Elevated high above the Kedron it looks but a short distance across the valley to the slopes of Olivet, where rest the remains of tens of thousands of the children of Abraham. This cleft was once spanned by a bridge—and according to Moslem belief will be so again on the final day of judgment. Instead of a foot-bridge, however, like the first structure, this last one will be a fine wire. Every soul will have to pass over this from the Mount to the temple wall. The faithful will accomplish the crossing in safety; all others will fall into the deep Kedron valley which will open into hell. A horizontal column sticking out of the wall marks the place where the western end of this bridge for spirits will end. The strange part of the story is that Christ will be on Mount Olivet to welcome the successful; Mohammed's position will be where the bridge starts on the Temple wall.

From this southeast corner the whole course of the Kedron valley, from the Tomb of the Virgin to the junction with the valley of Hinnom, can be traced. It is a giddy height now to look down from and must have been much more so before the immense accumulations of debris had gathered outside the wall. This corner is a famous one from an archæological point of view, and is subject of much difference of opinion. I see no reason for doubting its antiquity; I would even refer the immense stones here to the time of Solomon. The marvel is how any builders at any time were able to put these stones in position. On this corner was one of the strong towers, which the Jews always took special pains to erect of the largest and best material. The "chief corner stone" must have been an object of great care.

From this corner there is an entrance down some rude stairs to the substructures where we gain a good idea of the immense amount of labor necessary to bring this part of the temple area up to the required level. Could this southeastern slope of Moriah be cleared of all the works of human hands we should probably find that there was a rapid descent from the "holy rock" to the bed of the Kedron. The ancient levellers were good engineers as well as laborers, and in preparing the sacred enclosure, they rightly spared neither money nor labor to make it worthy to be dedicated to the worship of their God.

The corner stairs bring us first to a small praying place in which is shown the alleged "cradle of Jesus," which has on it the very marks that disprove the claim. It is a small prayer niche that has had its position changed. The Mohammedans treat it with great veneration. Our Moslem soldier kneels down beside it, lays his two hands upon it and rubs them over his face. Passing through a door to the west one gets his first view of the "Stables of Solomon," wonderful relics of an uncertain age, but certainly attesting the skill of those who laid their foundations. They are not stables and were never intended to be so used. However, the Crusaders did so use them and the holes pierced through the square corners of the columns show where their horses were tied. These columns belong to the time of either Herod or Solomon, and do credit to whoever built them; they are about a hundred in number and are the support of more modern arches upon which rest the large flag-stones on the surface above. One can wander around in these vaults and among this forest of imposing columns for some time and not grow weary unless, unfortunately for himself and his companions, he belongs to that lackadaisical class of people—too many of whom waste their "substance" in coming to Jerusalem—who can find no interest in anything. There are fragments of ancient columns and arches built in the walls. The place where the "single gate" and "triple gate" were, ancient entrances to the temple from the south, still have their foundations preserved. These large square columns may extend for some distance down into the ground. Many of them are exposed for twenty-five feet of their length. They are composed of large, square, smooth-faced stones with edges slightly bevelled. Interesting finds would undoubtedly result could permission be had to excavate here. But so long as the Turk has possession the world will be none the wiser and those who should like to know will continue to speculate.

We must return to the surface by the same way entrance was had, turn to the west, cross a large paved court and enter a side door of the Mosque el Aksa, now a holy structure of the Moslems where all their public services are held, but originally a Christian Church, or basilica, built by the Emperor Justinian in honor of the Virgin. In the conquest by Omar this was one of the buildings he considered would be useful to his co-religionists. Taking it he rededicated it and called it Jam 'i el Aksa. It is a mistake to call it the Masjid el Aksa for it is now nothing more than a mosque. Masjid is the term correctly applied to the entire temple area. This name, Masjid el Aksa, is taken from the Koran [1] which refers to the

---
[1] xvii. 1.

ascent to heaven of Mohammed from the temple of Jerusalem. The passage reads: "Praise be unto Him who transported his servant by night from El Masjid el Haram (*i. e.* the 'Sacred Place of Adoration' at Mecca) to El Masjid el Aksa (*i. e.* the Remote Place of Adoration at Jerusalem)."[1] Masjid is from the word "sejada," meaning "to adore." "El Aksa" means "the Remote" and is applied to Jerusalem because of its great distance from Mecca.

The Mosque el Aksa is notable for its size rather than any attractiveness of architecture or ornamentation. It is by far the largest single room in the city. To it every Friday comes the Turkish Governor of Palestine. At the same hour when His Serene Highness, the Sultan, is attentive to the services in The Palace Mosque, at Constantinople, his representative is enjoying the privilege of worship in a much more holy place. To one who knows nothing of the Moslem form of worship the genuflexions and prostrations of a company of the faithful are peculiar sights. There is a devoutness about it all that is to be commended. The immense oratory of the Mosque el Aksa is a splendid place in which to witness it, though on Friday, the day when most is to be seen, the visitor to the city is not admitted.

The Mosque was formerly cruciform. This form did not please the conquerors and in the restoration at the time of El Mahdi two aisles were added, one on each side, and thus the objectionable feature was altered to suit the taste of the advocates of "the Star and Crescent." Much old material has been worked into this edifice, and it would be hard to disprove the assertion—just as hard as it would be to prove it—that the pillars in nave and transept are relics of the Herodian temple. That they were not originally designed for this is evident, particularly in the transept where the lack of uniformity is very noticeable. To stop and inspect all the details of this Mosque would be more than any traveller does and much

[1] Besant & Palmer, "History of Jerusalem," p. 93.

more than any reader would wish to do. However, there are two features worthy of mention. There are several pieces of ancient marble worked into curious shapes which undoubtedly date from the long ago and may have been part of the wealth of marble with which the temple of Herod was adorned. The antiquary or admirer of the curious will not pass these by. The second feature is the pulpit. This stands at the eastern end of the Mosque and is composed of intricately and beautifully carved wood, the details of which are perfect. It is the work of an artist in wood, who lived in Aleppo several centuries ago, and gives an admirable illustration of the patience characteristic of the artist who is entirely faithful to his art.

Those who are interested in superstitious beliefs and practices will view with wonder the narrow space between two dark granite pillars just west of the pulpit. It was believed, and is yet by many of the "faithful," that any one who could not pass between these pillars could never enter Paradise. It was a matter on which there was no wish to be in doubt, and for centuries the effort must have been made, for the eastern column is considerably worn away with the attrition of human beings who have successfully passed through the "narrow way." Modern visitors or worshippers must remain in doubt, for an iron frame has been securely fixed between the columns.

Looking to the west from this point a long double colonnade may be seen, the vaulting of which is pointed. It is of little interest now and seldom visited. But here in the days of the Christian domination the Knights Templar lived. They felt that their location was an important one and called it Palatium Solomonis—the Palace of Solomon. They were the most aristocratic of all the orders of that time, and this may have been the secret of that success which resulted in their fall. Wealth poured in upon them and with its increase departed humility and consecration to the cause they had sworn to support. They were soon in open hostility to the Church and professed to have had a religious experience beyond that accorded to the vulgar Christian. A little more than a century after the institution of this order by Hugh de Payens and Geoffrey de St. Aldemar, in company with seven other Knights, it had grown until it numbered nineteen thousand. Each of these members was wealthy enough to support a knight in the Holy Land. And yet they did but little at any time to redeem the country from its Moslem possessors. They had a secret creed which confessed that there was no higher ecclesiastical power than the order itself. "It owned no bishop and would obey no pope."[1] This was a novel position for those days.

As we come out of the Mosque el Aksa by the main door at the western porch, a few steps to the right reveal a dark underground passage running south under the east side of the mosque; it is composed of heavy masonry on the sides and vaulted with smaller stones. An inclined plane leads down to another level where we perceive that we are in a double passage. Light from a small window in the southern wall shows us eight high steps which bring us down to another level and enable us to get a good idea of the substructions of El Aksa. The temple does not lack for solidity: two short, but very thick monolith columns support the arches, and appear able to carry the burden for many centuries yet. With an eye to preserving these great stones or perhaps adding to their rugged grandeur, the custodian has given them a coat of whitewash. The result awakens a desire in the bosom of the beholder to choke the unpoetic rascal who did it. There is no doubt about his rascality.

But the main points of interest here are the unquestioned and well-preserved remains of the old Double Gate, called in the Talmud the Huldah Portal. Three columns are visible and are of the size and workmanship that causes them to be assigned to the Jewish period. The lintels of the gates are still here and the sculptured capitals of the pillars. Time has

[1] Besant & Palmer, p. 279.

laid his hand upon them and the Moslem has done his worst with whitewash. These detract a little from present appearances, but not from their record as memorials of a more glorious past. Being the main entrance to the temple enclosure from the south we may be certain that more than once the Teacher out of Galilee with his unpretending pupils went by this way into "His Father's House."

Following the direction the Divine One would thus take, the cistern called the Well of the Leaf is passed. Moslem tradition holds that a gate to Paradise leads from this and that one of Omar's companions passed through it, and as proof showed a leaf from one of the unfading trees; nobody else has ever succeeded in finding the Paradise door. Here are also immense cisterns, the ones we read about in accounts of the ancient city, whose waters supplied the great demands of the temple service. Solomon was their builder, and into them through the tortuous aqueduct poured the stream from the "Sealed Fountain." Was this the "river, the streams whereof make glad the city of our God"? One of these hewn cisterns was called the "Sea," and, when its dimensions are known, the name does not seem inappropriate; it is forty feet deep and seven hundred and thirty-eight feet in circumference.

But the Holy Rock and the Dome that covers it must now attract us. By a flight of twenty-one steps we reach a broad platform whose sides face the cardinal points. A number of places of minor importance are here, connected with Jewish, Christian and Mohammedan traditions. To mention them all by name would be neither interesting nor instructive and to recount their improbable fables and fancies would be unprofitable.

Standing upon the summit of Moriah, a place made sacred by Divine appointment and by the prayerful veneration of the millions who believe in one only God, a height whence rose those temples—visions of snow and gold-emblematic of purity and consecration, a place from which ascended to heaven the smoke from the altar of offering illustrating the human consciousness that "without the shedding of blood is no remission," a place which has successively during three thousand years been in the possession of Jew and Christian and Mohammedan, a place now graced with one of the most exquisite structures on earth,—how little do the things of man seem here, how little man himself! It is a place for thought.

The present building is popularly called the Mosque of Omar, but it is not a mosque nor had Omar anything to do with it. This caliph does deserve credit for his reverence for the place and that he did erect a mosque near here is a matter of history. The account of his locating his building informs us that he asked a Jew where would be the best site and received the reply, "Place it behind the Holy Rock so that the two places of adoration, that of Moses and of Mohammed, may be identical." "Ah," said Omar, "thou art still a Jew and leanest to Jewish notions. The best place for the mosque is in front of the rock." So there it was built— a large, square, wooden structure capable of holding three thousand people. The present building called by the Moslems Kubbet es-Sakhrah, or "Dome of the Rock," is the most beautiful bit of architecture in Jerusalem. This is no great praise. Much more might be said in its favor, and as Professor Lewis in "The Holy Places of Jerusalem," says, "It is undoubtedly one of the most beautiful buildings existing." Mr. Fergusson, speaking as an architect, affirms that it is "unrivalled in the world." The latter opinion is at least extravagant.

The building is octagonal, each side being sixty-six and a half feet in length. It is faced from the ground to the window sills with slabs of marble peculiarly grained and placed so as to produce a very pleasing effect. That some of this work is from the days of the Crusaders, is more than probable. These Christian warriors took the city in 1099 A. D., and were wise enough not to destroy the work of the Moslems around the Holy Rock. They appropriated and added to it. Above the marble facing on the exterior walls are very fine tiles which took the place of marble and were placed by Sulieman the Magnificent in 1561. In fact a complete restoration was effected by this monarch and the Dome is to-day much as he left it. Visitors cannot but admire the marvellously executed inscriptions in tile work which run entirely around the building. Each tile had to be written and burned separately, but the result is certainly all the designer could wish. One cannot help noticing also that this gem of architecture—for such the Kubbet es-Sakhrah is—is being neglected by its owners. There are many signs of decay. Some of the marble slabs and tiles have fallen off and no effort is being made to replace them. There is even a suspicion that the religious heads of the institution will, for a sufficient consideration, cause them to be removed and find their way into the hands of "infidel" strangers. With all this neglect and vandalism it is one of the best preserved of religious buildings now in the possession of the followers of the Arab prophet. I have yet to see one that is not in decay.

There is beauty still here and grandeur, and one can come often without weariness. Within all is in good condition. Immense elegant rugs of Turkish design and manufacture, the gift of the present Sultan—hide the floor; their colors combining well with the other furnishings of the place. Two circles of variously colored concentric marble pillars divide the interior into three apartments. The shafts of the pillars are of different kinds of marble. That they were not especially constructed for their present positions is readily concluded from the fact that they differ in form, height and in some cases in design. The capitals of the columns are all gilded, but differ in size and design. On some of the capitals blocks of stone had to be placed in order to bring the entire height of the column to twenty feet. On these the arches are supported. The larger circle consists of eight six-sided piers

The Temple Hill

and two columns placed between each two piers, to assist in the support of the roof proper. The smaller circle of pillars, which supports the dome, consists of four piers, each with three columns on each side of it. The ironwork between the pillars is the work of the Crusaders and very artistic. The dome itself is of wood, covered with lead, and as black as paint can make it. From the ground to the crescent that surmounts the dome the distance is 115½ feet; the diameter of the dome is sixty-six feet and the vault thirty-nine feet. Within the dome is colored a beautiful blue and ornamented with gilded stucco in the Arabesque style. The whole design is pleasing and the execution faithfully carried out. Finally the magnificent colored windows were the gift of Sulieman and bear the date 935, which is 1528 of our era. Such a description as is here given leaves much to be told, but the interested reader can find it all in special works on the subject. The Dome of the Rock has never been lacking in enthusiastic admirers and no detail of its beauty has been omitted.

Just beneath the dome lies the rock, massive and rugged and silent. Would that it had a speaking tongue and could tell what scenes have been enacted upon it and about it! Tradition says that here Abraham offered Isaac. It is the general belief that on it stood the altar David built after the angel of destruction, that had been slaying thousands of Israel, had put up his sword. Later the great altar of burnt-offering occupied the site and there are markings upon the rock which bear out this statement. Traces of a channel that might have been used for carrying off the blood of the sacrifice, and a large opening leading down through the rock to a natural cave from which there is a subterranean passage, can be seen. The Holy Rock rises six-and-a-half feet higher than the floor of the Mosque and is fifty-seven feet long by forty-three wide. Marks of tools are plain on the western side and traces of steps are visible. These marks may be the work of the Crusaders who are known to have had an altar on the rock.

Besides the many Jewish legends that cluster about the Sakhrah, there are some Christian and a multitude of Moslem ones. No account of these will here be given, as the majority of them are wholly improbable and the rest silly. All those of the Moslems, except Mohammed's midnight visit and ascent, are fabrications of the prophet's successors who have sought in this way to give to this sacred place of the Jews a strictly Moslem setting. Because of its peculiarity mention must be made of their strange belief that on the day of judgment the sacred Kaaba will come from Mecca to the Sakhrah. This is explained by saying that the trumpet of the judgment will be here sounded and on the Holy Rock God will establish His throne. It is the desire of the faithful to pray once from this venerated spot, for did not " the prophet" himself say that one prayer offered here is better than a thousand from any other place?

On the south side of the Rock are eleven steps leading down into the cavern, concerning which there is a great deal of conjecture. There are four ancient altars in it named after Abraham, David, Solomon and St. George; how ancient they are will never be known. From this cave there is a rock-cutting, which is thought to be a passage leading down to the Kedron. The entrance is now closed by a tight-fitting marble slab and guarded so carefully that there is no chance of seeing into it. The Moslem guardians have no curiosity and a great deal of superstition, hence they either do not wish or are afraid to take off the marble covering. A thousand tourists every year enter this cave, every one of whom has curiosity enough and a sufficient lack of superstition to do the lifting and make the inspection; all they want is the permission. As the hole from the ancient altar led down into this cave and from hence the sacrificial blood was carried off into the Kedron, it is not at all unlikely that the temple service was in some way connected with it. But the cave itself is as much of a mystery as the rock-cut passage leading from it and which the Moslems, for lack of a better name, call "the well of souls."

Coming out of the Dome by the east door we see immediately in front of us a miniature copy of the Kubbet es-Sakhrah. It is known as Mehkemeh Dâûd, the Judgment seat of David, and is a graceful little affair; there is in it great variety yet pleasing unity. The bases and shafts and capitals of its columns are not at all alike and clearly prove that they were not originally intended for their present positions. It is held by the Moslems, and it may be true, that the architect of this and the larger structure was the same person and that the smaller was erected first and was the model for the more famous building. Turning to the west, crossing the limestone flagged court and passing under the graceful arcades which stand at the head of each of the main stairs leading to the lower level, we leave this, the cleanest and most attractive and most sacred part and are in the narrow dirty streets of the Old City—streets that once were paved with marble and on which the wealth and beauty of Judea could be seen; where later, the courtier of Rome and the austere priests passed and repassed, and where now is so much poverty and distress.

CHURCH OF THE HOLY SEPULCHRE

The Holiness of the Site—Location—Roman Conquest—Pella—Jews—Trajan—Hadrian's Reconstruction—Temple of Venus — Constantine — Eusebius — Macarius — Helena—The Basilica—Other Buildings—Bordeaux Pilgrim—Calvary—Chosroes II.—Destruction and Rebuilding—Omar—Hakem—Rebuilding by Nicephorous Crusaders—Saewulf—Saladin—Fire of 1808—Rebuilding—The Modern Church—Description Moslem Guard—Stone of Unction—Chapel of Adam—Calvary—Chapel of the Nailing—Rotunda—Holy Sepulchre—Chapel of the Angels—Chapel of the Sepulchre—Jewish Tombs—Chapel of the Apparition—Column of the Flagellation—Sword of Godfrey—Chapel of the Greeks—Small Chapels—Chapel of St. Helena—Finding of the Cross—Other Holy Places—Effect of it All—The One Sublime Fact.

X

CHURCH OF THE HOLY SEPULCHRE

NO place in the Christian world has been regarded with so much veneration as that occupied by the Church of the Holy Sepulchre. For more than fourteen centuries the faces of European and oriental Christians have been turned devoutly toward it, and their eyes have longed to behold its sacred relics. Whatever opinion we may hold as to the correctness of its location there can be no question that to the majority of those who profess the Christian faith this building covers the holiest ground of earth. Two-thirds of all Christendom love this spot above all others, because they believe it to be the sepulchre of their crucified Lord. They are not troubled by any questions as to location. Tradition and the Church say that here Christ was crucified and buried, and they ask no better reason for their belief.

The possibility—to me the strong probability—that the present building does not contain either the place of death or of sepulture of our Lord, cannot destroy interest in this historic monument. For it is historic, apart from the momentous fact from which its name is derived. It has been the scene of many battles for the faith, battles in which heroes fought, not for their own glory but for what they deemed honor to their Lord. Cold criticism of to-day may affirm that these warriors were a set of mistaken men whose abilities and time had been better employed at home in the pursuits of peace. No doubt the affirmation is true, but its truth does not tarnish the fame of those who considered that a Christian's first duty was to assist in rescuing his Lord's tomb from the possession of the "infidel," and who made this, the reputed place of that tomb the object of their tremendous efforts. But apart from these incidents of conflict and carnage, there are other reasons for interest in the place. To it have come, since the fourth century, pilgrims from all Christian lands to kneel in heartfelt prayer and weep at thought of the price paid for their redemption. These prayers and tears of the sincere in heart make this "holy ground" which all the deception and corruption of designing priests cannot entirely desecrate.

In treating of the subject of the Holy Sepulchre the question of location must necessarily arise. In this discussion personal feelings should have no part, facts and inferences from them should be our only arguments.

From the crucifixion of Christ until the destruction of the city by Titus the places of the cross and the tomb were well known, at least to those who had accepted Jesus as the Messiah. When the city fell into the hands of the Romans every building of importance was destroyed and every revered place altered. During the siege that preceded the overthrow the Christians escaped to Pella across the Jordan. The Jews who continued in the city, while they knew the site of Calvary as well as the Christians who had departed, had no regard for it. The Christians who returned would hardly recognize the fallen city as the one they had left; the heel of the destroyer had stamped out of it all semblance of its former glory. For sixty years it lay in ruins so complete that it is doubtful if there was a single house that could be used as a residence; during these years its history is a blank. When the Christians returned there is no record of their having sought out Calvary, or the tomb, or that they considered these sites as in any way to be preferred; there is nothing in the writings of the New Testament enjoining Christians to visit or to especially esteem these as holy places. In the absence of any record, and in the presence of the miraculous account of the recovery of the tomb and the "invention of the cross," the only reasonable

Church of the Holy Sepulchre 175

belief is that these sites, now so reverenced, were absolutely forgotten.

Though their city was in heaps of ruins the Jews were not yet completely subdued. The national spirit would flame out on occasions and the reign of the Emperor Trajan was marked by several serious insurrections on the part of his Hebrew subjects. Trajan's successor, Hadrian, determined to have a more peaceful reign and immediately set about devising means to render the Jews incapable of revolt. One of his plans, and one which he carried out, was to rebuild Jerusalem and by making it a thoroughly pagan city destroy every vestige of its former religious preëminence. It would likewise form a superior military centre, which, garrisoned by Roman troops, would keep this whole country in subjection and quell an insurrection on the first evidence of its outbreak. This reconstruction took place between 120 and 136 A. D., and when completed bore no resemblance to the former city. Out of the ruins of the Hebrew city Jerusalem rose the Roman city Ælia Capitolina. Where the magnificent temple of the living God had stood, rose another dedicated to the Roman Jupiter; and many other buildings in honor of various gods and goddesses of the Roman pantheon were erected. There seems to be no reason to doubt that on the site now occupied by the Church of the Sepulchre a temple to Venus was built. Those who seek to prove that the present church is correctly located assert that Hadrian chose this as a site for the Venus temple because it was the most sacred spot to the Christians, and he thought thus to dishonor it and them. Hadrian is said to have covered the rock containing the tomb with earth; this made surface was then paved and the temple erected.

The objection to such an assertion is that there is no record that the Christians at that time had any special regard for this place or that they considered it as the tomb of their Lord. The first writer mentioning this is Eusebius, who in an account written not earlier than 325 A. D., narrates the building of

Constantine's Church. This Church was located on the site of Hadrian's temple in the belief that that temple covered the place of Christ's entombment,—a belief for which there was neither history nor tradition. The whole story of Hadrian's attempted desecration of this place is at least questionable. Such a temple as a Roman Emperor would erect in honor of Venus would hardly be located on a mound of made earth. If Hadrian really had in mind to deprive the Christians of this, their sacred place, assuming that they so regarded it, it would have been easier and far more effective to destroy utterly the tumulus and its rock tomb. Labor in those days was too cheap to make such a piece of work serious. In a short time every vestige of the sacred rock would have been forever destroyed. This would have been equally effective in illustrating his contempt and would have afforded a much better foundation for his new structure.

When the Emperor Constantine succeeded in making himself master of the eastern world he began very materially to favor the Christians. After his vision of the Cross and his defeat of Maxentius, in 312, the Cross was made the standard of his army. In thankfulness for his continued victories, edicts compensating the Christians for their losses were issued. Among other deeds manifesting his appreciation of the divine favor was his effort to recover the Holy Sepulchre. Eusebius wishes to convey the impression that in this the Emperor was led by divine direction given long before he was able to follow it. It may seem a trifle presumptuous to question the assertions of one who wrote of the age in which he lived; but Eusebius did allow his personal prejudices to affect his pen, and what we know of the life of this royal patron of Christianity gives good reason for doubting that he followed divine impulses even if he ever had any. Biographers of royal personages are in the habit of ascribing to their subjects virtues which were never illustrated in their lives. But granting that Eusebius was not too eager to laud his subject it is not unlikely

Church of the Holy Sepulchre 177

that Macarius, then bishop of Jerusalem, used his position as bishop to increase the importance of his see. His great opportunity arose when the Emperor became interested in Christianity and favorable to it. The plan to recover the sepulchre and erect a Church over it could easily be carried out if once the sympathies and power of Constantine could be enlisted; this was done, the result hoped for followed, and in 336 the Church was dedicated.

Succeeding writers are not so loud as Eusebius in their praises of the part played by Constantine in this recovery. In fact they rather give him a secondary part in the affair and assign the first place to the royal mother, Helena. They were not so closely associated with the life and times of the Emperor as was Eusebius and their testimony may, for this very reason, be less open to suspicion. Nevertheless, we may accept as absolutely correct all that Eusebius says about this recovery and we are still a long way from satisfactory proof that Hadrian's temple to Venus was on the site of the sepulchre of our Lord.

Whether the localities were identical or not here Constantine's Church was built. In letters which he caused to be written to the governors of Eastern provinces, these governors were ordered to assist in the work of recovery and reconstruction. In his letter to Bishop Macarius, written in 326, and given at length by Eusebius, the Emperor expresses " his joy and gratitude and admiration," at the miraculous recovery and asserts his determination to ornament "the token of our Saviour's most holy passion" with magnificent buildings. The Bishop is enjoined to provide the necessary materials and workmen, and to inform him what may be necessary in the way of columns and marbles. The sacred cave was first cared for and was ornamented with marble slabs and finely wrought columns. Around it was a large free space, paved with polished stones and open to the sky. Cloisters, or porticos, surrounded this space on three sides, and on the fourth side, opposite to the cave, was the basilica which Eusebius thus describes: It was "an admirable work, raised to a mighty elevation and extensive in length and breadth. Its interior was lined with many colored marbles, and the outer surface of its walls decorated with polished and closely-jointed masonry, as handsome as marble itself. The roof with its chambers was covered with lead to protect it from the winter rains. The inner roof was decorated with sculptured panels and extended like a vast sea over the whole basilica; and being gilt with the purest gold caused the entire building to shine as if with rays of light" (Professor Willis' translation).

Other buildings grew up around this main one, just how many or how extensive cannot be told. Eusebius speaks of the entire group as the "Martyrium of the Resurrection," but his detailed description of them cannot be followed. There being no mention of Calvary made by this early writer it is altogether probable that the tumulus now so-called was not so considered by him. To argue that the very silence of Eusebius is expressive of the general belief, and that as nobody doubted it, there was no reason for his mentioning it, is rather a begging of the question. The Bordeaux Pilgrim who visited Jerusalem in 333 A. D. is the first one to mention this Golgotha. It was regarded by him as the real Calvary. His mention of the place makes the silence of Eusebius hard to understand, unless indeed, he expressed but his own opinion. A few years after this, or about the year 350, St. Cyril, who was ordained Bishop of Jerusalem in 335, makes frequent mention of this as Calvary. From this time on the acceptance is universal and simply shows how quickly the "invention" grew in favor and how subject the common people were to ecclesiastical power.

For two hundred and eighty years the Church of Constantine stood and was the pious resort of as many pilgrims as could reach it, while kings and prelates added to its possessions as they were able and inclined. Then it fell before the devastating Persian, Chosroes II., in 614, and was consumed by fire. In this sorry condition it was not allowed long to remain. Collections made in all parts of the Christian world poured in, and another structure rose on the ashes of the former. The new building was not equal in grandeur to its predecessor, owing to the fact that no royal treasuries were at the disposals of the builders. The plan of structure was altered in order to permit the embracing of the additional holy places that had been "invented." The honor of being the promoter of this second edifice is due to Modestus, the superior of the monastery of Theodosius. It lacked the symmetry of the one complete Church of Constantine and appears, judging from the account of Eutychius written in the tenth century, to have been three Churches not architecturally connected. This writer says that Theodosius "constructed the Churches of the Resurrection, of the Sepulchre, of the Calvary and of St. Constantine." The Sepulchre Church was included within that of the Resurrection.

This group of Churches remained uninjured for three hundred and fifty-five years. Jerusalem succumbed in 637 to the armies of Omar and remained for a time in Moslem hands. Omar and his immediate successors were not iconoclasts, and did little or no injury to any Christian buildings. It was not until the caliphate of Maez, about 969, that the order was given to destroy the Holy Sepulchre structure. The order was at least partially carried out, though it was not until the reign of the mad caliph Hakem, in 1010, that the work of destruction was completed. Then the Church was utterly destroyed. But the age of miracles had not passed; or perhaps we should say the age when it was thought necessary to strengthen or inspire faith by miracles, had not passed; contemporary chroniclers inform us that all the mad caliph's attempts to destroy the sepulchre itself were unavailing. Iron and fire were tried against the holy walls, but with no visible effect.

For thirty years the place was a scene of desolation—an evidence of the triumph of the Moslem and the humiliation of the Christian. In 1040 Monomachus, then emperor, gave permission, or rather concluded the negotiations which resulted in permission being granted to the Patriarch Nicephorus to rebuild the Church. Acting on this permission, the patriarch completed within eight years a structure not so grand as that of the first Constantine, though Monomachus, whose prenomen was also Constantine, assisted with artificers and funds. This was the Church of the Sepulchre which was standing when the Crusaders entered and took possession of Jerusalem in 1099. Using the work of Nicephorus as a nucleus these Crusaders, who were really wonderful builders, enlarged and beautified it. Sæwolf, who made a pilgrimage to the Holy Land in 1102, is the best authority for the condition of the Church before the additions and improvements of the Crusaders.

When the Christian occupation ceased after the conquest of the land and city by Saladin, the Church as left by the Crusaders, was allowed to remain unharmed, and it was that structure which fell in the great fire in September of 1808. For six centuries pilgrims had visited the place and made it the object of veneration and the recipient of their gifts. In spite of Mohammedan oppression, which was always more or less severe, the number of European Christians who made this pilgrimage was by no means small. The spirit which inspired the Crusaders never wholly died out, nor is it yet dead.

The fire of 1808 consumed many of the most sacred relics enclosed in the Church. Marble columns of great age and beauty crumbled in the flames. The rich hangings and pictures were burned, along with lamps and chandeliers and other ornaments in silver and gold. The lead with which the great dome was lined melted and poured down in streams. It was a great blow to the believers in the sacredness of the place, and yet there were some compensations, for the limestone tomb which had before come through fires and devastations unscathed, proved itself superior to this tremendous conflagration. So at least the faithful are told to believe, and so they do be-

Church of the Holy Sepulchre   181

lieve; only unbelievers doubt it, and they only have any desire to examine and see if behind the marble casings any limestone still exists. It would be a very easy matter to convince the doubters by removing one of the marble slabs, but this is just what the priestly guardians will not permit. You must believe the miracle! This fire began in the Armenian chapel; passed thence to the main rotunda, then to the Greek choir and to the chapels on Calvary. In five hours the great cupola fell with a crash upon the chapel of the Holy Sepulchre crushing in its fall the columns which supported this chapel and ruining the ornamental columns that stood around it.

Three accounts of this fire and its ravages are in existence, one made by the Greeks, another by the Latins and the third by a pilgrim named De Géramb. They agree generally, but when they particularize it is seen that each endeavors to prove that the part of the Church in which its author was interested was the part most miraculously preserved, while the parts belonging to other faiths were the objects of the divine displeasure.

Christian enthusiasm was again aroused to raise the means necessary to replace the structure and its attractions. Permission by special firman had to be procured from the Sublime Porte, and architectural plans made. An architect from Mitylene, Commenes by name, was employed and work begun. Then serious disputes arose between the various interested sects as to what portion of the new Church should belong to each. Further delay was caused by the opposition of the Moslems who wished to prevent the erection of the building. Bribes appeased these obstructionists. In spite of all these difficulties the new structure was completed and consecrated on the 11th of September, 1810, less than two years after the fire. The whole expense connected with the work amounted to nearly three millions of dollars, of which a third was eaten up by lawsuits and by bribes paid to Mohammedan officials.

This is the Church that stands to-day. How much of it is composed of materials used in former structures that stood on the same site could only be discovered by an expert who had abundance of time and full permission to make a careful examination. Even the opinion of such an one would not be allowed to go unchallenged; other experts would surely disagree with him—the more experts, the more conclusions, and archæological experts are in this respect not exceptional. There is no doubt, however, that very considerable remains of the more ancient structures are still here, and some of them yet in the original positions in which they were placed.

The church fronts on an open court surrounded on all sides by buildings. An arched street runs eastward from Christian street, makes a turn at right angles to the north, then to the east and passes along the eastern side of the court. It is a public street for all but Jews and for them so long as they can conceal the fact that they are Jews, not an easy thing for a Jerusalem Jew to do, as he wears conspicuously the marks of his race and religion. The Christians claim control of this thoroughfare and it is they who make it dangerous for any Hebrew to pass along it. As late as April, 1894, a strange Israelite, unacquainted with the unwritten law forbidding him to walk here, was set upon by several Greek Christians and, but for the timely interference of some soldiers of the Sultan, would have been killed; as it was he was severely injured. Nothing was ever done to punish his assailants.

A motley crowd of beggars and venders of tawdry religious wares lines this street. The court itself has been appropriated by these small merchants, who, about Easter time when the city is thronged with pilgrims, do a good business in crosses, rosaries and bits of holy relics. Their jangling voices, as they urge some reluctant pilgrim to purchase, do not add to the sanctity of the place. They are impostors who deserve the treatment accorded by Christ to their predecessors who made his Father's house a den of thieves. This court is paved with large slabs of light red limestone. It was once surrounded by pillars and was in the nature of a porch. Some of the bases of these columns are still *in situ* and are pieces of Crusader work. As one enters this court, or quadrangle from the west and faces north he will have on his left the Greek Chapel of St. James, next to it that of Mary Magdalene, then that of the Forty Martyrs. On his right, making the eastern boundary of the court, are the Armenian and Coptic Chapels and that of St. Mary of Egypt. This Mary was driven away from the door of the Church in 374 by some unknown power and on invoking the image of the Virgin secured admission. The Chapel of St. James, on the west side, commemorates the brother of Christ. That of the Forty Martyrs is the lowest story of the bell tower and was formerly the monastery of the Trinity wherein were buried the patriarchs of Jerusalem. Only three stories of the bell tower are now standing. That it was several stories higher is known from certain old pictures.

The south façade of the church proper exhibits some fine Gothic work. The main entrance is here and formerly consisted of two large portals, one of which is now effectively closed by masonry. Over the portals are large pointed arches. Ancient marble columns with Byzantine capitals and antique pedestals adjoin the doors. Over the left portal are bas-reliefs illustrating New Testament scenes, while over the right portal are vines, and flowers and fruits in the midst of which are naked figures and birds, the whole presenting an allegory of the contest between good and evil.

On entering the church the first thing that will attract the attention of the observing visitor is the Moslem guard which sits in a small elevated room to the immediate left. For this Christian Church has a Moslem guard whose duty it is to keep the peace between the various sects who profess belief in the Prince of Peace. This guard is composed of members of the oldest Mohammedan family in the city. They keep the keys of the main doors and open and close them when required by the Greek, Latin or Armenian Church officials. As each opening is paid for by the one desiring it quite a little revenue accrues. Formerly each person, pilgrim or visitor, paid an admission fee of one para—about an eighth of a cent. Coffee and cigarettes or narghilis are freely used by these custodians. The coffee is provided by that church party which has requested the opening and is made on a small earthen brazier just inside the door.

A great deal has been said and written against the persons constituting this guard for their disrespect to the place. But the truth is, they are no more disrespectful than one should expect them to be, judging from the example set by many of the Christian priests. At the time of the unholy exhibition of the Holy Fire this civil guard is increased by several hundred soldiers who line up around the inside of the church to keep the crowds in order and quell the disturbances that nearly always arise between the sects. With such a spectacle as is here continually given of "how these Christians love one another" the reason is very apparent why they have had so little success in winning the Jew or Moslem to belief in the religion of Jesus. It is a sickening fact that Moslem brute force must compel Christians to exercise, not charity toward each other, but common decency and decorum. But it is a fact, nevertheless, and will remain apparent to all, so long as priestcraft takes the place of New Testament Christianity and superstition supplants religion.

To read a detailed account of all the parts of this church and the adjacent more or less sacred structures would be confusing and uninteresting. Latin, Greek, Armenian, Syrian, Coptic and Abyssinian, each has his specially holy places. What matters it that the names and locations of most of these have been several times changed? What difference that some of the claims made for them are preposterous in the extreme and so ridiculously in error that only intentional fraud will dare assert and only dense ignorance will accept them? The patriarchs

Church of the Holy Sepulchre 185

and priests of these various faiths are by no means all ignorant men. They have some motives for their assertions about these places. To call these motives religious is to defame religion, which can have no part in a lie. Some have tried to soften the hard facts by calling these priestly impositions "pious frauds." When a lie may be justly called righteous a fraud may properly be termed pious, but until that time a religious fraud can be nothing but impious.

A few steps inside and directly in line with the main door is the "Stone of Unction," on which the body of the Lord was anointed in preparation for burial. Many times have I watched in admiration the devotion of Russian pilgrims, the privilege of whose life it has been to reach this sacred enclosure. The Stone of Unction being the first of the holy things to which they come gets a generous share of reverential prostrations and fervent kisses. They do not know that the stone they see and bow over is not even the reputed Stone of Anointing. The latter is covered and entirely concealed from view by a red limestone slab. This covering was necessary because the real stone was being worn away by the hands and lips of the worshippers. The fact that pilgrims about the time of their departure from the Holy City came to this stone to measure the shrouds in which they hoped to be buried will account for some of the wear. This practice is still in vogue; they now take the measure of the upper stone. Nor are they content to trust the word of a dealer in linen or cotton or depend upon a rule or tape measure; they bring the roll of goods, spread it out on the stone and then and there cut it off.

Over this place of worship are suspended eight handsome lamps belonging to the Armenians, Copts, Greeks and Latins; and large candelabra surround it. Some unbelievers doubt the genuineness of this real stone from the fact that the stone itself has been changed, and the correctness of its location from the fact that it has several times altered its position. Different religious bodies have at different times possessed it: the Copts owned it in the fifteenth century, the Gregorians in the sixteenth; from the Gregorians the Latins, for the consideration of 5,000 piasters (about $450.00), procured the right to burn candles over it; it is now Greek property.

The stone serves other purposes. Women place the pictures of absent loved ones upon it and pray over them; pilgrims lay their rosaries there that these may partake of its virtue; mothers bring their babies and think they do a holy act, beneficial to the little ones, by placing them on it and breathing a prayer to God or some favorite saint.

Toward the right from the stone a small door leads into the Chapel of Adam. Here our worthy progenitor, when his struggle with adverse nature was over, rested from his labors. According to a tradition, when the blood and water flowed from the side of the Saviour, it came down through the rock, touched the inanimate dust and Adam came to life again. This tradition accounts for the placing of a skull at the foot of the cross.

The whole church and all its separate chapels are associated with these ridiculous stories. A chapter giving them all would be curious but unprofitable reading. A recent American visitor having gone the rounds of the Church, examined its alleged attractions and listened to the nonsense of his guide, remarked as he came out, "That is the completest museum of religious horrors I know anything about." And his remark was true. There is certainly nothing that can in any way compete with it. You are seriously shown the exact centre of the earth, the very spot where the Creator procured the dust to make the first man; the place where Abraham was about to sacrifice Isaac and where the ram that became the real sacrifice was caught in the bushes; a marble slab on which the tears of the Virgin fell when she saw her divine Son die, each tear making a deep imprint and all together forming a cross. The majority of travellers who see and hear all this are usually content with one visit; in some it works sadness, in others disgust. Whatever previous opinion they may have had as to the correctness of the church's location, many go away with a prejudice against it, really glad that there is a reasonable doubt about it, and hoping that some discovery will warrant a settled belief that it does not cover the sites of the real Calvary and the real sepulchre.

The Calvary here shown is on an elevation a little less than fifteen feet above the level of the entrance to the church. It is reached from this entrance by two flights of stone steps. There are two small chapels each richly ornamented with lamps and candelabra, images and pictures. The one on the left, as one faces the east, is the Chapel of the Raising of the Cross. This is Greek property and is adorned in characteristic Greek fashion, with showy artificial flowers, brilliantly colored figures and faces. Its chief ornamental attraction is a large representation of Christ suspended on the Cross. This is done in silver and gilt. Its other attractions are those coming to it through the tradition that it is the place where the Cross was erected on the day of crucifixion.

Under the altar in the east apse is a circular opening faced with silver where the cross was placed in the rock; five feet from each side of this according to mediæval tradition stood the crosses on which the thieves were hanged. A little less than five feet to the right of where Christ's cross stood is a narrow metal slab which can be pushed aside if one wishes to see where "the rocks were rent." There is a cleft in the rock and you are seriously told that it reaches clear to the centre of the earth. As there is no way to disprove the statement without going to considerable trouble, most people have preferred to reserve their opinion; nor is it always safe here to express audibly what one thinks.

Just a few feet further to the right is the altar of the Stabat. This forms the thirteenth station of the Via Dolorosa and is where the Virgin received the body of her Son after it was let down from the cross. Just above this altar is an image of

Mary hung around with gold and precious stones, the offerings of devout Catholics who have thought by these to win her favor. This is Latin property. Just adjoining this on the south is the Latin Chapel of the Nailing to the Cross. It is more simply and hence more appropriately adorned. Over its altar is a representation of the act of crucifixion, before which candles are continually burning. Near the centre the place of the actual nailing is indicated by some pieces of marble fitted into the floor. This chapel is usually very dark and in order to see its main attraction visitors must have a good supply of candles. This attraction is a very fine picture showing Mary holding in her lap the head of the dead Christ. This is considered the finest picture in the whole church and deserves a much better location than it has. The light is never sufficient to give one a satisfactory view of it. The face of the Virgin Mother is most expressive, while that of Christ is one of the very few artist's conceptions of the Divine countenance that does not make an unpleasant impression. It is a manly countenance in peaceful repose. There is in it no trace of the previous agony, no suggestion of defeat, nothing but the expression of a gentle, manly soul who has finished the work that was given Him to do. The mother face bending over it is tender with a great sorrow; not hopeless, but as if she were in the presence of a mystery which she could not solve, and which still could not overthrow her faith in her divine Son and His mission, or diminish the love which overflowed with every beat of her heart.

From an architectural standpoint the Rotunda of the Sepulchre is the finest and most interesting part of the entire structure. The foundation of this belonged to the ancient structure. The dome is now supported by eighteen large pillars. These pillars are diverse in form and irregular in their location. Some are round and have pedestals and capitals, while others are square and perfectly simple. In fact there are three styles of piers, those on the east being of a decidedly

Church of the Holy Sepulchre 189

complex character and sustaining a wide arch which reaches to the triforium of the church and forms a passage leading from the floor of the rotunda to the choir. This choir was the work of the Crusaders, though the rotunda was erected before their day by Monomachus. The dome is sixty-five feet in diameter, and before the great fire in 1808 was roofed with cedar which had been gilded. This furnished a ready fuel to the flames which were very fierce in their destructiveness to this part of the building. The present rotunda is not so fine nor so large in diameter as its predecessor, for in the repairs the old masonry was allowed to remain and was encased by the new.

The dome for several years preceding 1868, was in a precarious condition and threatened to fall in. The jealousy between the sects who were joint owners of it was so great that they could not come to an amicable agreement as to the terms on which it was to be repaired; finally an international conference was held in which Turkey, France and Russia were represented; the findings of this council were followed, and in 1868 the repairs were made with the result now to be seen. The vault of the dome is colored a sky blue which forms the background for numerous gilt stars. From the ground-floor this gives rather a pleasing effect. Just now the blue and gilt are coming off and the vault has rather a shabby appearance. It is to be hoped that it can be repaired without resort to another international committee of arbitration; but there is no promise of any such peaceful settlement in the present feeling of the sects for each other.

In the centre of the rotunda, facing the east, is the Chapel of the Holy Sepulchre, the most revered place in the Christian world. The whole church structure is sacred, just as the whole temple was sacred to the Jew; but this spot is the Holy of Holies. The pilgrims who come here to bow in holy awe, to murmur their earnest prayers, to solemnly and sincerely make upon themselves the sign of the cross, believe as much in the sacredness of this spot as any Hebrew ever did in the sanctity of the Most Holy place. The most absolute unbeliever in the religion that these people profess, the most positive rejector of the site as the true sepulchre cannot observe these devoted souls without a feeling of respect for them and of something very akin to admiration for their fealty to their convictions. Such devotion as they manifest and such tears as they shed cannot be feigned; to them all is real, as real as if they had seen the Divine One crucified on the neighboring Calvary and laid in this tomb. How abjectly they prostrate themselves before the entrance to this holy place; how solemnly they enter and how reverently, as though this were the supreme moment of a privileged life, they kiss the marble slab above the reputed place where their God was buried! If the present Church of Christ, irrespective of creed, were made up of men and women possessed of a faith like this, but intelligently directed, long ago would "all nations" have heard the Gospel of Redemption preached, and seen it lived.

The Chapel of the Sepulchre resembles a small church. It is built of Santa Croce marble and looks very durable with its columns and pilasters. In shape it is an oblong square though it has not always had this form. In Crusader time it was circular and had a small tower. Later on it was described as polygonal. The fire destroyed the tower, but did not seriously damage the rest of the chapel. Nevertheless, in the reconstruction of the totally destroyed portions of the church, it was thought best to rebuild this. It is now twenty-six feet long and seventeen and a half feet wide. Numerous pictures are hung around the outside of the chapel, all very inferior as works of art. Nearly every available spot is utilized as a receptacle for candles and little oil lamps of many colors. Immense candelabra stand in front of the chapel where is an antechamber having stone benches where Oriental Christians sit to remove their shoes before entering.

Church of the Holy Sepulchre

Going through the small door the visitor comes first to the Chapel of the Angels. A stone set on a small box elevated on a stand is pointed out as the veritable stone which the angels rolled away from the mouth of the tomb. The Armenians have a stone in their parish church on Mount Zion for which they claim a similar distinction. A doubt as to the genuineness of either could, under these circumstances, hardly be termed heresy. Greek, Latin, Armenian and Coptic lamps swing from the ceiling and add to the heavy odors of the small room. The walls of this chapel are very thick and are lined with marble. Two large circular openings pierce the sides, one on the north and the other on the south wall, through which on the afternoon of the Saturday preceding Easter, the "holy fire" is passed out to the runners and to the assembled thousands standing as near as possible to the Sepulchre.

From the Chapel of the Angels a low door, necessitating considerable stooping as one passes through it, leads into the little Chapel of the Sepulchre. This, the chapel proper, is very small, being only six-and-a-half feet long by six wide; and it is the Holy of Holies of the entire structure. It is said that six persons can be accommodated with standing room in it at one time, though I should not care to be one of the six. When the chapel is open for visitors a priest is always on guard; no vandalism is allowed here. On the north, east and west walls are reliefs, while just on the inside of the door can be read in Greek the following inscription: "Lord, remember thy servant the royal builder, Kalfa Komnenos of Milytene, 1810." On the right of the entrance, occupying nearly one half of the floor space is the tomb. It is five feet long, two high and three wide. Swinging from the ceiling are forty-three very costly lamps. The Latins, Greeks and Armenians each own thirteen of these, while the remaining four are Coptic property. The tomb is covered by a large marble slab which is often used as an altar, for here every day in the year the Mass is celebrated. This is, we are told, the very place where the Christ, He who "brought life and immortality to light in the Gospel," lay in the embrace of death. Those who believe in the tradition claim to experience a peculiar thrill when they lay their hand upon the marble-covering of the tomb; those who doubt the tradition never feel the thrill.

Every day during the tourist and pilgrim season rosaries and crucifixes are brought here and laid for consecration upon the marble slab. The attending priest pronounces his blessing upon them and they become specially holy. Thousands upon thousands of rosaries and crosses are thus treated every year and find their way to countries and homes most remote from the Holy City. In April of 1894 a Catholic priest from one of the large inland cities of Ohio, purchased fifteen hundred rosaries, had them all blessed in this way—one for every member of his congregation; he was a wise pastor in thus showing no favoritism. Every year, also, thousands of cards, having on them pressed flowers of the Holy Land, are treated in the same way. The superscription on many of these cards announces that they bear flowers from the Garden of Gethsemane, but the statement cannot be always true, for this little garden spot does not grow flowers enough to supply the demand. The only way to know positively that you have flowers from Gethsemane is to go yourself and pluck them; and this is not an easy matter, for the priestly custodians guard their charge with jealous care. Nor have articles, which are supposed to have been laid on the tomb and blessed, been always so honored. And what does it matter whether they have or not? If contact with any particular place makes more holy, it should suffice that the thing has been in sacred Jerusalem. But as residence in the city does not have any such effect upon persons, it is not probable that it has any holier action upon cards or rosaries. It is a sort of idolatry—an idolatry which to a greater or less degree affects us all—that this locality or that is more sacred than some other and transfers its sacredness to thing or person touched by it.

Church of the Holy Sepulchre 193

Just back of the sepulchre and seemingly a part of it is a wretched little chapel belonging to the Coptic Church, and just across the circular aisle that surrounds the sepulchre is the Chapel of the Syrians. Neither of these is in itself deserving of mention and they are only here mentioned because they are in line with a small recess in which are two interesting rock-cut tombs. Nor are these tombs interesting in themselves; they are important, however, in that they prove beyond a doubt that this part of the church was once without the walls. For they are old Jewish tombs and we know that, with the exception of the royal tombs, none were ever within the city. There are two ways of accounting for the existence of these. One is that they date from the time of David or Solomon, were without the north wall at that time, and when the Second Wall was built, were brought within the city. The other and more recent theory supposes the First Wall to have included these tombs and thus makes them as they were on the slope of Zion, none other than the remains of the royal tombs themselves. Whatever may be said about them one thing is sure, that there is no basis for the sixteenth century story which assigns to them the names of the Tomb of Joseph of Arimathea and of Nicodemus, who came to Jesus by night.

Coming out from the Syrian Chapel into the rotunda, again we pass through an antechamber where Christ appeared to Mary on the first Easter morning, and enter the principal Chapel of the Roman Catholics. A fourteenth century tradition, which affirms that here Christ first appeared to His mother after His resurrection, has given this plainly furnished enclosure the name "the Chapel of the Apparition." Its special treasure is the Column of Flagellation, which is kept in a cabinet just at the right of the entrance. The column cannot be seen except during one day in the year, on which day every pilgrim in the city kisses it. During this ordeal two Latin priests guard it and no worshipper is allowed to remain long before the sacred relic. When each one's time is up he or she is rudely pushed along to make room for others. It is a religious act on the part of the pilgrims, but on the part of the priests seemingly a purely business one, which, the sooner over the better. Ordinarily the stone can only be felt with a stick about two feet long, which is provided for the purpose. Pilgrims enter the chapel just to touch the column, and having put the stick against it, kiss it and make upon head and breast the sign of the cross; they have thus performed a meritorious act at which they will rejoice on their return to their native lands. Different pilgrims at different times have given descriptions of this column. If these accounts are correct it is like the other holy stones in having several times changed its form and color and position.

A few steps to the left from this chapel entrance bring one to the Latin Sacristy. It is not a very important place judging from its size and the disorder in which it is usually kept; but it contains three important relics, the sword, cross and spurs of Godfrey de Bouillon—the first Christian king of Jerusalem. These relics are probably genuine. The sword is a long straight blade having a cruciform handle; the spurs are cruel implements eight inches in length with barbs long and sharp enough to inflict absolute torture. When this church was the place of investiture of the knights of St. John, this sword was used in the ceremony of initiation. It is now employed by the Order of the Sepulchre in inducting new members, but as this order is a small one, the sword is not often required for this purpose.

Coming again to the rotunda one can enter under the imposing Arch of the Emperor, the Catholican, or main chapel of the Greeks. This forms the nave of the Cathedral and is ornamented in almost barbaric style, with highly colored decorations, brazen lamps and pictures. It surpasses in size and ornamentation the chapels of any of the other sects, but gives the impression of abundance rather than taste; to the Greek

Church of the Holy Sepulchre 195

or Russian, however, this wealth of gilding and paint is no doubt very impressive. We are told that this chapel stands where formerly was the garden of Joseph of Arimathea. If so, I should much prefer that the garden had never been destroyed. It has the further honor of being situated right in the centre of the world; the exact centre is indicated by a rounded stone covered with netting and lifted from the floor on a low stand. On each side of the chapel is an episcopal throne, the one on the south being for the use of the Greek bishop of Jerusalem, while that on the north is for the bishop of Antioch. The Greek body being the richest of all here, of course has the finest vestments and most costly jewels. These are kept in a place called the Iconoclaustrum and are exhibited on special occasions to sufficiently distinguished visitors.

Near this part of the church are numerous small chapels having no attractions sufficient to commend them to the interested visitor and very doubtful ones for the pious pilgrim to consider. Fortunately the pious pilgrim does not consider; he accepts; and, accepting, reverences, and no unpleasant doubts assail his mind. There is an altar having in it two round holes. Here Christ's feet were confined during the preparation for the crucifixion. Then there is the Prison of Christ, the altar of Saint Longinus, the centurion whose spear pierced the Saviour's side as he was suspended on the cross. A tradition, quite as credible as the others, records that Longinus had but one eye; when the blood and water followed his spear some of it fell into his empty eye socket and immediately a new eye replaced the lost one; he accordingly became a Christian and was promoted to sainthood.

Then comes the chapel where the soldiers cast lots for Christ's garments; the Chapel of Derision and altars almost too numerous to mention. The passage-way here is quite in gloom and it requires some acquaintance with the arrangement in order to find one's way. Among these niches in which the altars stand is a stairway of twenty-nine steps leading down into the Chapel of

St. Helena, sixteen feet below the level of the church floor. This is Abyssinian property, but this sect being poor in worldly goods in Jerusalem and, having more need of the money than of the chapel, rents it to the Armenians. It is rather a desolate place and has the appearance of poverty, its altars and ornaments being sadly in need of renovation. On this site Constantine's basilica originally stood and early Christians considered it the place where the true cross was unearthed. It gets its present name from the belief that here Saint Helena sat during the excavations which resulted in demonstrating the correctness of the location of the Church of the Sepulchre.

Traditions are a little mixed just here, and one of about the year 1400, mentions another place which is here also. So, by going down thirteen high steps, some of which are cut in the native rock, one can stand in what is now known as the Chapel of the Finding of the Cross; this chapel is modern, was formerly a natural cave in the rock or a cistern, and has no claims to serious regard, but for all that it is seriously considered by all the pilgrims who visit it. Here they murmur a prayer, or if they feel able, will buy a candle from a young Greek in charge and place it in a hole in the marble slab that marks the place where the crosses were found. Three crosses were discovered here, and though it was known instantly that they were the three used on the occasion of Christ's crucifixion, there was no way of telling on which one the Saviour had hung. But Bishop Macarius saw the way out of this difficulty. A very pious lady was lying at the point of death; one by one the three crosses were presented to the sufferer. No effect was noticeable on presentation of the first two, but when her eyes beheld the third and her hand felt it, the recovery was instantaneous. This was a demonstration that left no room for doubt. And yet some do have very serious doubts about the whole story; they can see no reason for the angelic visitation to Helena informing her where to look; they cannot understand why it was necessary for the cross to be found because

Church of the Holy Sepulchre 197

there was no purpose to be served. To assert that it was to prove the correctness of the site chosen for the sepulchre rather weakens than strengthens the argument, for if that site was as well known as its advocates insist it was in the time of Constantine, there was certainly nothing to be gained by a miraculous interposition.

Many other places called holy, connected with which are traditions of the miraculous, are included within the compass of this cluster of buildings. How genuine the sites and how holy, how much of truth there is in the traditions and how much of miracle in the miraculous, each must estimate for himself, unless he is satisfied to accept without question the dicta of the custodian priests. If reason and probability be allowed to figure in the estimate the great mass of tradition and miracle must be rejected as fraudulent and productive of no possible good. Some of the more preposterous sites have been passed without mention.

These many holy sites and attendant fables were not originated at one time. They are the growth of centuries, being added to from time to time as the ecclesiastical authorities deemed advisable. Venerated and worshipped by the ignorant, priest-ridden pilgrims, these holy sites are a scandal to intelligent Christians, and the objects of derision to unbelievers. The Christianity of Christ is outraged by such pretensions, and when this Christianity takes possession of the people, as it will, they will break away from this priestly thralldom and worship God only.

The Church of the Holy Sepulchre gives to the non-Christian world the very worst possible illustration of the religion of Him in whose name it stands. That religion was simple, spiritual and productive of love; whereas the religion exhibited by this church is as complex as can be devised, as material as any form of idolatry and annually productive of as loveless sights as can be imagined. Between the different sects represented here there is positive enmity. The followers of Moses and Mohammed will never leave their faiths to embrace the type of Christianity seen in this, which they have reason to regard as the leading church of the followers of Christ. They know what it stands for—the death and resurrection of Him whom the Gentile world has accepted as its Messiah. They know of no other Christianity than this. No wonder they reject it and all its pretensions. And they do so on a principle enunciated by Christ and universally accepted as correct, "By their fruits ye shall know them." A brief glance at the history of this church convinces us that it has produced nothing attractive; it has been a curse rather than a blessing; it has been a house of war instead of a house of peace: it has stood for bigotry, envy, falsehood, strife and murder, instead of witnessing for peace, liberty, truth and love. True religion would lose nothing if this church and its record could be expunged from the pages of history.

But the church does stand as a witness for one stupendous event. The truth of her testimony is not affected by her mistaken location, her senseless traditions or her warring sects. Greek may differ from Latin, Latin from Armenian, Armenian from Syrian, Syrian from Copt and Copt from Abyssinian and each from all the others; they may have their disgraceful strifes and in asserting their preëminence show their loveless characters; they may differ as much as they can on the minor points of belief, but on the great essential there is unanimity. Christ died for men and rose again. The old Church stands for this—the truth of God which human error and ignorance cannot destroy—the truth that shall live and influence for eternity the lives of the followers of the Risen One.

Photograph by E. Warren Clark.
THE CITY AS SEEN FROM THE SUMMIT OF THE NEW CALVARY.

THE NEW, OR GORDON'S, CALVARY

Religious Prejudices as to Holy Sites—Questions of Locality—Untrustworthiness of Tradition—Known Facts about the Place of the Crucifixion—Support for the Traditional Holy Sepulchre—Eusebius—Korté's Opposition to the Tradition—Dr. Robinson—Remains under Frères' College—Conder's Opinion—Holy Sites and Christian Faith—The Green Hill—Circumstantial Evidence—Place of Stoning—Roman Methods—Topographical Requirements met by the New Calvary—Main Roads—Real Via Dolorosa—Conspicuous—Shape of the Hill—Jeremiah's Grotto—Size of the Hill—The New Tomb—Church of St. Stephen—Rock Tombs—Within the New Tomb—Conder's Tomb.

XI

THE NEW, OR GORDON'S, CALVARY

THE localities in and around the Holy City have occasioned many a hot dispute. Absolute identifications are the exceptions, and the contested field is wide. In the contests passionate expression of mere personal opinion is all too common. Such expressions are general from persons who are too interested in one or the other place to speak without prejudice. Prejudice distorts truth, or so affects the mental medium through which truth passes that it is distorted in the expression. No prejudice is so violent as that which touches religious matters. Many advocates of the present holy places consider that great religious importance attaches to them and that to express disbelief in them tends to rob men of their faith in that which saves. Hence the passionate verbal assaults upon those who refuse to accept the traditional site of the Holy Sepulchre and of Calvary. But passionate assaults are not arguments and followers of Christ will insist that the genuineness of this or that locality in its relation to the life or death of the Saviour has nothing at all to do with salvation.

Education is broadening and in all matters of religion young men and women are being taught to think for themselves. In the more enlightened countries a statement is not accepted as truth simply because it is made by priest or preacher. It must be reasonable, must be in harmony with known facts. But the "holy places" are not in an enlightened country, nor do their possessors represent an enlightened type of Christianity. Patriarchs and bishops say the places are genuine and therefore holy, and the people for the most part accept without question their statements. Until very recent years there has been no expressed doubt about most of these places, but lately the almost universal acceptance has been negatived by many intelligent investigators who demand something more than the opinion of an individual, it matters not how distinguished in any branch of learning that individual may be, something more than an ancient tradition in support of any locality for which pretentious claims are made. They are demanding good reasons for such claims, are questioning those incapable of proof and rejecting any that are plainly in opposition to the known facts.

Concerning the holy sites of the Holy City any one has the right to ask why this one is located here or that one there. If the answer given is not satisfactory he has the right to doubt or disbelieve. For instance when one sees hundreds of Russian pilgrims kneeling devoutly and kissing reverently a spot on the rock on the eastern slope of Mount Moriah, just near where the Jericho road turns to cross the brook Kedron, and is informed that here is where Saint Stephen was stoned, he has a right to question the reason for this localization. The evidence of an old tradition proves nothing. The place of Jewish capital punishment being known and Saint Stephen having suffered that punishment there is no reason to seek another place for his death than the one used commonly in his day. How or when the tradition assigned the event to the spot outside of the present St. Stephen Gate is a matter of no moment. The tradition is groundless.

A tradition just as groundless has for fifteen centuries affirmed that the two most momentous facts in Christian history took place on the site now occupied by the Church of the Holy Sepulchre. To the one whom tradition satisfies this is enough. The one who accepts the dicta of the Church without dispute reasons that, as the Church has maintained these two sites during these centuries, he has no right to doubt their genuineness. Had the Church never been mistaken; had she never been compelled to change her position such acquiescence might be given by even a greater number than now.

The New, or Gordon's, Calvary

But so long as the Church is made up of human creatures dependent upon human judgment there are those who will refuse absolutely to acknowledge her infallibility. This will be so especially in matters unessential to salvation, to which class certainly belongs the localization of any event connected with the life or death of our Lord.

There are certain things positively known about the places of the crucifixion and burial of Jesus. They were outside the city walls at that time and not far from one of the gates. (Heb. xiii. 12.) The places of death and sepulture were near each other, the latter being in a garden. (John xix. 41 and 42.) The crucifixion took place on a conspicuous site near a public road. (Matt. xxvii. 39 and 55; Mark xv. 29; Luke xxiii. 35.) Any place laying claim to being the site of these two events must meet these three requirements, it must have been without the walls, near one of the gates and conspicuous. Failing in any of these particulars its claims are untrustworthy, no matter how old the tradition favoring it or how great the ecclesiastical authority supporting it.

No locality could have better traditional or ecclesiastical support than the present Church of the Holy Sepulchre. For sixteen hundred and seventy years the tradition has been accepted as true by the great majority of Christians. True, there was a period of nearly three hundred years previous to the birth of the tradition when it was at least doubtful whether anybody connected these events with this place. During the sixteen hundred and seventy years, however, all the Oriental Christian Churches, together with the great Roman branch, have repeatedly pronounced in favor of the truth of the tradition. The fact, and it is a fact beyond question, that there is no record pointing to this as the place of the crucifixion and burial before the origin of the tradition might be overlooked, were there no other arguments against it. Other things being equal, strong traditionary evidence must be accepted. But in this instance other things are not equal. When the tradition began the places of death and burial had been lost. Nothing is more certain than this. Nobody at the time of the conversion of Constantine knew where Christ had suffered or where His pierced body had rested from that Friday of death till the Sunday of resurrection. The assertion of Eusebius to the effect that while clearing away the ruins of a heathen temple the Holy Sepulchre was found "most unexpectedly," would never have been made had he known just where the Lord had been buried; and he would have known had that knowledge been possessed by anybody. A certain tomb was found, not one only, but several, and the assumption was immediately made that one of these was the lost tomb of the Saviour. Beyond a doubt these were old Jewish tombs and probably the last resting-places of some of Judah's royal families. Archæologists date them from a time anterior to Christ. No man speaks with greater authority on this question than Major C. R. Conder, and it is his opinion that is here given.

The recovery of the cross is nowhere mentioned in the writings of Eusebius. Cyril first speaks of this "invention" in a sermon preached in the basilica that was erected over these then newly discovered holy places. This basilica was completed in 335 A. D. Cyril began to preach in 347 and in the sermon above mentioned speaks of pieces of the true cross having been distributed throughout the world. Thus in a quarter of a century this tradition began and had met with general acceptance. Were it not thus positively known that there was no previous history connecting this place with the crucifixion the necessity of introducing the miraculous into the narrative would suffice to convince that there was no such history. The knowledge that this was the actual place where that event occurred would have required no miracle to substantiate it. We are thus compelled to believe that the Christians residing in Jerusalem at the beginning of the fourth century were not cognizant of the places of the death and resurrection of their Lord.

Nevertheless, this was the place fixed upon by ecclesiastical authority, believed in by the unthinking laity and fought for by those, in many ways unique warriors—the Crusaders. Unquestioned, at least publicly, for fourteen hundred years it was honored by prelates and enriched by kings. Religious bodies before the Reformation and since have vied with each other in many unholy ways to gain possession of the ground within the holy enclosure. Altars stand in nearly every nook and corner, each one professing to cover some place where some event connected with the history of the Christian religion, but more especially with the passion of its Founder, occurred. To protect these and maintain the supremacy of Christianity kings sent their armies, and knights of various degree, and for various reasons, followed. None but the Omniscient knows how many lives were sacrificed in that century of struggle which ended in defeat for the Christian arms. None but the same All-knowing One can tell how many devout souls have come on peaceful pilgrimages to weep where they thought their Christ had suffered and pray the prayers deemed doubly efficacious because offered from this "holy ground." And the pilgrimages were not without spiritual blessing to those who made them nor the invocaters less efficacious because the suppliants were mistaken.

The first person who publicly expressed his doubts as to the genuineness of the sites covered by this Church was a certain German bookseller named Korté. He made a visit to Jerusalem in 1738, and whether what he witnessed in and around the Church disillusioned him as to its sanctity, or his study of the topography convinced him that the founders of the Church were mistaken; at any rate, on his return to Germany he sought by every means to assure his countrymen that the claims made for it could not be sustained. This was the beginning of the present wide-spread disbelief.

Since Korté's day there have been many who have thought and expressed themselves as he did. But the cause lacked a vigorous champion until it was advocated by Doctor Edward Robinson, the great American name associated with the explorations and discoveries in and near Jerusalem. In 1856 Doctor Robinson proved to every mind free to accept proof that the traditional site of the Holy Sepulchre must have been within the walls at the time of the crucifixion. Any doubt that might have been entertained as to the sufficiency of this proof was removed a few years ago by the discovery of the remains of the old north wall near the northwestern angle of the present wall. These remains called the Castle of Goliath, can be seen in the basement of the Frères' College. They appear to be the ruins of three large towers and were part of the Second Wall. They have *in situ* at least ten layers of masonry of the same massive form, peculiar level and rough face as the old masonry at the Damascus Gate and at the southwest angle of the temple area near Robinson's Arch. This permits only one conclusion, and that is that the locators of the Church of the Holy Sepulchre were very much mistaken.

The only other possible theory, and it is highly improbable, is that the Church, now two hundred yards south of this north wall, was left on the outside by the wall making a great detour to the south in the form of a horseshoe. As the city could grow only toward the north and as this detour would necessitate more than double the labor and expense of a straight wall, besides losing to the increasing city a very valuable building section, the theory is absolutely untenable. As Conder says, speaking of these bits of wall under the Frères' College; "'This last discovery is the death blow to the claims of the traditional site and a final settlement of a bitter controversy.''

Would that it were "a final settlement!" But this discovery has not had that effect upon those who favor the traditional location. They have held it too long to confess now to centuries of error. Leaders of religious thought who could be mistaken for so long on a matter so important as their followers believe this location of Calvary to be, are likely to be just as much in error on other questions relating to belief and practice. The leaders know their followers will thus reason and so they hold all the more tenaciously to the traditional site and treat with as much contempt as they can command any one assailing it. The "death-blow" may have been given, but those upon whom it has fallen are making a desperate and so far successful effort to keep alive. "The final settlement of a bitter controversy" has been reached only by those who accept facts regardless of their effect upon venerable opinions, and who feel that the religion of Jesus is in no way dependent upon what men believe about certain localities, if they but believe in Him.

Bearing this in mind, it will matter but little to the intelligent Christian if the place where Christ was crucified remains forever unknown. The divine knowledge of the proneness of men to idolatry and their tendency to worship the place to the forgetting of the Person and His work may be the very reason for the present uncertainty. Let us hope that this uncertainty will continue, if thereby the spiritual part of the religion of Jesus be enhanced.

However, no account of modern Jerusalem would be complete without a brief mention of a hillock, just north of the city, which has recently been brought into prominence as a claimant for the distinction of being the true Calvary. Other sites have been selected and advocated by writers, but I cannot regard any of them as worthy of serious consideration. No positive proof can be furnished that this "New Calvary" was the actual site of the great tragedy; the circumstantial evidence is very strong and is here presented for what it is worth. Even tradition is not lacking.

The eminence we are describing is the only prominent hillock north of the city and yet near enough for any event happening upon it to be witnessed by persons viewing it from the walls. It is the northern extremity of the hill on which that part of the city called Bezetha stands, and has been artificially separated from the rest of the hill by a deep moat about a hundred yards wide. This moat was made to assist in the defence of the north wall and out of it was taken much of the stone used in the process of city erection. Just when it was cut through is not known, but certainly it was done long before our era began and at the time of Christ would meet all the requirements of the "Place of the Skull." The hill is called El Heidemyeh to-day by the native Arabs, a name meaning "the place of Heidem," who, Mohammedans assert, belonged to a princely family, was also the leader of a strong religious sect and at his death was buried on this hill. The Christians refuse to accept this tradition and instead claim that El Heidemyeh was in the fifteenth century written El Heiremyeh, meaning Jeremiah. In favor of the Moslem account is the fact that the hill is covered by one of their oldest cemeteries, while in favor of the Christian is the old Jewish tradition which informs us that in a cave in the hill the Tearful Prophet wrote his book of Lamentations.

Among the Jews it is known as the Place of Stoning, where those condemned to death under their law met such punishment as the law prescribed. Nor was the punishment here meted out limited to the Jewish method of stoning, as is manifest from a passage in the Talmud, (Sanhedrim vi. 1–4), from which it appears that crucifixion was also practiced at the "House of Stoning." "They sunk a beam in the ground and a cross beam was stretched from it, and they bound his hands together and hung him up." There is some uncertainty as to the date when the above selection was written, but certainly it was previous to 200 A. D. In this passage it is also said that, "The place of stoning was the height of two men." These are important as showing that at the time they were recorded crucifixion took place here and that a precipice similar to the one now seen was then in existence.

The fact that Jesus was executed according to Roman methods has nothing to do with the place of execution. The

Photograph by E. Warren Clark.   SOUTHERN VIEW OF NEW CALVARY.

opposers of the New Calvary insist that it is not at all likely that the Romans would use the place the Jews were in the habit of using—why is not easy to understand, for the Romans were not likely to neglect any suitable thing or place simply because others had previously employed it. The House of Stoning was well adapted, it was conveniently located and it is more than likely that the Roman governors found it very useful in troublous times as a place of execution and warning.

Topographical requirements are well met by the New Calvary. It is outside the present city wall and the ancient masonry at the Damascus Gate assures us that here at least the present wall occupies the identical position of the wall existing in the time of Christ. This old wall is called the Second Wall. Calvary was outside of that wall. The New Calvary is also near two gates which lead northward from the city. A road from the Damascus Gate followed the present miserable pathway to the north and passed so near the knoll now regarded as Skull hill that any event occurring there could be easily witnessed by those who "passed by." The other road proceeded from the Tower of Antonia, and formed the military highway to Cæsarea, the Roman capital of the country at that time. This latter road skirted the eastern base of the knoll within easy speaking distance of the summit. Travellers to and from the city would be continually going and coming along this important road. If Christ were led direct from Pilate's judgment hall to the place of execution this is the way He would most likely have taken and so this would be the real Via Dolorosa.

Further, the site of this Calvary is most conspicuous. From every direction it can be plainly seen. It is the only prominent hill anywhere in the neighborhood. There is nothing to prevent such a crowd as assembled on the day of the crucifixion from gathering on the slopes of the hill and viewing every act connected with that triple scene of death. Thus it will be seen that this position meets all the requirements of the Gospel accounts, being "without the gate," yet "nigh unto the city"; capable of being seen "afar off," and close enough to two main roads for those who "passed by" to "revile" the Crucified.

The shape of the knoll has by some been thought to contribute an argument in its favor. The site of the crucifixion for some reason was known as "the Place of a Skull." Whether it was given this name because it really resembled a human skull in form or because the unburied remains of malefactors who had met death for their crimes could frequently be seen on it cannot be now definitely known. Some visitors to the hill profess to see in it a resemblance to a human skull, but I must say that it is only by the exercise of much imagination that I have been able to observe this. Two small caves in the face of the southern cliff do look a little like empty eye sockets, but to base anything on these would be presuming too much, for their date is very uncertain. The part of the cliff in which they are formed in a very soft limestone and these small apertures may be one of Nature's many freaks in the Judean hills. The several caves in this vicinity were formerly the residence of Moslem and Christian hermits, and too many changes are likely to have taken place during nineteen centuries to permit much weight to attach to a fancied resemblance.

A much larger cave exists here and goes by the name of Jeremiah's Grotto. A Christian Apocrypha, dating from 136 A. D., a part of which is read every year by the Greek Church on the anniversary of the destruction of Jerusalem, informs us that in this grotto the book of Lamentations was written.

Major Conder was the first real authority who advocated in print the claims of this New Calvary, though Doctor Selah Merrill, present United States Consul at Jerusalem, certainly shares this honor with the English explorer. The name of neither of the gentlemen is ever applied to the hillock, but another name more widely known for other reasons is often given it.

The New, or Gordon's, Calvary 211

General Gordon, of Chinese and African fame, a year or two before his last campaign, visited Jerusalem and was so impressed with the belief that the New Calvary was the actual one that he wrote and spoke much in its favor. An enterprising photographer named his view of the hill Gordon's Calvary, and it is to-day probably better known by this than by any other title.

The surface of the hill covers an extent of about three acres. It slopes rather abruptly to the west, but gently on the east and north. The summit is almost flat and affords a good place for religious meetings. The Moslems whose dead are buried here make no serious objections to their tombs being used as seats by Christians. That they would prefer the absence of these infidels is well told on the faces of any Mohammedans who happen to be on the hill when a Christian service is being held. American Christians have thus far been usually the ones who have assembled here, and some very profitable meetings have been held by them. Mr. Moody and Doctor Talmage have preached on this suggestive place; and an occasion not to be forgotten by any who were present was a service held by the Congregational Party on the Sunday of April 21st, 1895. Nor will Easter of 1898 when Rev. P. Cady preached on "The Resurrection" be forgotten.

Equal in importance with Golgotha was the tomb of Joseph in which the Crucified was laid. The two places were near each other. "Now in the place where He was crucified there was a garden; and in the garden a new sepulchre wherein was never man yet laid. There laid they Jesus, therefore, because of the Jews' preparation day: for the sepulchre was nigh at hand" (John xix. 41, 42). Certainly there can be but one conclusion from a statement so definite. The places of the cross and the grave were so near each other that little time would be consumed in transferring the body from the former to the latter. If the New Calvary be the real Calvary, where is that rock tomb? Diligent search has been made for it, but, as usual, with no certain result. One writer says here, another says there, and the interested reader may take his choice. In the meantime the war of words goes on. We hope the only outcome of it all will be to have the matter remain undecided. This will avoid any likelihood of a repetition of the idolatry and sacrilege that goes on around the traditional tomb.

In the vicinity of the New Calvary there is no scarcity of rock tombs. It has been a burying ground for ages, and each new excavation brings to light the forgotten resting-place of some former resident of Jerusalem. In the multiplicity of these tombs it is not at all probable that one will be finally agreed upon as the garden sepulchre of the wealthy Joseph of Arimathea. Excavations whose object was the recovery of the "new tomb" began in 1873. In 1881 the ruins of an ancient Christian Church were unearthed. The Dominicans, who are now the possessors of this ruin, claim that it was the work of the Empress Eudoxia. Around it are many rock-cut sepulchres. From inscriptions found in these it is known that they were the tombs of deacons of the early Church, but just how early cannot be known positively. At whatever time these tombs were cut it appears that this locality was regarded as a desirable place for Christian burial. It may have been because Saint Stephen here met his death at the hands of the infuriated Jews, or because a Greater than Stephen here finished the work He was appointed to do. If the latter be true, the surmise of a recent writer may be correct. Rev. Haskett Smith says in effect that these Christian tombs manifest the desire of the early followers of the Crucified to be buried "near their Lord."

This New Calvary has had its northwestern slope cut away and the exposed rock has been worked to a smooth, perpendicular face. The accumulated debris of centuries had hidden from view this work of the masons, until modern explorations, in quest of the secrets the earth contained, removed the debris

The New, or Gordon's, Calvary 213

and exposed the face of the rock. A ditch thirty-five feet long and from twelve to fifteen in depth has been sunk, but so far only one tomb has been discovered. This now goes by the name of the New Tomb. No one can question that in point of locality it fulfills all the requirements of the Gospel narrative. It is only a few rods from the summit of Calvary and is within the enclosure of a very ancient garden. The dispute as to its genuineness hinges on its form. In the rock tombs around Jerusalem two distinct styles are noted. There are those which have a sort of vestibule or chamber. From this chamber openings are cut in the walls just large enough to insert a body lengthwise. Such are called Kokim and are the older form. In the later style, known as loculi, the places for the reception of the bodies were rock-cut sarcophagi and were parallel with the sides of the chamber. This New Tomb belongs to the loculus form and was the kind in which Christ was interred. This kind only would have permitted the view that Mary had of "two angels in white sitting, the one at the head and the other at the feet where the body of Jesus had lain." Such a description could not apply to the older style.

A descent of ten steps is necessary below the level of the garden before the door of the sepulchre is reached. Just recently a guard has been stationed here and no one is admitted except by him and under his surveillance—a precaution made necessary by the vandalism of visitors, many of whom in their desire to obtain a fragment of the rock did not hesitate to deface the tomb itself.

The low door at which the visitor enters leads into a vestibule, whence two steps lead down into the tomb chamber, in which are three receptacles for the dead ranged around the three sides and even with the floor. The receptacle on the left as one faces the south is by many considered the "place where the Lord lay." On the south wall of the tomb chamber can be traced an ancient cross painted on the rock, but as this is in the Latin form it is argued that it cannot be older than the fifth and may date from the twelfth century. This cross and the accompanying inscriptions, IC. XP. A and Ω are regarded by Major Conder as mediæval. But the cross and inscriptions have nothing, necessarily, to do in attesting the age of the tomb. They simply prove that at the time they were painted this was considered Christian property and may indicate that there was once a small chapel or praying place in this quiet retreat.

The Rev. Haskett Smith is very strong in his belief in the genuineness of this tomb and has succeeded in arousing so much interest in it that a company of English protestants has purchased the garden in which it stands. The price paid the former owner was very much more than the actual value of the land, but in such cases sentiment is reckoned at its full value by the seller. An imposing wall now surrounds the garden. Let us hope that the sentiment of the good people who have recently come into possession of it will carry them no further and that they will allow the tomb to remain without ornamentation of any sort.

The inconclusive nature of the evidence in favor of this being the New Tomb of Joseph does not affect the strong proofs that the hill above it is the real Golgotha. Further excavations in the neighborhood may bring to light another tomb about whose antiquity there will be no doubt. Major Conder claims to have found such a tomb, but there are too many objections to this because of its location. This was hewn in a rock which as the advocate of it says: "Became the foundation of the corner tower of the 'Third Wall' about forty years after the crucifixion."

Certainly, of all the sites advocated, this hill just north of the Damascus Gate offers the most convincing evidence of its identity as the true place of the crucifixion. In fact there is no argument against it. Let us hope that it will continue as it is, undesecrated.

SOME PLACES OF SPECIAL INTEREST

The Citadel of David—Commanding Position—Herod's Work—Diversity of Opinion as to Age—Phasælus—Dimensions—View from the Tower—Tomb of David—Questionable—History of the Site—Moslem Property—Coenaculum—Traditions—Via Dolorosa—Important Street—Church of St. Anne—First Station—Scala Sancta—Ecce Homo Arch—Various Stations—A Modern Tradition for this Via Dolorosa—Pool of Hezekiah—Christian Street—Uncertainty—Dimensions—Moslem Reconstruction—New Topography—Pool of Bethesda—Dimensions—Sheep's Pool—Five Porches—Pool in Property of St. Anne Probably the Real—Explorations—Tombs of the Kings—Rock Tombs—Queen Helena—Description of Tombs—De Sauley—Solomon's Quarry—Location—Recovery—Danger—Quality of Stone—Method of Quarrying—Of Masonic Interest.

XII

SOME PLACES OF SPECIAL INTEREST

    I. Tower of David.
   II. Tomb of David.
  III. Via Dolorosa.
  IV. Pool of Hezekiah.
   V. Pool of Bethesda.
  VI. Tombs of the Kings.
 VII. Solomon's Quarry.

IN the preceding pages brief mention has been made of certain places that have been important in the city's past and add to the interest and appearance of its present. To omit a description and illustration of these in a work of this kind would be neglecting the most conspicuous objects of the city's architecture, and passing by as unimportant, places and things which thousands of pilgrims and tourists come every year to see.

The Citadel of David.—The first building that meets the vision of one approaching Jerusalem from the south or west is that known as the Citadel of David. It occupies a commanding position and was originally chosen for its natural advantages as a place of defence; from the day of its first choosing it has been so used. Perhaps the early Jebusites had a stronghold here, and what they had erected David improved when he made Jerusalem the capital of his kingdom. It stood in the northwest corner of David's city and doubtless then as now commanded the principal entrance. It was the site of some of Herod's greatest works of fortification and is zealously held to-day by the forces of the Sultan.

The massive stones in the base of the tower would settle a

disputed question if they could tell just when they were placed in their present positions, for they are *in situ*. There is great diversity of opinion as to the date to be assigned to masonry,—there being no marks which prove beyond doubt the age when the builders wrought. So the large ancient-looking stones in the Tower of David, with their marginal drafts of from four to five inches wide are as mysterious as many another feature of this strange old city. They are certainly as old as the Herodian period. We know from Josephus that Herod built three large towers in this part of the city and called them Hippicus, Phasælus and Miriamne. Parts of three towers still stand, the one now called after David's name being identified as that of Hippicus or Phasælus. Herod's towers were not destroyed when the Romans under Titus took and demolished so much of the town; the Saracens and Crusaders also permitted them to stand; they were partly demolished in 1239 A. D. by Daûd of Kerak, but this conqueror left the base of the tower under discussion undisturbed, and this was used as a foundation for later buildings.

From the description and measurements of the ancient masonry in this tower Sir Charles Warren and Major Conder may be correct in identifying it with Phasælus. The present dimensions—fifty-four feet north and south by sixty-eight feet east and west—approximate the dimensions of Phasælus as recorded by Josephus. The present battlements correspond to Josephus' description of them as they were in his day. A sloping escarp of smooth-faced stones leads up to these battlements. This escarp was no doubt magnificent masonry when first constructed and for centuries afterward. Ages of exposure to the weather and severe treatment by the weapons of assailants have caused it to crumble in places, and modern repairers have been very careless. In spite of its age, bad treatment and the indifference of its present owners it is a commanding structure and is the finest of the ancient towers.

Within the chamber of the tower is an immense cistern

whose water partly supplies the needs of the "Sultan's children." It is filled by surface drainage and by a conduit from the Birket Mamilla, or Upper Pool of Gihon. Josephus tells us of the existence of such a conduit, through which "water was brought into the tower of Hippicus."

A climb to the top of the tower gives us a commanding view and a good notion of the carelessness of those who have charge of Turkish military affairs. There seems to be no order about the barracks. The soldiers are untidy, but not more so than their quarters. The cannons in the tower are genuine antiques, but during the Moslem feasts are sufficiently powerful to satisfy any one chancing to be in the vicinity of their noise. If the garrisons' ordnance consists of the pieces visitors are permitted to see, they could offer little resistance to an attacking force modernly equipped. The view from the top is the best to be had from any point in the city. An uninterrupted prospect in every direction can be enjoyed. The observer is above an historic spot, and his range of vision includes as many places whereon history has been made as any view-point on earth.

Tomb of David.—A few rods south of the Zion Gate is a cluster of buildings the largest of which is called Nebi Daûd —the Prophet David. This is the site of the sepulchres of the early kings of Israel, or is believed to be by Jews, Moslems, and the majority of Christians. In recent years, however, the effort has been made to locate the "royal tombs" on the eastern hill, or Moriah. All depends on the position of the City of David. If that city stood on the low hill south of the temple area, then somewhere in that very limited space David and his successors were buried. If, as has been advocated in the chapters of this work, the western hill must have been the city's real location, then here we must look for the royal burial-place. At all events this is now called the tomb of David and for present purposes that is all we require.

As David is considered by Moslems one of the greatest of

the prophets, this is an especially holy place, guarded more zealously from "infidel" defilement than even the sacred cave at Hebron. The site was formerly Christian property and before the building of the Church of the Holy Sepulchre a church stood here. It was called the Church of the Apostles and marked the place of the descent of the Holy Ghost on the day of Pentecost. In the seventh century it was affirmed that here also the Last Supper was held. When the Crusaders had possession of Jerusalem this church was known as the Church of Zion, or of St. Mary. In the fourteenth century the Franciscans acquired title to this property, and the building in its present form is as they constructed it. In 1547 the Moslems expelled the Franciscans considering that their occupation was a sacrilege. It has since remained a Moslem sanctuary. Christians are never welcomed, and indeed are forbidden to enter any place except an "upper room" which members of the Latin and Oriental Churches regard as the chamber in which the Lord's Supper was instituted. This room, which is called the Coenaculum, was originally part of a Christian Church. Its pillars and ceiling are interesting, but not ancient, probably dating from the fourteenth century. In the southeast corner a stairway leads into a smaller room where the guardian of the place points out a monument of modern design and informs you that it stands directly above the sarcophagus of David, which still exists in the cave beneath. A door is shown which is said to lead into this cave, though whether any such cave really exists is a question. No living person has looked into it. Christians and Jew cannot; Moslems will not. If permission were given to make an inspection the question of the "City of David" and so Mount Zion might be settled.

Apart from its connection with the burial of the kings an interest attaches to Nebi Daûd from the fact that tradition has assigned to the space it includes so many of the events of early Christianity. It is said by Dean Stanley that the Coenaculum "contains within its four walls a greater confluence of traditions than any other place of like dimensions in Palestine." Besides being the place of the Last Supper, it is claimed that it was the scene of Christ's sudden appearance among the disciples after His resurrection; of the descent of the Holy Ghost at Pentecost, of the residence and death of the Virgin Mary and of the burial of Saint Stephen.

This is certainly one instance in which a superabundance of traditions detracts from the probability of each one. It is not at all likely that a residence should have been permitted in Christ's time immediately above the Sepulchre of David. The centering of all these traditions on this spot may be traced to a statement in the writings of Cyril, that the only building which survived the destruction of the city by Titus stood here. It would be easy to infer that a structure so spared must have been divinely protected, and if so, for what better reason than its connection with sacred events? Such events, the places of whose occurrence had been lost, would be readily assigned to this locality; there was no intention to deceive; they wished by thus localizing an event to make it more real. Perhaps it may be said for all such places located since, that their locators had no intention to deceive, but the method of locating many Holy places and the purposes for which they have been employed make one suspicious of the motives.

Via Dolorosa.—Entering the city from the east through the Gate of St. Stephen we are on one of the most important streets—the most important if estimated by the number of Holy Places that line it. Just within the gate is a doorway leading to the Church of St. Anne, the mother of the Virgin, on a site which has been held sacred to the memory of this saint since the seventh century and was kept by a sisterhood in the time of the Crusades. Saladin after his conquest established a large school here, and it was held by the Moslems until 1856, when it was presented by the then reigning Sultan, Abdul-Mejid, to Napoleon III. The present church, remodelled in the twelfth century, has been little disturbed by its different owners.

Following this street, which is known as that of Our Lady Mary, we soon come to some very ancient masonry regarded as formerly belonging to the Tower of Antonia. A little further to the west is the Chapel of Scourging, a marble slab let into the wall on the right indicating the place. This is Franciscan property, having been presented to that order by Ibrahim Pasha in 1838. Below the new chapel, which was built in 1839 by the generosity of Duke Maximilian of Bavaria, the Column of Scourging was found.

The Via Dolorosa proper begins a little further west or in front of the entrance to the Turkish barracks. This is the first of the fourteen stations of "the way of pain"—a way believed by the faithful pilgrims to be the identical road trodden by the foot of the Son of Man, as He went to His death.

This first station marks, according to recent tradition, the place of the House of Pilate, which until the time of the Crusaders was supposed to be somewhere on the western hill. The holy steps—Scala Sancta—now in the Church of St. John Lateran, at Rome, were taken from this place. The second station, where the cross was laid upon the shoulders of Christ, is near the steps leading up to the barracks. A little further on is the fine school and church of the Sisters of Zion, and the Ecce Homo arch where Pilate called the attention of those who were crying for the blood of an innocent Person in the words "Behold the Man." This arch dates from the Roman period and has frequently been repaired; it was probably originally an arch of triumph, and it received its present designation in the tenth century.

Beyond the arch the "way" passes the Austrian Hospice, makes a right angle to the left and then to the right, and ascends the western hill by a succession of steps, passing under gloomy vaults, till it reaches the northern end of Christian street, near which was formerly an entrance to the Church of the Holy Sepulchre. There is nothing about this way which distinguishes it from any other street in the city; it is as tortuous and narrow and unattractive as any. But the very places are shown where each incident in the progress of Christ from the judgment hall to Calvary took place. Here the Saviour sank under the weight of the cross; here Simon of Cyrene was compelled to assume the burden; here is the house of Lazarus as well as that of Dives; here is the house and tomb of Veronica, the saint on whose handkerchief was imprinted the likeness of the Christ when she wiped the sweat from His brow.

The last five stations are in the Church of the Holy Sepulchre. They mark the places where Christ was disrobed, where He was nailed to the cross, where the cross was raised, where He was taken down from the cross and where He was buried.

Thousands of pilgrims come every year and visit time and again all the places marked as holy along this "way." For them it is all very real. Their tears are tears of sorrow and their prayers prayers of faith. They never doubt the accuracy of the locations, and do not know that these sacred sites were not so considered until the fourteenth century, nor that there is not the slightest historical evidence to sustain their genuineness.

Pool of Hezekiah.—Christian street is the cleanest and most attractive in the city. The shops along it are superior in appearance and in fact. Going into almost any one of these on the left as one approaches the Holy Sepulchre, a view can be had of the most important pool in the city—the pool of Hezekiah. The good king is supposed to have constructed it, and for centuries its identity was not questioned. An aqueduct leads to it from the Mamilla Pool, or Upper Pool of Gihon, which is in the large Moslem cemetery, northwest of the town. If this Mamilla Pool was "the upper water course of Gihon," which "Hezekiah stopped,"[1] then there is no doubt about the identification of this pool as Hezekiah's; if it is not, the points

[1] 2 Chron. xxxii. 30.

of resemblance are at least striking. But this is one more instance where certainty is not possible.

Hezekiah's Pool, as it now appears, is eighty yards long by forty-eight wide and three deep, estimating the depth from the level of the street. In winter, after the heavy rains, it is quite an artificial lake, though in midsummer it is generally dry. Its waters are used by the people living near it and supply also the large "Bath of the Patriarch" near at hand; hence it is often called the Pool of the Patriarch's Bath. According to Mejr-ed-Din, an Arabic historian, it was known to the early Moslems, and for long time after, as the Birket Iyad. This Iyad was one of the Prophet's companions; he entered Jerusalem with Omar, and having reconstructed the Pool, he was honored by having it named after him. It is generally regarded as the Amygdalon Pool—the tower pool—of Josephus.

The new theory of Jerusalem topography—which relieves none of the many difficulties—asserts that this pool has no right to the name by which it is popularly known and informs us that what is now called the Pool of Siloam is the real Pool of Hezekiah.

Pool of Bethesda.—Just outside the north wall of the Harâm may be seen the traditional Pool of Bethesda, or rather where the Pool once was. It was 372 feet long, by 126 feet wide, and its depth, measuring from the level of the Mosque area, is sixty-eight feet. This Pool was situated in a valley which anciently extended in a northwesterly direction till it joined the Tyropean. This valley has been filled with debris and the Pool is suffering a similar fate, in some places being already on a level with the street. Only after a heavy rain will any water be seen in it, and then only covering a small place close to the Harâm wall.

In calling this by the ancient name Bethesda we are following an old, but by no means universally accepted, tradition. Early pilgrims also called it "the Sheep Pool," erroneously believing that the present St. Stephen's Gate occupies the site of the Sheep Gate. Recent discoveries have led to the belief that the real pool of this name was in the grounds of the Church of St. Anne. That the Crusaders regarded this latter as Bethesda is argued from the fact that they built five "porches" about it, thus making it correspond to the description of John v. 2. These "porches" still remain and seem to have been rebuilt on ancient foundations. A picture of an angel troubling the waters still remains, the wings and part of the body being easily made out.

The traditional pool is now called Birket Israel. In and near it Captain Warren made some interesting explorations— interesting in that they revealed in the lower courses of the northern Harâm wall masonry similar to that in the southeast angle. Characters in red paint were also found here, which certainly indicate great antiquity. A passage-way was also discovered leading into an aqueduct which formerly carried the water from the pool, underground, through part of the temple enclosure, and discharged it into the Kedron valley. The existence of such an aqueduct points to a time when water was abundant in this pool, for its exit is twenty-five feet above the bottom. The water in the pool could consequently never rise higher than this.

There are interesting discoveries awaiting the pick of the explorer in this northeast angle, just as there are in every part of the Harâm area. But the explorer has to wait, for this is one of the very holiest places of Mohammedanism, and as long as it remains so no permission to excavate will be given, nor will its owners do such work themselves.

Tombs of the Kings.—It may not be pleasant to contemplate, but is, nevertheless, a fact, that the city of Jerusalem stands in the center of an immense cemetery. There are tombs on every side; hardly a building is erected in the newer parts without discovering in the excavations for the foundation the rock-hewn resting-place of some former resident of the ancient city. It is difficult to assign the date to many of these tombs in the rocks, though there are marks which indicate that they cannot be later than a certain time. But many of these tombs have been repeatedly used and during the ages may have been altered to accord with the ideas of sepulture which prevailed at the time.

The most interesting as well as the best preserved are those known as the Tombs of the Kings, situated about half a mile directly north of the Damascus Gate. A French inscription just over the door of entrance tells us that these are the tombs of the Kings of Judah. Ignorance or deception placed this notice where it is and indifference keeps it there. The place is interesting enough without ascribing to it any fictitious value. The tradition calling these the Tombs of the Kings is not older than the fourteenth century.

These tombs are now generally considered as those of Queen Helena, of Adiabene, and her family. Josephus locates the burial-place of this queen here. She was a convert to Judaism, having while in her own land, become convinced of the truth of that religion. On the death of her husband, Mombaz, in 48 A. D., she removed to Jerusalem with her son Izates and resided here for some years. On a visit to her country she died, but her body was brought to the city she loved and buried here. It is said that Izates was the father of twenty-four sons, which, if true, would account for the number of resting places in the tomb.

A flight of twenty-four steps cut in the rock leads down to the level where an entrance to the tomb proper is effected. At the foot of these steps are several large cisterns where the ablutions preliminary to burial were no doubt performed. Passing then through a door on the left which pierces a wall of native rock one is in a large rectangular space fronting the façade of the tombs. On this façade is some of the very finest ornamental carving that remains from ancient times. The character of this and the subjects depicted—such as clusters of grapes, so common on Jewish coins—has assisted in identifying the tombs as Jewish. De Sauley did most of the work of recovering and planning these tombs. In his work of excavation several beautiful sarcophagi were found, which were transported to Paris and may now be seen in the Louvre.

A doorway on the left, some feet below the level of the vestibule, conducts into the main chamber. From this low passages—not easy to follow—lead off in three directions to the smaller chambers where the loculi—places where bodies were laid—may be seen. The evident care which was taken in the making of these tombs, together with the variety of ornamentation, leaves no doubt that they were intended for persons of great wealth and importance.

Solomon's Quarry.—A hundred yards east of the Damascus Gate is a high cliff made by a wide excavation which separates Bezetha from the New Calvary hill. Just at its base where the cliff is highest is a small door leading into the largest cavern near the city. The name given to this by the Moslems is "The Cotton Grotto" because of the unusual whiteness of rock in which it is cut. The common appellation for it is Solomon's Quarry, assuming, and not without reason, that it was here that royal builder procured the stone for his great works. For centuries all knowledge of the existence of this artificial cavern was lost. Since it was recovered, in 1852, it has been a place all visitors wish to see. And it is worth seeing in itself apart from any connection it may have with any of the great builders of antiquity.

The quarry extends southward under the city for nearly seven hundred feet. At some places the roof is so low that one has to stoop in order to pass; in others so high that the light of the candles is swallowed up in the darkness. Here and there large natural pillars are left to support the roof, but these have not prevented the loose rock from falling and as one passes a spot where such a fall has occurred it sends a shudder through him at thought of the possibility of a similar catastrophe occurring during his visit. But none has occurred that has proved fatal to visitors; through carelessness persons have been seriously injured and at least one death has resulted. As there are dangerous pitfalls from which the rock has been taken and which have never been filled up, a person well acquainted with the "cave" should accompany every party.

The stone to be had in this quarry is exceedingly white and beautiful. It is soft and hence can be easily taken out. By the markings in the rock the ancient method of quarrying may be understood. By means of a pick, or similar tool, a deep groove was cut in the face of the rock to the width desired. This was followed by parallel grooves. It was then an easy matter when one stone was removed for all the rest in its tier to be taken out. This was done by making a small niche in the rock, driving in a wooden wedge and then pouring water on the wedge which, as the wood swelled, split the stone. All through the quarries are small shelves on which stood the earthen lamps that gave light to the laborers.

This cavern is of special interest to the Masonic Order. Small and large parties of this fraternity visit the city every year and seem to find their chief delight in the gloomy recesses where they hold, many of them, that Masonry was instituted by King Solomon himself. Many a bit of the white stone, large enough to be worked into an emblem of the Order, finds its way into the trunks of the brethren and is carefully guarded till it takes its place among the sacred relics of the home lodge. Several large blocks have been lately shipped to various cities in America, destined to be worked into some Masonic Temple.

From descriptions of the temples, which at various periods of Jerusalem's history have graced the Mount Moriah, it seems but reasonable to believe that the stone that formed them was procured here. There is no stone like it, none so beautiful, in the vicinity. The quarry is very near the place where the temple stood and by making a surface opening in its southern extremity the distance of transportation would be very short. We are told in 1 Kings vi. 7, that the temple was erected without sound of "any tool of iron heard in the house," and was "of stone ready made before it was brought thither." This preparatory work could easily have been done in the quarry, almost on the very site of the Holy House, and yet no sound be heard within the sacred enclosure. There is no good reason for doubting that here the whiteness was procured that helped to produce the "vision of snow and gold" that stood on Mount Moriah.

EXCAVATIONS IN JERUSALEM

Constantine's Labors—History of Early Explorations—Dr. Edward Robinson—Canon George Williams—Ordnance Survey—Conrad Schick—Topographical Certainties—Uncertainties—Unanswered Questions—Sir Charles Warren—Results Satisfactory—Rock Levels—Tyropean Valley—Mount Moriah—Kedron Valley—Ophel—Siloam Aqueduct—Siloam Inscription—Palestine Exploration Fund's Work—Dr. Bliss and Mr. Dickie—Excavations on Southern Brow of Zion—Walls—Jewish Cemetery—At Siloam Pool—Siloam Church—Endocia's Wall—Other Excavations.

XIII

EXCAVATIONS IN JERUSALEM

SINCE the days of Constantine, when that which is now called the Holy Sepulchre was brought to light, many efforts have been made to reveal the secrets which the debris of many centuries had kept so carefully. Doubt rests upon Constantine's results and upon those of many later delvers in and near the city. But the uncertainty of results has not chilled the ardor with which explorers of more recent times have entered upon their tasks.

A brief list of the lovers of Jerusalem who visited the city since it became prominent as a center of Christian activity and who have left a record of what it was in their time may be of interest.

The Bordeaux Pilgrim was in Jerusalem in 333. In the "Itinerary" he gives us his account of what the city then was. Eusebius, a contemporary of the Pilgrim fully describes the Church of the Resurrection in his "Life of Constantine." Arculfus about the close of the same century gives very distinct testimony as to the sepulchre, and there are many allusions to localities in the Letters of Jerome and in the Homilies of St. Cyril. In the fifth century (427–440) the important tract of Eucherius and several notices in the works of Ephanius were written. Procopius and Theodosius are the authorities for the sixth century. Toward the close of the seventh century (680) Arculfus recorded the impressions received during his pilgrimage. St. Willibald belongs to the eighth century and Bernard the Wise to the ninth. These, with Soewolf (1102), describe the city's appearance before its rebuilding under the Crusaders.

In the history written by William of Tyre Jerusalem topography is frequently alluded to, and in the twelfth century Fetellus (1150) and Theodoricus (1172) give their accounts. The same century furnishes us with some Jewish tracts, the most important of which is that of Benjamin of Tudela.

Brocardus in 1283 is an authority for his time, and Sir John Mandeville (1322) was, until recently, highly regarded. Mejr-ed-Din, the historian, about 1495 gives the best account from an Arab standpoint, while in the same century, though somewhat earlier, John Poloner recounts his impressions from a Christian point of view. In 1616 a Latin monk, named Quaresmius, wrote an account based on tradition. Henry Maundrell's account written in 1697 is considered a valuable document. Reland (1714), Pococke (1737) and Chateaubriand (1807) bring us to the beginning of this century and the inception of critical and scientific investigations concerning the topography of the Holy City.

The above list by no means gives the names of all those who during these centuries have left on record what they had seen in Jerusalem or heard from those who had seen. It comprises simply those upon whom modern students generally rely. A work of unknown authorship, dating from 1190, and first published in Count Beugnot's "Assises de Jerusalem" in 1843, gives a topographical description of the city as it was when Saladin finally wrested it from the Crusaders.

The honor of the first real scientific exploration of sacred sites in Palestine belongs to the American scholar and traveller, Dr. Edward Robinson. He began his work in this line in 1838, and soon became so dissatisfied with the proofs that were presented to him that he was compelled to regard as utterly worthless the entire mass of monkish traditions that were adduced in the support of localities. His results were conclusive to the great majority of Bible Land students, though he found a worthy opponent in the English traditionalist Canon George Williams, whose work "The Holy City"—a monument of history and topography—appeared in 1849. German scholars, notable among whom are Thrupp (1855), and Tobler (1845–1855) added to existing information. Other names of prominence about this time are Fergusson, Willis, Barclay, Stanley, De Sauley, Vandevelde and the Duc de Vogüe.

While the labors of all these are important and their writings are authoritative, the later explorations conducted by the Ordnance Survey at the expense of Lady Burdett-Coutts, and published in 1866, have rendered the work of all but Dr. Robinson and the Duc de Vogüe, to a greater or less extent, obsolete. Since then the society known as the Palestine Exploration Fund have been the principal workers in this field. The most indefatigable individual worker is Dr. Conrad Schick, who has resided in Jerusalem for fifty years and is probably better acquainted with the city than any other living person. Along with these must be mentioned the excavations on Ophel made by Dr. Guthe, in 1881, and the exploration of the well-known Zion scarp by Mr. Henry Maudsley in 1874. The clearing of the Muristan by the German Government in 1873 disclosed this part of the city. While these practical explorers have been at work seeking to increase our knowledge of Jerusalem and its environs by actual excavations, there has been a class of theorizers, no less numerous, who have advanced opinions as to the city's topography, some of which are ingenious, some absurd. The number of this latter class and the confusion resulting from their numerous hypotheses have led the general reader into the belief that there is nothing certain in modern localizations of the ancient famous places and buildings. While a great deal of uncertainty really does exist, it is an unwarranted statement to say that there is nothing sure.

We are certain that the ridge facing the Temple Hill on the east is the Mount of Olives; that the valley between these two hills is the valley of the Kedron. There is no reasonable doubt that the hill within the city, and known as Mt. Moriah, is that on which the temple stood. The valley that separates

Mt. Moriah from the modern Zion is conceded to be the Tyropean of Josephus. No one questions that the Pool of Siloam is properly named, or that Ophel is the southern slope of Mt. Moriah. The east wall of the Haram enclosure is recognized as being part of the wall of the ancient city, and the present southwest corner of the Haram enclosure marks the limits of the ancient temple area in this direction. The modern citadel, known as David's Tower, is located in the immediate vicinity of the royal fortresses built by Herod. The Zion scarp in the Protestant cemetery is the old southwest angle of the city.

These are settled points. They are not numerous, but it is some satisfaction to know that concerning them there is a harmony of opinion among writers on Jerusalem. The unsettled points are many. At the same time they may be included in four main questions. First, Where was the City of David, on modern Zion, or on Ophel, just south of the temple area? Second, What was the extent of the city at its greatest prosperity, or just before its destruction by Titus in 70 A. D.? Third, What was the area included within the temple walls and just where within this area did the temple itself stand? Fourth, What is the true site of Calvary and of the Holy Sepulchre?

On all these questions authorities differ. The only key to the solution of the first will be the discovery of the Tomb of David. This we know was in the city of David. Efforts have been made to locate these royal sepulchres, but without success. Of late authorities have been inclining to accept the eastern hill south of the temple area as the true site of the ancient city. The difficulties in the way of such an acceptance are many. To recognize the summit of Zion as being the place selected for his city by Israel's warrior king is not without its objections either. While I hold to this latter opinion, it is only an opinion whose tenure depends upon the pick of the excavator.

The answer to the second question depends upon the discovery of the ancient walls. On the south the wall is now fairly well known. The recent excavations of Doctor Bliss, conducted under the Palestine Exploration Fund during the years 1893 to 1897, have traced this wall from the scarp at the southwest corner, in the Protestant cemetery, along the southern brow of the Zion hill, eastward to and including the Pool of Siloam. There is still some doubt as to whether the wall thus traced was ancient, but there is no room for dispute that at some time in its history the city extended thus far in this direction. Nor is there any doubt that the wall—a double wall—exposed south of the Siloam Pool is ancient.

The east wall as far as the northeast angle of the temple enclosure, and the west wall as far north as the present Jaffa Gate are regarded as occupying the positions of the ancient city walls. But the walls to the north, of which there were three, erected at different periods, are under consideration and will probably remain so for a long time. The most important of these, and the one that has given rise to the greatest discussion, is the Second Wall. Its importance is due to its relation to the site of the Holy Sepulchre Church.

Concerning the third question as to the area of the temple enclosure and the exact position of the Holy House we must wait for answer upon the result of explorations yet to be made. The excavations of Sir Charles Warren, which resulted in the discovery of the large wall on Ophel, favors those who believe that the temple area was a square measuring one thousand feet on each side. The line of this wall discovered by Warren joins the Haram wall at the southeast angle and thus corresponds with a statement in Josephus, which informs us that the Ophel wall joined the east cloister of Herod's Temple. The opposite opinion is that the temple area was a square of about six hundred feet on each side.

The actual site of the temple itself is not known and as long as the Moriah hill remains a Moslem sacred place will not be known.

As regards the fourth question, namely, the true site of Calvary and of the Holy Sepulchre, it has been sufficiently dwelt upon in the chapters on "The Holy Sepulchre" and "The New Calvary."

Concerning the rest of the city and its immediate environs there is hardly a square rod that has not been examined by some enterprising student of topography; excepting only sites considered holy by the Moslems. Unfortunately these exceptions cover most interesting places, as for example, the Mosque area and the traditional site of the Tomb of David. In all firmans granted to individuals or societies, giving permission to excavate, absolute prohibition against touching these sacred places is invariable. It will thus be seen that the most interesting exploring is still to be done.

And yet, in spite of these prohibitions and of other hindrances and inconveniences the results of recent explorations have been numerous and satisfactory. It will be possible to mention these only in a general way; in the various volumes published by, and in the Quarterly Reports of the Palestine Exploration Fund they may be found in detail.

A very important preliminary to the proper study of Jerusalem was the ascertaining of the levels of the rock foundations upon which the city was built. This work was done by Lieutenant-Colonel Conder principally, though he was assisted by the previous labors of Doctor Schick and Sir Charles Wilson. These rock levels give an idea of the contour of the hills and valleys of Jerusalem before they were selected by men as suitable ground for the building of a city. They reveal the depth of the debris that has been accumulated during the city's history.

Having once obtained these levels the explorer could easily see how much change had come over the surface contour, and how necessary it was to take this alteration into account in considering the descriptions of the city's topography as recorded in the Bible and in Josephus. It gives us the approximate height of the hills, the depth and width of the valleys as they were in earlier days. One of the results of seeking for these levels was the revelation of the important valley that began near the Jaffa Gate and descended into the Tyropean. There has been so much accumulation here that this valley, which many consider the true commencement of the Tyropean, was quite forgotten. It was originally a considerable gorge and gave to the lower part of the northwestern hill a "gibbous" form.

The main part of the Tyropean valley has been partially excavated. The accumulations of rubbish here are of great depth. Vaults and pools and passages constructed of large and well-dressed stones exist beneath the present surface. The modern Street of the Chain crosses this valley on a causeway, beneath which is a long passage that has been called the Secret Passage. North of this are two parallel rows of vaults dating from pre-Saracenic times as is seen from repairs evidently Saracenic. When these vaults were constructed their course was hindered by a large building made of drafted stones. This structure is no doubt one of the oldest pieces of masonry in Jerusalem and is called the Ancient Hall.

And so following the whole course of this Tyropean Valley until it merges into the Kedron valley the excavator has found a most fertile soil. Foundations of buildings, cisterns and drains show the immensity of the work that has been expended upon it at various periods of the history of the city. A large part of it is outside the present walls, as in fact is a large part of the ground covered by the ancient city.

There was also in early times a considerable valley north of the temple area which assisted in the protection of the sacred enclosure. This commences north of the present wall of the city, descends in a southerly direction and turns to the east just west of the Church of Saint Anne, shortly afterward merging into the Kedron. This valley is mentioned by Josephus in the Antiquities xiv. 4, 2, and in the Wars 1, 7, 3. Pompey sought to fill up this valley and found it a serious undertaking. The great reservoir, commonly called, though erroneously, the Pool of Bethesda, lies in this valley. The natives term it Birket Israel, or Pool of Israel. It extends along the north wall of the Mosque enclosure for 360 feet and has a breadth of 126 feet and depth of eighty feet. It is, however, rapidly being filled up by refuse and part of it, never covered by water, is being used as a vegetable garden.

The excavations just outside the walls of the Mosque area, and the several examinations of the cistern within the enclosure which have been permitted by the Moslem custodians enable us to have a reasonably correct idea of the original contour of Mount Moriah. The summit was the sacred rock now under the Dome. From this the rock shelved off on all sides, except at the northwest corner where the rock was prominent and on which now stands the Turkish barracks occupying the old site of the Tower of Antonia. A neck of rock formerly joined Mount Moriah to Bezetha, but this was artificially cut through at an early date.

The Kedron valley has witnessed many attempts at excavation. Great difficulties were experienced here and owing to the loose nature of the debris always will be. Mixed with the soil is an immense amount of stone chippings, which prevent the soil from cohering and make deep excavating dangerous. Unfortunately only deep excavating is of any value here for the depth of the debris, which is all comparatively modern, is great and any discoveries that will throw light upon ancient times are found beneath this.

The original bed of the Kedron is forty feet west of the present. The unstable nature of the debris has gradually forced it thus far to the east, at the same time filling up the bed and raising its surface about twelve feet. A wall built for the purpose of retaining the accumulations on the west has been uncovered just west of the true bed. It has long been overcome by the moving mass, which has forced itself eastward until it threatens to cover and hide from view the many tombs of the Hebrews that were thought to have been buried at a safe distance from the winter brook.

This eastern wall of the sanctuary has been already examined and some of the results of subterranean investigation mentioned. But what is known, compared to what is yet to be revealed, is very little. The cause of this ignorance is the presence of what is always a bane to explorers, a Moslem cemetery. This extends over a large part of the ground between the southeast corner of the wall and St. Stephen's Gate. North of the Golden Gate, however, it is known that the depth of the debris is 125 feet, and that the wall is built up from the native rock foundation. This was learned only after most laborious excavation by Sir Charles Warren. Perhaps, as Warren has supposed, if excavating could be done in the Moslem cemetery and along the wall the huge stones—twenty cubits long by six cubits thick—which Solomon placed on this side would be uncovered.

The Ophel hill, which is but the southern slope of Moriah, is very different in appearance from what it was when it was within the city proper. It is now covered by gardens that are tilled in rich soil that overlies the houses of former Jerusalemites. And where the solemn priests once wended their way to the temple and its services the Fellahin now delve and guard their small patches of ground. Amid the gardens Warren discovered the Ophel wall which has a width at its base of fifteen feet and at its top of twelve feet. This wall was followed southward for seventy-six feet where it turned to the west and continued for 700 feet. Several towers of great strength were observed. Among the many interesting antiquities that were found within this wall was a cavern containing fullers' vats, very near to the traditional place where Saint James was thrown from the temple wall and killed by a fuller's club.

The Siloam aqueduct is interesting in showing the early engineering of the Jews. This aqueduct extends from the Virgin's Fountain through the spur of Ophel to the Pool of Siloam. The distance between the Fountain and the Pool is, in a straight line, about 900 feet. But the course followed by the conduit makes it 1,708 feet. Why this tortuous route was taken has given rise to conjecture, some supposing it was taken intentionally in order to avoid the tombs of the kings. But there is no evidence whatever that these tombs are on this ridge of Ophel, and it is more likely that the great length of the aqueduct was due to the ignorance of its makers in subterranean engineering. This belief is supported by the fact that openings have been found from the tunnel to the surface, indicating in all likelihood that they were made in order that the excavators might thus get their bearings.

Modern explorers have managed with difficulty to crawl through this aqueduct. Doctor Robinson was the first of these. Doctor Barclay also succeeded before the Palestine Exploration Fund's workers under Colonel Warren were on the ground. To the latter, however, belongs the credit of having made a careful survey of the route. With their great care, however, the most important secret the tunnel contained was not discovered. This is what is now known as the Siloam Inscription, and is the oldest Hebrew inscription in existence. It was found in 1880 by a Fellah working under the direction of Herr Conrad Schick. This laborer fell into the water of the tunnel accidentally and happened then to notice some lettering on the wall cut in the solid rock. Later inspection showed that the face of the rock had been smoothed into a tablet form of about twenty-seven inches square. This was found about fifteen feet from the Siloam end of the tunnel, on the right side as one would enter it.

Several men of prominence in Jerusalem exploration worked upon this inscription. During the centuries of its existence a deposit of lime had formed over it. This Doctor Guthe, the

Excavations in Jerusalem 243

German authority on Jerusalem topography, removed by washing the tablet in a weak solution of hydrochloric acid. A "squeeze" of the inscription was taken by Major Conder under great difficulties, he and his assistant Lieutenant Mantell having to remain in an uncomfortable position partially in water for several hours. Professor Sayce had seen the original inscription *in situ*, but used as the basis of his study of it the squeeze made by Conder. The following is Sayce's translation of the text:

1. "(Behold the) Excavation. Now this is the history of the excavation. While the excavators were still lifting up
2. "The pick, each toward his neighbor, and while there were yet three cubits to (excavate, there was heard) the voice of one man
3. "Calling to his neighbor, for there was an excess (?) in the rock on the right hand (and on the left?). And after that on the day
4. "Of excavating the excavators had struck pick against pick, one against another,
5. "The waters flowed from the spring to the pool for a distance of 1,200 cubits. And (part)
6. "Of a cubit was the height of the rock over the head of the excavators"

Each verse of the above translation represents a line on the tablet. The characters are in ancient Hebrew resembling closely those on the Moabite Stone. Their existence sets at rest the ignorant assertion that the early Israelites were unable to write.

The most recent scientific exploring has been done by the Palestine Exploration Fund, with Doctor Fredrick J. Bliss as the man in charge. Excavating is not easy work and the Fund soon found that an assistant to Doctor Bliss was necessary. Mr. A. C. Dickie was the assistant selected. These two able and enthusiastic explorers spent the working seasons of three consecutive years mostly on the southern slope of Mount Zion and in the Tyropean valley. Full reports of their labors and "finds" are given in the Quarterly Statement of the Fund. Work was begun in the spring of 1894.

Commencing at the so-called Rock Scarp of Zion this scarp was followed for a considerable distance. Inside the scarp a long line of fine masonry *in situ* was found. A massive gateway in the wall was uncovered, which is thought to be the Dung Gate of Scripture. A paved street led up to this gate and beneath the street was found a large drain. This gate must have once been the main exit from the city to the south.

No evidence of a wall on the scarp was found. But the wall within was definitely traced for 1,050 feet, and the tracing then had to be discontinued because it led through the ancient Zion burial-place of the Jews. In the wall thus exposed five different styles of masonry are recognized, viz:—rubble foundation, roughly-dressed stones, smooth-faced stones, drafted stones with flat centres, drafted stones with projecting bosses. To what period to assign these various styles no one knows positively, and no key is given by the stones themselves, as none bore any inscription or ornamentation. The masonry was all small, but this fact tells nothing about the date. The probability is that this wall represents several reconstructions. In the time of the city's greatest prosperity and extent a wall certainly stood here, and that it was a single wall we learn from Josephus who gives as a reason for it the exceeding steepness of the valley beneath it. In all probability Hadrian's southern wall ran on this line, as did also that of the Crusaders', judging from Marina Samito's map.

As the age of masonry in Jerusalem cannot be positively told by the dressing of the stones, the assigning of the building of this southern wall to any particular age or century is impossible. This much is certain, that it reveals the work of at least three periods when walls were built, or rebuilt, on this line; also that it marks the city's greatest possible extent in this direction. The inference is safe that at the time of the greatest prosperity of Jerusalem it extended as far south as at any time and that at that time—the reign of Herod the Great —there existed a wall on this site. That Doctor Bliss in following the ruined south wall was tracing the route of a wall that was standing at the time of Christ there can be no reasonable doubt.

No excavating was done in the Jewish cemetery already mentioned, so the wall for a distance of 700 feet was not examined. Just east of the cemetery it was rediscovered and followed, not without great difficulty, past a tower and gate, along the brow of Mount Zion to the Pool of Siloam. In the side excavations that were made while the wall was being followed ruins of houses, pools, streets, drains and stairways cut in the rock of Mount Zion were unearthed.

But perhaps the most interesting work was done in the immediate vicinity of the Siloam Pool. There was a great stairway to the west of the pool consisting of thirty-four steps "arranged in a system of wide and narrow treads alternately." Some of these steps are cut out of the natural rock and are much worn by the feet of former generations. These steps were the means of ascent and descent to the waters of the pool.

Of considerable importance was the recovery of the ruins of an ancient Christian Church, whose south aisle was "built over the north arcade of the ancient pool." A church was known to have been built here and the ruins were thought to be hidden under the debris, but to Doctor Bliss and architect Dickie belongs the honor of unearthing and describing and depicting the ruin. The lower parts of the building were in a good state of preservation and the length and breadth of the original structure were easily determined. It was eighty-four feet in length, fifty-one feet six inches in width, and the width of the nave was twenty-five feet ten inches.

This church was probably built under the direction and by the patronage of the Empress Eudocia. When the Bordeaux

Pilgrim visited Jerusalem in 333 A. D., there was no church here, or he certainly would have noted it, as he does describe the pool and mentions its having a four-sided portico. Arculfus in 670 was in Jerusalem and is recognized as the authority for the city's churches as they then were. He does not mention this church at Siloam. He does say, however, that Eudocia extended the walls of the city so as to include the pool. It is known that this Empress, who died in 460, spent the last ten years of her life in Jerusalem and that she occupied her time in building churches and strengthening the city walls. It is probable that when she built the wall to include the pool, she intended it also as a protection for her Siloam Church.

The ruins of this wall which Eudocia built were those found just south of the old, or lower, Siloam pool, which is just at the junction of the Tyropean valley with that of Jehoshaphat, and is now always polluted by the refuse water from the city. But another thing was assured by the excavations here, namely, that Eudocia was not the first to bring the Siloam pool within the walls of Jerusalem. In the debris, thirty feet under the present surface, were found the remains of an ancient wall, many of the stones of which are *in situ*. Perhaps when the Siloam tunnel that made the pool possible was excavated, the city authorities built this including wall to protect this important reservoir.

Other excavations on Mount Zion and on Ophel were made under the direction of Doctor Bliss, which revealed that the parts of these hills now outside the walls of the city and given over to gardens were once built over with houses. The results of these excavations are of interest to the special student of Jerusalem topography, but not to the general reader. They are found in detail in the Quarterly Reports of the Palestine Exploration Fund.

CLIMATE AND HEALTH

Great Variety of Climate in Palestine—Causes—Temperature of Jerusalem—Sudden Changes—Lack of Forests—Two Seasons—Rains, Early and Latter—Heaviest Rains—Winter—Spring—Snow—Summer—Disadvantages of Climate—Annual Rainfall—Increased Necessary—Mists—Dews—Winds—Sirocco—Jerusalem a Healthful City—Sanitary Violations—Odors—Cholera—Quarantine—Nature's Provision for Health—Fever—Water Supply—A Summer Resort—Spring Water—Mortality Among Children—Children's Hospital.

CHAPTER XIV

CLIMATE AND HEALTH

NO country on earth has at once so limited an area and so great a variety of climate as Palestine. Though not under the tropics, the Jordan valley enjoys tropical heat and vegetation. Mount Hermon is just beyond the northern boundary of Palestine proper, and from the perpetual summer of the Ghôr, or Jordan Valley, can be seen lifting up its head to a height where the snow remains throughout the year. This diversity of climate is due to the physical features of the land —features peculiar, indeed unique. The Dead Sea lies 1,30c feet below sea level. Mount Hermon rises 9,050 above sea level. Between these two extremes there is variety enough to satisfy the most exacting. A Jerusalem resident can reach the region of continual summer by making a journey sixteen miles to the east, during which journey he will descend nearly 4,000 feet; he can reach the orange groves of Jaffa, with their soft Florida climate, after a journey of forty-three miles; he is only one hundred and fifty miles from the summit of Hermon. In midsummer one can stand on the shore of the Dead Sea with the thermometer registering the almost insufferable heat of 140° Fahrenheit and, looking up the Ghôr, or Jordan valley, see the snow fields on the top of Hermon. In his own city, 2,600 feet above the Mediterranean, and 3,900 feet above the Dead Sea, the Jerusalemite has in summer a temperature seldom rising above 95° Fahrenheit in the shade, and in midwinter seldom going lower than the freezing point, and that only at night.

The position of the city, between the high mountains on the north and the hot desert lands on the south and east, renders it subject to rather sudden changes of temperature. Only occasionally, however, are the changes severe enough to cause suffering even among the lightly clad denizens of the place. These changes are now more frequent and more severe than they once were, owing to the denuded condition of the country as regards forests; there is practically no timber in any part of Palestine. There are some districts that might be called woodland in a country where woods were not abundant. These woods, a low copse-like growth, are found only on Carmel and in Gilead; and they can have no affect upon the rainfall or temperature. And yet there are those[1] acquainted with the land in its present condition and with the descriptions of it contained in the Bible and other ancient records who assert that "we may safely conclude that the land was never very much more wooded than it is to-day." Whether this view be correct or not, certainly under present conditions there is no prospect of any increase in timber growth. With an utter disregard of the future the inhabitants have in most quarters stripped the hills of every tree. What little fuel is necessary is procured by grubbing out the roots of the ground-oak and the fragments of olive-trees. As for tree culture there is nothing of the kind practiced. The fact that in Bible times the rainfall was more abundant and the natural springs more numerous and copious would lead to the inference that at that time the forests covered a considerable part of the land. One other thing is assured, namely, that Palestine could never have supported the population accredited to it at certain periods of its history, had it always been in its present condition as regards moisture.

Jerusalem and the neighboring districts have but two seasons—the wet and the dry. One has only to pass a year in the city to be convinced that these two are plainly marked. "Seed time and harvest, cold and heat, winter and summer," are the Biblical names. And each term is exact. The wet season is the "seed time, the cold, the winter"; the dry sea-

[1] George Adam Smith in "Hist. Geog. of the Holy Land," p. 81.

son is "the harvest, the heat, the summer." There are likewise two periods of rain called in our English Bible "the former," or "early," and "the latter rains." The early rains usually commence late in October or early in November. Until the first or middle of December the fall is not large, but its effect is very beneficent. It opens the agricultural season, softening the earth that has been dried hard by the long summer and making it possible for the husbandman to use his rude plow, an implement which has been in no way improved since the days of the patriarchs. During the early rains the weather is very changeable. One day will be warm and clear with no sign of cloud or suggestion of winter; the next day rain will be falling, perhaps mingled with snow or sleet; and on the third a cold bitter wind will be blowing out of the north, sending the clouds flying across the heavens and making half-clad humanity draw its clothes more tightly around it and seek the shelter of some friendly building or wall.

Between "the early" and "latter rains" there is usually a period of a week or two during which fair weather prevails, though it is not to be counted on. In January and February the heaviest showers fall. In March and April come the "latter rains" of Scripture. These are very important, being necessary for the maturing of the crops and preparing the land and people for the long rainless summer. Frequent mention is made in the Bible of the "early and latter rains," and the impression is gotten by some that there are two distinct times of rain, viz, at the vernal and autumnal equinoxes. But the truth is that the rainy season lasts during all the winter months. Their importance is the cause of their frequent mention. By the time the heavy showers of March and April set in Nature has begun to put on her beautiful garments, and by the middle of April "the winter is past, the rain is over and gone, the flowers appear on the earth, the time of the singing of birds is come, and the voice of the turtle is heard in the land." This is the balmy time of the year and those who can visit the city and land at this season cannot but have delightful remembrances of it.

During every winter there are usually a few days of freezing weather; a thin coating of ice forms on small pools during the night, but it disappears before the following noon unless in a very protected place. Snow is an occasional, and to the natives a very unwelcome, visitor. It has been known to fall and remain for several days at a time, but conditions admitting this very seldom arise. Three heavy falls of snow occurred during the months of January and February of this year, 1898, when the winter was exceptionally cold and much suffering was endured by the people.

Summer begins about the middle of May and continues until the last of September or well into October. During this time hardly a drop of rain falls. The sky is generally perfectly free from clouds, though occasionally soft fleecy ones are blown up from the Mediterranean, linger for awhile and then disappear. "Clouds are they without water."[1] By the middle of June the flowers and grass have perished for lack of moisture; only the olive and fig trees and the low grapevines show any sign of green. A haziness fills the atmosphere and limits the circle of vision. Often for days at a time the Moab hills cannot be seen. This is due to the effect of the sun upon the naked hills, heating the lower stratum of the air and causing it to rise rapidly. But here in the Judean hills the climate in midsummer is much more endurable than in New York or in any city south of it on the Atlantic seaboard; it is more agreeable than that of any American inland city, whether in summer or winter. Its great disadvantage is the length of its rainless period and consequent scarcity of water and abundance of dust. If the rains could be distributed throughout the year this disadvantage would be overcome, for in the five winter months more rain falls than in most places in the United States during twelve months; the average annual precipitation

[1] Jude 12.

is about thirty inches. There is some indication that the rainfall is increasing and this to many is regarded as a strong proof of the fulfillment, in the near future, of certain prophecies relating to the land. If the land ever recovers its former glory such as it had when it was characterized as "a delightsome land," [1] "the glory of all lands," [2] "an exceeding good land," [3] "the land flowing with milk and honey" [4] or "the land which the Lord thy God careth for," it will have to be more blessed with water during the summer than it now is. This lends some weight to the opinion [4] that there was still another rainy season which occurred just after the harvest was all gathered in, a period of moisture which would make up just what is lacking, for a rain then would refresh the entire land, blessing the mountain pastures where the sheep and goats now hunt almost in vain for a few spears of grass, and laying the dust in the city and suburbs.

In the summer morning mists are occasional and oftentimes so dense as to prevent an observer in the city from seeing the Mount of Olives. I have been on some of the high points around the city early on a July morning and had face and hands made quite wet by a mist that would do credit to a Scotch highland; but when the sun rises above the Moab hills the fog and mist vanish rapidly. From this sudden disappearance the Hebrew writers drew many of their figures illustrative of the frailty and brevity of life. "What is your life?" [5] asks James in his epistle and answers it by a reference well known. "It is even a vapor that appeareth for a little time and then vanisheth away." The dews at night are often quite heavy and on the streets and surrounding roads in the early morning one might imagine that a modern sprinkler had passed; were the

---

[1] Mal. iii. 12.   [2] Ezek. xx. 6.
[3] Numbers xiv. 7.   [4] Ex. xxxiii. 3; Lev. xx. 24; Numbers xiv. 8; Jer. xxxii. 22; Ezek. xx. 6.
[4] Barclay, "City of the Great King," p. 54.
[5] James iv. 14.

resident of experience not quite incapable of conceiving so useful an engine in the hands of Turkish officials.

The belief that the annual rainfall is increasing is well founded. Records at hand for the years succeeding 1861, if estimated in decades, will show this. From 1861 to 1870 the average annual rainfall was 21.87 inches; from 1871 to 1880 it was 24.60 inches, while the decade ending with 1890 averaged annually 27.69 inches, an increase of 3.09 inches over the decade ending with 1880 and of 5.82 inches over that ending with 1870. During this entire period the smallest precipitation for any one year was in 1889, when the registration amounted to 13.79 inches. Thus far during the present decade the fall has been abundant each year and gives support to the frequently made statement that the rainfall of Palestine is increasing. For the figures here given for the present decade I am indebted to the Rev. A. Hastings Kelk, rector of Christ's Church, Jerusalem:—

	1890	1891	1892	1893	1894	1895	1896	1897	1898
January			6.30	4.65	3.65	.69	7.85	13.31	4.40
February			3.50	1.43	5.15	2.86	7.2	6.39	5.74
March		22.71	1.45	9.52	7.18	4.77	4.93	7.41	5.76
April			1.34	.28	1.67	1.83	2.14	.04	
May			.84			.23	.42	.25	
June								.01	
July									
August									
September									
October		.035	.03	.11			.04	9	
November		2.41	5.08	.49	5.75	9.67	2.08	3.03	
December		9.56	7.25	6.25	6.68		4.37	6.34	
Yearly Total	35.51	34.72	27.78	22.73	30.08	20.05	29.03	37.68	

Jerusalem is decidedly a windy city. Her winds, while sometimes exceedingly boisterous and careering over the mountains at a rate that would do justice to a Dakota breeze, are her best friends. The sultry and sickening winds from the desert are fortunately infrequent. In every part of the city but the low underground hovels of the Jewish quarter and some of the narrow, arched streets, fresh air can always be enjoyed. I confess that it is not always enjoyed, for the denizens of some parts of the city are so vile in their habits of life that they seem to prefer the odors of decaying vegetable and animal matter to the combination of fresh sea and mountain air. This preference on their part gives the casual visitors of a day or two a wrong idea of the city, because in order to see many of the interesting places they have to pass through these villainous alleys of putrefaction. In winter the prevailing wind is from the west; it blows up fresh from the Mediterranean and drives the welcome clouds, heavy with moisture, before it, until, reaching the cooler altitude of the hills, they drop their refreshment upon the thousand-mouthed earth. It is not always true now, as our Lord's assertion would lead us to believe it was in His day, that "When ye see a cloud rise out of the west, straightway ye say 'There cometh a shower and so it is,'"[1] for very often the winds drive before them heavy threatening banks of leaden clouds having every evidence of "abundance of rain," only to have them pass away without leaving a blessing on the waiting fields. "Clouds are they without water, carried about of winds."[2] In summer the prevalent winds are from the northwest. They are not shower bringers, but are welcome because of their coolness. Nearly every morning they commence to blow and continue their cheer through most of the day. Occasionally they increase to violence, and gathering the dust in their embrace sweep it along in such quantities as to be a great discomfort to men and animals. This northwest wind performs good service for the native threshers who winnow their grain against it, throw-

[1] Luke xxii. 54. [2] Jude 12.

ing the mixed wheat and chaff up from the threshing floor on some hilltop and letting the wind carry the chaff away.[1]

With the exception of these winds from the northwest "the wind bloweth where it listeth." But winds from other quarters are not very desirable. The east and south winds are not frequent, but are very effective; they are hot and enervating and their departure is most welcome. True it is that, "when ye see the south wind blow ye say, There will be heat and it cometh to pass"[2] these south winds are called "sirocco" by European residents and "sherkiyeh" by the Arabs. Discomfort to man and beast and injury to vegetation result from them. Fine sand accompanies the sirocco and sifts into every part of the house, so that it is literally true that you can "see" it. Isaiah must have had some experience with this unwelcome visitor, but drew certain consolation from the fact that it was attended by nothing worse. "He stayeth his rough wind in the day of the east wind."[3] I have known the temperature to rise 30° Fahrenheit as a result of one of these siroccos between sunrise and noon, and the spirits to sink correspondingly. One would suppose that the natives, who have been accustomed to these winds all their lives, would not notice them much. That they do notice and are affected by them fully as much as are Europeans or Americans is the fact. When a "sherkiyeh" is blowing they do nothing except to get as much as possible out of it, draw their loose garments about their faces and make the best of it by sleeping. The sirocco never brings rain and is of no use to the thresher. Jeremiah[4] may have it in mind speaking of it as "A dry wind of the high places in the wilderness toward the daughter of my people, neither to fan nor to cleanse."

Not only does the sirocco depress one's spirits and, as Barclay says,[5] "cause a feeling of perfect good-for-nothingness," it

[1] Psalm i. 4; Dan. ii. 35; Hosea xiii. 3; Luke iii. 17.
[2] Luke xii. 55.   [3] Is. xxvii. 8.   [4] Jeremiah iv. 11.
[5] "City of the Great King," p. 61.

also induces fever, and a low type of malaria is sure to make its appearance when this wind is frequent and continued. The coolness and refreshment of the breezes from the west and north fortunately overbalance any evils brought by those from the opposite direction; without them Jerusalem would be a most unhealthy place of residence. I question if any city in the world of its size violates more flagrantly the primal laws of sanitation. Regardless of these laws and indifferent to their surroundings the people in some parts throw all the refuse of their living into the narrow, unventilated streets and allow it to lie there exhaling its poisonous vapors, until the street-cleaning brigade, consisting of a couple of donkeys and as many boys, with little more intelligence than their long-eared helpers, come along and carry it off to the common dumping grounds. To a foreigner—even to some whose own cities are by no means models of cleanliness—the odors from some of the Holy City's side streets are excruciating. The wonder is that such utter disregard of sanitation does not frequently result in fatal epidemics. But it does not. Cholera is a frequent visitor to some parts of the Turkish dominions, but for thirty years Jerusalem has escaped its ravages. On the first reports of its approach in the Levant, Jaffa quarantines against every vessel coming from an infected port. This protects Jerusalem from the sea. Every road leading into the city is guarded and no one admitted in this way. All goods are quarantined for some days and then fumigated. I have seen them washing money in the sea at Jaffa in order to free it from any clinging cholera bacilli, while at the same time in the streets of that city and in Jerusalem were unnoticed piles of decaying, cholera breeding matter, a great deal more likely to work injury to the inhabitants. There are two reasons why disastrous results do not follow such negligence, the power of the sun to dry all putrefying matter and the continual breezes that carry off the poisonous gases.

Nature has made this a healthy city in spite of the filthy

habits of the majority of its inhabitants and the puerility of its official class. Its high altitude and deep encompassing valleys counteract this carelessness and childishness. Had Jerusalem been built on a plain and its people had the habits of its present population it would long ago have been depopulated or at least sunk to the condition of the wretched villages of the Maritime plain. It has a sewer system of most primitive construction, which any sanitary engineer would pronounce more destructive of than conducive to health. The streets and sewers could not be flushed if the authorities had any inclination to resort to such modern novelties, owing to the lack of any kind of waterworks. This condition of affairs is the wonder and disgust of visitors and civilized residents. Often have I heard this or similar remarks, "Well, of all places I was ever in this is the filthiest and can produce the most villainous odors. It must be one of the most unhealthy places on earth." The sights and smells of some quarters are as bad as the most vivid imagination can conceive them, but the conclusion usually drawn is incorrect. Nevertheless this carelessness does not pass unpunished altogether. During the summer months there is a great deal of what is commonly known as Jerusalem fever. This is a low type of malaria, and while seldom leading to fatal results does produce an intense longing in the bosom of its victim—a longing to be in a city less renowned for holiness, and more distinguished for cleanliness.

One great cause of this fever is the condition of the water supply. Standing for months in ill-kept cisterns the water has become tainted and the free use of it for drinking purposes, especially in August and September, is apt to result in this fever. Other causes assist, but this is the most fruitful source, and cleaning the cisterns each year would produce good effects. But year after year, without so much as a thought being given to their condition, these cisterns are used and one year's corruption is added to another's. This fever has a deterrent effect upon summer visitors. Reports of it have spread abroad and the wily tourist keeps far distant. He does not want to be scorched externally by the Judean sun or burned internally by the Jerusalem fever, so he comes in the winter and exposes himself to the rains and chilly winds, has difficulty in keeping dry and greater difficulty in keeping warm and risks pneumonia, all to escape the heat and the fever.

And yet, as has been said, the climate in summer is preferable to that of the majority of places in the temperate zone. The city's altitude, dry air and proximity to the sea and the mountains, make it something of a summer resort. Many missionaries residing in the surrounding districts and in Egypt spend their vacations here, coming up from the plains and cities along the Syrian coast and from neighboring villages. And they find what they seek, rest and a change of climate.

No matter what the day is, though it is seldom hot enough to be uncomfortable indoors, the nights are always cool. As soon as the sun dips into the western sea coolness comes that would be the envy of our American cities even in the Northern States. If New York and Philadelphia and Chicago could enjoy the same temperature at night fewer of their citizens would need to "waste their substance" in paying the high rates of seashore, lake and mountain resorts, where they think they must go in order to make existence bearable.

But the water; its impurity and scarcity is the great objection. Still nobody desiring a daily bath need go without it, and good, pure water, as healthful as any water on earth, gushes out in living springs from the limestone hills near enough to the city to admit of its being brought in and sold at the not too exorbitant figure of three cents per gallon.

There is one thing that must be mentioned, and that is, the great mortality among children. To one acquainted with the conditions this is not surprising. The wonder is that any of the native children of parents of the lower classes survive.

After living for two years near Doctor Sandreczky's Children's Hospital; after seeing children in the homes of native Christians, Jews and Moslems, I am certain that had the children of America and Europe the same treatment, very few of them would reach years of maturity. Often have I seen unweaned babies munching away at green cucumbers and other vegetables raw and equally indigestible. Among a number of cases I have known brought to Doctor Sandreczky's Hospital was that of a boy twelve years old who never in his life had had a bath. Before he was born his mother had made a vow to this effect and the worst of it was she was faithful to her vow. The first thing that happened at the hospital was to break the vow so far as it affected the boy. This with a little careful treatment was all he needed.

What has been said of the climate and health of Jerusalem ought certainly to correct some false impressions, usually hastily received, and take away from the old city some unmerited reproach.

PASSION WEEK AND EASTER

A Comparison—Easter Week Generally—In Jerusalem—Pilgrims—Inconveniences—Passover Conditions—Passover and Easter—Religious Metropolis—Variety of the City's Guests at Easter—Easter of 1895—Palm Sunday—Pilgrim Ignorance—Procession Around the Sepulchre—Greek Patriarch—Tourist Discourtesy—Religious Disturbances—Church Jealousy—The Washing of Feet—Miracle Plays—Latin Service—Good Friday—Midnight in the Church—The Holy Fire—Scenes at the Fire—Soldiers—Riot of 1834—A Trivial Difficulty—Responsibility for the Holy Fire—The Procession—The Chapel—The Riot of 1895—Cause—America's Contribution—The Coming of the Fire—An Offensive Delusion—Antiquity—Origin of the Ceremony—Easter Morning.

CHAPTER XV

PASSION WEEK AND EASTER

AS a general statement it is true that the further away one is from Jerusalem the less ceremony he will see in connection with Easter and the days of fast and feast that fall near it. There is more ceremony in the Greek and other distinctively Oriental Churches than there is in the Latin, more in the Latin than in the established Churches of Germany and England, more in these established Churches than there is in the independent Protestant denominations of America. Furthermore it is true that there is more ceremony in the Latin Church in Italy than there is in the same body in France and Spain and the Latin-American countries; more in these last than there is in the same Church in the United States. In spite of the Church of Rome's assertion that she is "semper idem"; she differs in different lands; not in essentials it is true, but in matters serious enough to be noticeable. This remark is not made by way of detraction; it is true of all branches of the Church and merely goes to prove that as an institution the Church of Christ in the world is not beyond being influenced by the conditions which surround her. She may have a superior organization and triumph where other merely human institutions fail, but so long as the human element enters into her, it will affect and in some measure control her. This dependence upon conditions will account for the varieties of church government and for the difference of forms in different churches having the same government. In this respect as in others variety is life.

Easter week is the most important week in the ecclesiastical year, and it is celebrated in Jerusalem with greater pomp than in any other city on earth. Nor is the reason of this far to seek. In Jerusalem Christ spent the days of Passion week; and on each day he performed some memorable act. In Jerusalem the great tragedy of the crucifixion was carried to its eventful close; in Jerusalem the Crucified One triumphed over His enemies and over death itself by His glorious resurrection. Never can locality and event be more inseparably united than the places in Jerusalem and the events of Passion week and that first Easter morning. Human uncertainty as to the exact location is immaterial; the events took place in Jerusalem, and to Jerusalem, as to the place most appropriate, Christians come to commemorate these events. Opinions of the truly pious may differ as to the necessity and benefit of such commemoration, but two-thirds of the Christian world care nothing for opinions on such matters. They believe in the power and appropriateness of such observances, and if they cannot in person participate in them hope for the time to come when they may. Thousands do take part; the narrow streets are full of pilgrims and tourists, the former actuated by motives of religion, the latter by a laudable curiosity to see the ancient city and the sights of Easter week. The many hospices of the various churches and religious orders are crowded; the hotels have doubled their sleeping accommodations and are often compelled to refuse desirable guests. Visitors have to put up with many inconveniences and do so generally without complaint, very glad that there is any place for them. In the olive groves around the city many tents are pitched, where people unable to obtain hotel apartments and some who prefer tent life are making themselves as comfortable as possible. If the weather is favorable the tent-dwellers are really better off than those in the hotels; but this is the season of the latter rains.

This crowded condition of the city and its suburbs is something as it must have been in the long ago when the Jews came up from all lands to celebrate their great Passover feast in their ancestral holy city. Then as now the houses were

Passion Week and Easter

filled with guests and the various hostelries were taxed to their utmost; then as now tents and booths took shelter under the olive trees in the valleys or along the hillsides, furnishing rest at night to their occupants who spent the day within the walls; then as now every nation was represented, only now the variety is greater, for Gentile nations then unheard of send their thousands to participate. Then as now one great past event was commemorated—in reality the same event—for the symbolic meaning of the slaying of the Paschal lamb found its fulfillment in the sacrifice of Christ.

Easter is the Christian Passover and Jerusalem is a very appropriate place to commemorate it. The city has changed much for the worse during these Christian centuries, but its power of suggestion is not lost. Its glorious temple and wonderful palaces have crumbled before the shock of the ram or the power of the flame, but it is Jerusalem still. The palaces and walls and temples were the pride of the ancient inhabitant, but if the city's fame depended upon these it would be to-day like the cities of the Nile or Mesopotamia. What has made Jerusalem known more widely than any city of antiquity is her spiritual preëminence; she is the world's religious metropolis. Other places are recognized as the centres of the religious life of a nation or some particular branch of the Church, but in the streets of the Holy City they all unite. The Jew comes from countries most remote to dwell for a time within the city of his fathers, to weep because his sacred place is in the hands of the heathen, and to pray here on holy ground to that Jehovah who so miraculously established his people in this land, and who, he believes, will restore it to them in His own good time. The swarthy African Christian, member of the ancient Coptic or Abyssinian Church, meets on these streets, or around the traditional tomb of their common Saviour, the fair-faced European or American Christian. They rejoice in the possession of the same blessings from the same God and Saviour and in the same hopes of immortality through the finished work of the same Redeemer. They may differ in a thousand other respects, but they meet here on the same level and honor Jerusalem for the sake of its association with that Divine Person whom all acknowledge as the Founder of their faith. The Moslem, too, comes here on his holy pilgrimage and about Easter time many strangers holding the faith of the Prophet may be seen. The latter calls Jerusalem "El-Kuds," the Holy. Next to Mecca it is his heart's desire. His pilgrimage is not complete till he has visited it and bowed in prayer beneath the Dome of the Rock.

Thus if one wishes to see Jerusalem at the most interesting time of the year he should come at the Easter season. The variety of costume is endless; the variety of methods of worship likewise. As the Greek and Latin calendars differ, the Easters of these two Churches usually fall on different dates. As nearly all the Oriental Churches follow the Greeks, the crowds are larger and more enthusiastic, and religious and other sights novel to the Occidental are much more numerous at the time of the Greek Easter. Occasionally the calendars of all agree, and the following account is descriptive of the scenes and incidents of such a year, namely Easter week of 1895. There was nothing very distinctive about this particular week of this particular year, however; it differed little, if at all, from the same week of other years.

For several days preceding Palm Sunday the dealers in palm-branches did a rushing business. No pilgrim was too poor to be furnished with some emblem of the Lord's triumphal entry, or too modest to show his token of rejoicing on the anniversary of that event. Some were satisfied with a plain straight branch of this tree, others who could afford it had theirs woven into various shapes with gay-colored ribbons intertwined. A visitor from another sphere, had he landed in Jerusalem on that Sunday morning, would have known that some great celebration was being held. Every pilgrim was out, going to or coming from some church service. Each one was dressed in his best apparel and carried the palm-branch indicative of rejoicing. In every church that morning there was a special service, though in the Latin churches it does not equal in splendor and consequent interest what can be seen in Rome on the same day.

The Crusaders used to represent the Christ's triumphal entry, carrying it out in detail. A priest personating the Saviour rode on an ass from Bethphage; others as his disciples followed or went before him crying "Hosanna," and a crowd with palm and olive branches came out from the city to meet them. Now, however, the entire service is conducted in the Church of the Sepulchre; this is more quiet and orderly, but it is not an uncommon sight on this Sunday afternoon to see that many of the Russian pilgrims, both men and women, have allowed their excess of joy to steal away their senses. Too freely have they imbibed of that which intoxicates, and while as a general thing they are not boisterous in their words or actions they do illustrate a phase of life far removed from the Christianity of Christ. But Christianity comes to them very much adulterated by human opinions, very much distorted by ecclesiasticism and priestly innovations. They cannot read and so religion must be taught them by pictures. They have no conception of the spiritual and to "worship in spirit" is impossible for them. The Church to which they belong tells them that this is a great feast day, a day on which they are to rejoice, and they do so in the way they most relish. This is not to be understood as applying to all classes; there are Russian pilgrims just as intelligent and just as decorous as come from any other land, but their proportion to the entire number is very small.

The centre of interest for those desiring to see the church services is, as usual, at the Holy Sepulchre. This is one of the days on which the richest vestments of patriarchs, bishops and priests may be seen, in the procession made around the tomb. At ten o'clock on Palm Sunday morning we edged our way through the crowd around and in the church, climbed a series of stairways and took a position in the Franciscan convent from which a good view of all the proceedings could be had. Singing began in the Greek chapel some minutes before there was any sign of singer or of priest. Then from this chapel, which is directly east of the Holy Cave, came eight young men carrying banners on which were painted appropriate scenes. The first member of the procession was a lad carrying an immense olive branch. Immediately after the singers came the priests in double file to the number of seventy, each with his ordinary garb hidden by a long robe that reached to the feet and which was stiff with gold embroidery. Then came the censer-bearers and just following them was the Greek Patriarch of Jerusalem—a man with a fine, intellectual face and dignified bearing. His robes were princely in their magnificence, but the most striking feature was his crown, which was encrusted with sparkling jewels of great value. His see is one of the richest in Christendom. Money can be procured for the Church in Jerusalem even when there is great lack of it in other places, so that the patriarch can maintain his position as becomes a prince of the Church. It is one of the sights of the city, permitted to very few, to have a glimpse of his treasuries.

The tomb is encircled three times by the procession. Every few steps the censer-bearers turn toward the patriarch and swing their censers so that the fumes pass over his person. When the patriarch has passed once around and has come in front of the entrance to the sepulchre he does obeisance and makes the sign of the cross. The crown he has been wearing is then removed from his head and another supplied, no less rich in appearance, but evidently of lighter weight. The procession is then continued, and by the time the remaining two rounds are made over an hour has been consumed. The singing has never stopped, and as the notes are few and have been repeated over and over again, has become very monotonous. But the crowd below has no doubt appreciated it, and as it was intended for them the disapproval of outsiders is of no consequence. They have seen a wonderful exhibition of pictures and candles, of vestments and jewels and it has made an impression upon their minds not soon to be forgotten. It is part of their religion; they have endured hardships to witness it. On this occasion a number of devout Russian women had by remaining all night in the church secured good positions just in front of the Holy Sepulchre. But priority of possession gives no title in such a case. A party of tourists had come in just a few minutes before the procession began; they had come to see, and like most tourists of every nation they were not solicitous about the rights or the feelings of others. The Turkish guard of the church was "seen" and a couple of soldiers put at the disposal of this party; a way was forced through the crowd to the door of the sepulchre; the Russian pilgrims were rudely thrust aside and made to stand where they could not see the long-desired sight, and the tourists, to whom the whole affair was merely a matter of curiosity, quietly and unconcernedly took their places. A little "bucksheesh" goes a long way with the average Turk, but nothing can go far enough to justify the behavior of some tourists.

The Latins, Armenians and other Churches have their special services on this day in this place. When Easter falls on the same day for all, some prearrangement as to time must be made. For several reasons no two of the sects could have their religious exercises going on at the same time. The crowds would be too great and confusion follow, and, more serious than this reason, the participants in the service could not preserve the peace. By mistake, or intention, one party might infringe upon the rights or do something contrary to the wishes of the other; in which case an altercation would be begun at once, regardless of the disturbing effect upon the service. And the altercation might not cease with words.

More than once in recent times this great Cathedral church of Oriental Christendom has witnessed proceedings most un-Christian-like. Each Church, we are informed, must be jealous in the assertion and protection of its rights, or it would soon have none to assert or protect. Each wants as much of this sacred ground and edifice as it can obtain and is not always above suspicion of dishonesty in the methods used to acquire possession. A precedent counts immensely and if one sect were this year to permit another to enjoy its privilege or to trespass on its part of the church, next year the sect thus favored would just as likely demand this as its right. The aggressive spirit manifested in efforts to own parts of the church would be commendable and beautiful if it were expanded in illustrating and advancing true Christianity. As it is the energy is used without benefit to the one exercising it and without blessing upon anybody.

After the Palm-Sunday processionals there is little of interest, religiously speaking. Services are held every day in some of the churches so that none so inclined need suffer from lack of religious opportunity. But when Thursday arrives there is considerable that to an Occidental is novel and interesting. At eight o'clock on the morning of this particular day the court in front of the Sepulchre Church is filled with a solid mass of reverent or curious humanity. Every available nook and corner of the old church is occupied. The steps leading to the Chapel of the Agony, the roofs of neighboring buildings and of the church itself, the balconies and windows overlooking the court are thronged with people of many nationalities. Side by side with the Christian from some Fellah village among the hills of Judah or Benjamin is a polite Greek from Athens, a stolid German from the Fatherland, a dapper Frenchman and smooth Italian, while conspicuous among all is the indifferent and typical Englishman in his suit of grey tweed, and the professional globe-trotter from the land of great travellers—the United States. Some of the audience—

Passion Week and Easter 271

especially the religiously inclined—took up their positions the night before and kept them during the long watches before the sun showed himself above Olivet. In the midst of a sea of faces an elevated platform is seen, with stands for candles at its four corners and seats for a dozen or more persons. A chair of state occupies a small elevated position at the western end of this platform, facing the east. In front of the platform on the wall of the building a temporary pulpit has been erected. A stranger would know that some important ceremony was about to take place. About eight o'clock a procession of Greek priests files out of the main door of the church. The shouting of the multitude that has been going on for hours ceases, and the Turkish soldiers who have been trying to restrain the mob enjoy a rest. The patriarch ascends the platform and takes the conspicuous chair, and twelve priests, representing the twelve apostles, arrange themselves along both sides and in front of him. Their robes are splendid and, as the morning sun strikes upon them, they emit a glitter that is dazzling to the eyes; but the robes of the patriarch himself are the centre of attraction. The richest of materials adorned with the most delicate needlework cover his entire person, while his head dress is resplendent with jewels.

A relic of the old miracle plays is about to be enacted. It is a play in which Jesus and His disciples are to be personated, though there is nothing in the manner or garb of the patriarch and priests to suggest the appearance or actions of the Originals. It is more like an ecclesiastical dress parade, whose design is not to call to the minds of the observers the solemn occasion in the " Upper room " when the Master, laying aside His garments and girding Himself with a towel began to wash His disciples' feet, so much as it is to impress upon them the richness of the clerical vestments and the importance of the wearers. A choir in attendance sings and sings well. The passage in John, thirteenth chapter, is read by a priest standing in the temporary pulpit. Then the patriarch lays aside his gorgeous outer robe, a priest takes his bejewelled crown, while another rolls back his rose-colored satin sleeves and lays a towel over his arm. From a stand an immense silver wash bowl is taken and partly filled with rose-water. Then the actual ceremony of the feet-washing begins. It is carried out in detail though it has nothing about it suggestive of that humility which Christ wished to illustrate before, and thus encourage in, His disciples. While this is going on it requires every effort of the soldiers of the Sultan to keep back the crowding, crushing mob. Each one is anxious to have his handkerchief or some small possession dipped into the basin of rose-water that is being used. It is said that a handkerchief thus treated becomes a very precious thing and is highly prized by its owner. On the two occasions I witnessed the performance many handkerchiefs were thus elevated in value. As soon as the owner received his from the hand of one of the obliging priests he immediately rubbed it over hands and face, and became blessed above his fellows. For though there was seemingly no scarcity of rose-water the supply would not have sufficed to gratify all the devotees.

This part of the service being completed a brief rest is taken and then the people are transported in imagination to the Garden of Gethsemane. There is no change of scenery nor of costume, the acting and imagination must supply any lack in these respects. Just at the foot of the stairs leading up to the platform the patriarch and three priests represent Christ in the agony of prayer in the garden and His three drowsy disciples. Here, too, the dress of the modern portrayers of this solemn "night scene" in the Saviour's life was in strange contrast to what we have been taught, and rightly, to believe was the condition as to apparel of our Lord and His followers. In strange contrast, also, to the midnight stillness of deepshaded Gethsemane, when no eye but the Father's beheld the praying Christ, was this curious myriad-eyed throng, straining in the garish light of day to see this tawdry imitation of a sacred scene.

Passion Week and Easter 273

This part being ended the patriarch and priests again took their places on the platform. Robes were arranged and crown donned and then, while this spiritual head of the Greek Church in Jerusalem stood clad in his robes and the insignia of his high office, a photographer in a neighboring window was quietly signalled to and the camera preserved the scene. The great ceremony of the washing of the feet is over and the procession files back into the church. As he goes the patriarch dips a large bouquet he is carrying into what remains of the rose-water and sprays it over the throng, the majority of whom reverently bow their bared heads to receive it.

On the afternoon of the same day the Latins have a similar service, but it is done quietly and inside the church. The uproar that characterized the morning observance is agreeably absent at that of the afternoon. The costumes of the officiating Latin priests do not compare in richness with those of the Greeks, but the effect upon the worshippers is equally good, if there is any good whatever resulting from these portrayals of the scenes in the Saviour's earthly life. There may have been a time when such things were helps to faith, there may be some minds yet which can receive impressions only in this way, but that time certainly ought to have passed long ago, and has passed in those countries where Christianity has not been throttled and supplanted by sacerdotalism. At the door of the church that tolerates it must be laid the blame for that condition of ignorance which demands such exhibitions in order to keep its faith alive.

The one notable event of Good Friday—notable in the sense of being out of the ordinary—is the mystery play representing the scenes that were witnessed just previous to, during, and immediately after the crucifixion. A small figure of the Christ is brought into the Chapel of the Nailing to the Cross by the Franciscans—the order which has entire charge of this performance. The figure is less than half life-size and is hideous in the extreme. In the Chapel of the Nailing it is crucified and a crown of thorns placed upon the head. Over the image, as it lies upon the floor surrounded by priests and spectators, one of the Franciscan brothers delivers a sermon in German. The procession then moves a few feet to the west and is in the Chapel of the Crucifixion. This is Greek property, and Latin intrusion is tolerated within certain limits. The cross bearing the image is erected just back of the altar that covers the "hole in the rock," where tradition asserts that the "true cross" stood. Then a brother preaches a sermon in French, appropriate to the occasion, after which with much pomp and an appearance of solemnity the figure is taken down from the cross, placed upon a richly embroidered cloth and carried through the closely packed crowd on Calvary down the stairs to the Stone of Unction. Here the procession halts awhile, the figure is anointed and a sermon in Arabic given. After this linen grave-clothes are wrapped about the image, and it is carried through the vaulted passage to the sepulchre and laid upon the marble covering of the traditional tomb of Christ; there it remains until the following Sunday morning, when it is quietly removed.

There is little to be said in commendation of this mystery play. A relic of semi-barbarous days, it is neither interesting nor edifying. If it were not that the subject of the play is so sacred the whole affair would be ridiculous. It is an ancient practice begun in an age of ignorance, but is certainly an anachronism in the closing years of the nineteenth century even in the unchanging Orient.

After this mystery play is over the curious are glad to wander through the secluded chapels of the old church and along its vaulted passages. It is nearly midnight and the deep shadows are intensified by the flicker of the almost consumed candles and glimmer of the little oil lamps with their floating wicks. The throng of Latin worshippers has gone and the Moslem guard will soon close the church for the night, but there is an evident intention on the part of many to pass the night within the sacred enclosure. In out of the way places, on the narrow stairways leading to the dome, along the gloomy, unventilated corridors, heavy with the poison exhaled from a thousand lungs, are to be seen the sleeping forms of many Greek and Russian pilgrims. They have had no part nor interest in the evening's performance, but have taken the opportunity to come in and secure a place to pass the night so as to be ready in the morning to take up a position near the Holy Sepulchre to witness what is to them the most convincing proof of divine communion with men. This is the "miracle" of the Holy Fire, scheduled to take place between three and four o'clock on Saturday afternoon. The suffering these people endure in order to witness this greatest of frauds is deserving of more consideration than it gets. For at least sixteen hours they remain in the church possessed of one desire, namely to witness the descent of the "holy fire" and to light their candles from it. During at least eight of these hours they stand in one place, crowded to suffocation and moving only when some convulsion moves the entire mass or when the Turkish soldiers force them aside to make a way for some civil dignitary to pass through.

Pilgrims are not the only ones who are willing to put themselves to great inconvenience to behold this strange spectacle and the cause of it. American and English ladies and gentlemen have gone here early on the morning of this day, taken their lunch with them, and securing the best place they could find, there stayed through the long stifling hours, crushed and crowded; and treated to the continual din of a mob whose shouting would drown the voices of the brokers on the floor of the New York Stock Exchange on an exciting day.

No one can describe the scene that is enacted at this time. It has been attempted many times, but without success. There is nothing to which one can compare it, for there is nothing on earth like it. Dean Stanley[1] tries to convey it to the

[1] Sinai and Palestine, p. 466.

minds of his readers by saying "A succession of gambols takes place which an Englishman can only compare to a mixture of prisoner's base, football and leap frog, round and round the Holy Sepulchre." It is all this and much more. Added to the shouts of men are the screams of women and the cries of babies. One pities the babies and wonders at the folly of the parents who bring them to such a place at such a time. Here and there are men standing upon the shoulders of others or walking about from shoulder to shoulder over the heads of others, wildly gesticulating and yelling under the frenzy of religious enthusiasm. The Greek and Arab Christians are much more vociferous than the Russians. It was formerly believed that unless they ran around the tomb a certain number of times the fire from heaven would not come. There is no such running now. Humanity is wedged together too closely, and the bulwark of Turkish soldiers prevents it.

As the hour approached on Easter eve of 1895 when the procession of Greek priests was expected to make its appearance the noise was almost deafening. With wild shouting, frenzied hand-clapping and blowing of horns the crowd amused itself and the spectators in the galleries of the Latins, where each consul is given an alcove to which he can invite his male friends to the number of ten or more. The burden of the shouting can be made out by practiced ears. A knot of a dozen or so men stationed near the entrance of the sepulchre are repeating in chorus and incessantly, "This is the tomb of Jesus Christ." Not far from them are others vying with them in loudness of tone, but their strain is "This is the day the Jew mourns and the Christian rejoices." Another lot repeat "Jesus Christ has redeemed us." Amidst it all can be heard occasionally, "God save the Sultan." For a professedly religious exercise this is wondrously inappropriate. The stolid Turkish soldiers, no doubt wondering at these unseemly acts and cries of Christians in this their most sacred cathedral, stand around the sepulchre ready when the signal

Passion Week and Easter 277

is given to clear a passage for the patriarchal procession or to obey any command of their superiors. Strange as it may seem these soldiers are a necessary adjunct to the affair. The performance could not go on without them and yet their only object is to keep the peace and prevent Christians of different sects from shedding each other's blood. At this time more than any other the feeling of bitter sectarianism runs high and all it needs is for some brainless fanatic to transgress the rights of some other than his own sect and a riot will be on in a minute. This happened in 1834 and is likely to recur at any time. On that occasion a disturbance took place and an order was issued to suppress it. The soldiers were only too willing to obey, and in a short time the floor was strewn with three hundred bodies of those who had been slain by Turkish weapons, or trampled to death during that short reign of terror. The present soldiers look like men who would not hesitate to repeat that scene with this generation of Christians for their victims.

When two o'clock arrived on this particular afternoon Bedlam was equalled by the commotion and noise. All were in suspense waiting for the signal for the procession to begin. Time wore on till half-past two and there was no sign given. A little difficulty had arisen about which the multitude knew nothing. It was so trivial as to be childish, and yet it was considered so serious that the patriarchs of the Greek and Armenian Churches took it up, the Moslem Pasha of Jerusalem was appealed to as an arbiter and it looked for a time as if the coming of the "holy fire" was to be indefinitely postponed. Seated as I was near the Pasha the whole by-play was plain before me. First would come a Greek, then an Armenian, each endeavoring to persuade His Excellency as to the justice of his presentation of the facts. It was all over a miserable little oil lamp worth a few cents, but it was Greek property, and the Armenian had blown out its light by mistake or touched it, or done something equally heinous, and deserved instant and severe punishment. The point was finally decided, but not to the satisfaction of the Armenians, and the unholy farce proceeded.

In former times all the Churches participated in this ceremony. The Greeks now assume entire responsibility for it though the Armenians and Copts are represented in the procession. Up to the sixteenth century the Latins were eager participants in it, but now the enmity existing for centuries between these two Churches finds vent in the ridicule heaped by the Latin priests, on the Greek fire. In "The Annals of the Propagation of the Faith" they show their present estimate of it by terming it "a ridiculous and superstitious ceremony."

Several bells in the Greek chapel begin ringing vigorously and the crowd knows by this and by the voices of singers that the first scene is about to be presented. Immediately room is made by the double line of soldiers, as shoulder to shoulder they back against the apparently solid mass of humanity around the sepulchre and the walls of the rotunda. But the way is cleared; the banners, taking in the ritual the places of images, are borne in front, and just after them is a double line of singers and chanting priests, in all about fifty. For a time the noise of the rabble ceases, but as the procession moves slowly and with evident solemnity it again breaks out, and along with the chanting is heard the shriek of the half-savage Arab Christian.

One thing now noticed is the Holy Sepulchre chapel itself. There it stands grim and silent and dark amid that sea of faces and roar of voices—a quiet protest, one can almost imagine, against the whole nefarious business. Every candle and lamp has been extinguished. On ordinary feast days there are hundreds of these burning. On the morning of this day is the only time in the year when they are put out and new candles and flesh oil supplied, all to be lighted again by the fire from heaven. This absence of artificial light makes the chapel have a neglected look. One sees it just as it is,

Passion Week and Easter

with the exception of the cheap pictures which are hung around it, and which look all the cheaper now. But this absence of light within and without is necessary. There must be no visible suggestion of imposture, no matter how much actual imposture there may be.

The procession moves very slowly around, along the passage flanked on both sides with soldiers. There is a tremor in the crowd and in the very air itself as though something unusual were about to take place—something more than the coming of the fire. A number of Armenian priests having looks of determination in their faces are standing on the south side of the sepulchre near the wall of the rotunda. When the procession is making its third round and the patriarch is about to ascend to the little platform in front of the Holy Cave, there is a grand rush on the part of the Armenians. It was a movement that would have done honor to the rush line of a 'Varsity football team. They forced their way through the crowd of pilgrims, through the line of soldiers and placed one of their priests right beside the Greek patriarch. Some such action on their part was expected, and when it came Greeks and Turks were partially prepared. Then there was war. It was a mass of wriggling, struggling, shrieking priests and soldiers, each apparently endeavoring to do all possible injury to whomever he could reach. No respect was shown the patriarch. He was pushed and pulled by his own and the opposing priests and was only with difficulty saved from severe treatment. His episcopal dignity was gone, his heavy crown almost rolled on the floor and he himself was quivering with fright when they finally got him out of the reach of harm. But the fight went on. Greek trampled on Armenian, and Armenian on Greek, and Turk on both. Though doing his very best the commanding officer seemed unable to separate the combatants. The bugle rang out time after time and detachment after detachment of soldiers plunged into the mêlée. At times they seemed to have it under control and then it would break out with renewed vigor. This went on for fifteen minutes. Just how much damage was done nobody will ever know. There were a number of bruised faces and broken heads, and a report was current that two pilgrims had died from the effects of injuries received. An incident like this shows just how necessary the soldiers are on these occasions. Had they not been on hand these frenzied fanatics would have killed each other, and there would have been little cause for regret if they had.

The trouble arose because of a desire on the part of the Armenians to have two of their priests go with the Greek patriarch as far as the Chapel of the Angels. The Armenians generally regard the holy fire as a fraud and their patriarch at Jerusalem will have nothing to do with the perpetration of it. He sends one of his ordinary priests to represent him. This priest and a Coptic delegate have the right to go as far as the above mentioned chapel, while the Greek patriarch goes alone into the Sepulchre Chapel proper. This year, report says, the Armenians tried to have two priests go in, not that they cared thus to honor the "fire," but simply to annoy the Greeks. This is what started this disgraceful row—the worst for years—so say the Greeks; the Armenians refuse to speak of it; which goes to prove that they were in the wrong, or else are justly ashamed of having been party to the shameful occurrence.

The Armenians failed to carry their point. America contributed largely to their defeat. Just here the Greeks showed their foresight. Anticipating trouble they had secured the services of an American professional boxer and wrestler, fitted him up in the garb of a priest and made him one of the patriarch's bodyguard. He did good service for the cause for which he had been retained. As soon as the patriarch was in danger the American seized him, forced his way through the crowd and helped him into the sepulchre. Then he stood guard at the door and as fast as any of the opposition came in the way made them feel the force of his ponderous fist. It

Passion Week and Easter

was a beautiful exhibition of professional skill, but not of a profession usually associated with priests or exhibited in holy places.

Quiet was finally restored. The patriarch was in the little Chapel of the Sepulchre. The runners were at the openings through which the fire would come if it came at all. Tourists and pilgrims were on the alert to catch the first view of it. In a few moments the hand of a priest reaching in drew out what appeared to be a large torch all aflame, first on the side of the Greeks and then on that of the Armenians. Off dashed the runners with it to light the lamps and candles in the various chapels near. A horseman carries it to Bethlehem and the lamps in the Greek Church there and in the Grotto of the Nativity are relighted. It is carried north, and the churches and convents through the land as far as Nazareth get the fresh fire. In an incredibly short time the whole floor of the rotunda is a mass of moving flame. Pilgrims and tourists had candles which they lit as fast as they could pass the fire from one to the other. Every pilgrim believes that this light is caused by the descent of the Spirit upon the tomb. Every intelligent priest and tourist believes it is caused by the patriarch with the assistance of a match. The patriarch and priests say nothing about it. They allow each to have his opinion.

In a recent conversation with one of the Greek priests, one very near to the patriarch, I was informed that the Church did not hold that this fire really came down from heaven. "But," I replied, "do not the ignorant pilgrims, and in fact the great majority of the membership of your Church, so believe; and does the Church through its spiritual leaders do anything to let them know the truth about it?" He acknowledged that it did not and gave as a reason that it dared not. The shock this information would give to the faith of the pilgrims in their Church would be fatal. Their Church is their religion and it has allowed them to believe, if it has not actually taught them, that this fire is of divine origin, really the visible manifestation of God Himself. What ignorance on the one hand; what wretched weakness on the other!

In ten minutes after the first appearance of the fire every candle and lamp has been lighted. The pilgrims have held their hands in the flame of their tapers and not been burned, have let the melted wax run onto their hands and then rubbed them over their faces and through their hair. Up the stairs, through the dark passages, into every chapel and alcove the fire has been passed. Everything is rejoicing in fresh illumination except the Latin chapels and that part of the rotunda in the second story belonging to the Franciscans. In this latter place are the consuls of the various powers with their friends. In that part assigned to the American were a couple of gentlemen who wished to take away some memento of the occasion and had brought candles to light, let burn awhile and then extinguish. Not knowing the absolute enmity of the Franciscans against the recent proceedings they took the fire from some Greeks in a near apartment which communicated with theirs by a grated window. In an instant an infuriated creature in the garb of a monk rushed in, seized the candles in the hand of one of the party and before the owner of them knew what was going on had torn them from his grasp. Then turning to another whose candles were still burning he seized these and extinguished them. This person had recovered from his surprise and resenting what looked like an uncalled for insult treated the monk to a specimen of true American resentment. The surprise was now on the other side and when the brother gathered himself together he immediately appealed to the French consul who is the protector of the Latins. Matters were soon explained between the two consuls and peace restored for the time. This incident proved that the Latins are just as violent in their fanaticism as the Greeks whom they ridicule on this account. And no less a personage than the president of the Franciscan convent was the chief actor in this scene.

Passion Week and Easter 283

As soon as all have received the fire the wild enthusiasm ceases so suddenly as to excite wonder. All the curious visitors leave the church, glad the weird, wild ceremony is over and rejoicing to be again in the fresh air. They have seen the "holy fire" once, and once is enough for all time. But the pilgrims do not leave the church. For them there is yet something of importance, and they are to spend another night within the sacred enclosure. When the shadows deepen they can be seen—men and women—as on the previous night, sleeping in every available corner except the Latin chapel. They are preparing themselves for the midnight office, when the services of Easter morning begin.

With the coming of the "holy fire" the main part of the Greek Easter is over. Surely no one ought to be more thankful that it is passed than the patriarch himself. To be conscious of having played the chief part in a stupendous fraud, a part he must play or be deposed from his patriarchate,[1] must belittle a man in his own estimation. Taking everything into consideration, the place, the time and the attendant circumstances, this so-called "miracle of the holy fire" is as Dean Stanley characterizes it, "probably the most offensive delusion to be found in the world."

The perpetrators of this unprofitable and inexcusable fraud claim for the practice a very great antiquity; and justly, for it is mentioned by a traveller[2] as early as the ninth century. It has been continued ever since during Christian occupation of the city; it was one of the causes that led to the destruction of the church by the Caliph Hakam. On the reconstruction of the building the "holy fire" rite was revived and just before the Crusaders entered Jerusalem one of the Fatimite

[1] Van Egmont gives an account of an exile he met at Mount Sinai who had refused appointment to the Jerusalem patriarchate because of his unwillingness to take part in what he regarded as a fraud. See Sinai and Palestine, p. 470, *note*.

[2] Bernard the Wise 870 c. Early Travels in Palestine.

caliphs of Egypt is said to have tested the genuineness of the miracle. Instead of permitting the use of ordinary wicks for the lamps, he had iron ones prepared, rightly inferring that if the fire was from heaven the quality of the wicks would not affect its appearance. We are informed that the fire appeared as usual and the iron wicks immediately ignited.

Just when or why this ceremony was first performed no one can say positively. It may have been one of the earliest of the miracle-plays in which was represented the descent of the Holy Spirit on the first Pentecost after our Lord's ascension, when "There appeared cloven tongues like as of fire and it sat upon each of them."[1] Or it may be a continuation into Christian times of a belief that was prevalent in ancient days among most peoples—a belief in the miraculous appearance of fire. The modern Moslems assert that on every Friday this dazzling heavenly light appears in the tombs of their saints. On a visit[2] to the Mosque at Hebron I was informed by one of the sheikhs that the reason the cave where the bodies of the patriarchs lie buried is closed up by masonry is because of the powerful light within which would immediately strike with blindness or even death any one who was unfortunate enough to behold it.

Whatever was originally symbolized by this Greek fire has been so long lost that nothing now remains but the superstitious idea of the pilgrims that it is the manifestation of God. How long this idea will hold them depends upon the power of the Church to keep the people in ignorance. The ceremony is not the same in every particular as formerly; certain features have been omitted, as, for instance, the letting out of a dove from the sepulchre just before the fire appeared. The continuance of the whole observance is a sacrilege and an evidence of great weakness in the Church that is responsible for it.

By ten o'clock on Sunday morning Easter is over. In the grounds about the Russian buildings a general moving day has

[1] Acts ii. 3. [2] May 13th, 1895, in company with Minister Terrell.

come. Hundreds have their bundles and boxes packed and are waiting for porters and wagons to carry them to the station near the colony of the German Templars, half a mile southwest of the city. A special train takes the uncouth, but exultant pilgrims to Jaffa, where after many tribulations they are transported from the shore to a Russian ship that is waiting to convey them to Odessa. On arriving there they separate and seek their various homes in the land of the Tsar.

THE JEWS IN JERUSALEM

The Jew and Civilization—Religion and Culture—Unfair Estimate of the Hebrew—Peculiar—Persecutions—Number of Jews in Jerusalem—A Census—Variety of Jews—Increasing—Causes of Increase—Prohibition—Departures—Racial Purity—Divisions—Ashkenazim—Sephardim—Persians—Yemenites—Caraites—Chassidim—Bond of Religion—Rabbis—Synagogues—Wall of Wailing—Visitors—Wretched Homes—Suffering—Jewish Colonies—Home Life—Respect for Parents—Jewish Women—Resemblance to Arabs—Education—Schools—Unwisdom of the Jew—Marriages—Divorce—Religious Feasts—Day of Atonement—Purim—Tabernacles—Superstitions—Messianic Beliefs—Christian Missions—A Charem—Opposition to Missions—Haluka, or Charity Funds—Kolil America—Jewish Nationalism.

CHAPTER XVI

THE JEWS IN JERUSALEM

THE features and the habits of the descendants of Jacob are known in every part of the civilized world. The Jew has been the agent of civilization. His proverbial acuteness has led him to reap the benefits of civilization; while in his world-wide dispersion he has carried the advantages of civilization with him to quarters where its benign influence had not been felt. Whatever the popular view may be, the Jew has undoubtedly been an advance agent and a continuing force in the spread of civilization.

When the legions of Titus destroyed Jerusalem and drove its inhabitants into exile, the homeless ones carried into strange lands their religion and their culture. Of their religion historians have told us again and again. But of their culture we are not so well informed. The historians of this people give an undue weight to their religious beliefs and practices. There is a large volume yet to be written concerning their intellectual and æsthetic beliefs and practices. To the lack of such accounts is due the great ignorance among people otherwise intelligent as to the Jew's contribution to the present state of the civilized world. We have estimated the race long enough from what we have seen of a few specimens of peddlers and dealers in old clothes; or perhaps from that sleek and sly representative who is always on the alert to benefit himself at the expense of others regardless of the method. It ought to be remembered that these are exceptions, the dregs, as it were, of a people, which, in whatever land it has been, has contributed largely to its moral, intellectual and political advancement.

With these few preliminary remarks we turn to view the remnant of this people, which, in its wanderings, has found its way back to its ancestral city.

Wherever the Jew is he is worthy of intelligent consideration. He has always been regarded as peculiar; and justly so. Because of this peculiarity he is doubtfully regarded in most communities and in some looked upon with a disfavor so decided that it results in persecution. The Anti-Semitism, which is disgracefully conspicuous in some parts of the world even now, is directed against this peculiarity. To my mind it is but the expression of envy and is a method which meanness takes to injure a successful rival. It has been the cause in times past and now of bringing back to Jerusalem the descendants of its former inhabitants.

In the days of Ferdinand and Isabella, when the Jews were driven from Spain, some of the refugees never rested permanently till they found protection under the Sultan and made homes for themselves in the then poor little city that occupied part of the site of the once glorious capital of their nation. There are families here now who can trace their descent in unbroken line from these victims of Spanish oppression.

Many cities of America and Europe have larger Jewish populations than has this—the world's capital of Judaism. London and New York each has more of these people than can be found in all Palestine. The superiority in population of these cities does not, however, detract from the religious preëminence of the City of Zion, nor can it give them the place in the hearts or the prayers of this scattered people that Jerusalem holds.

Of the 85,000 Jews in Palestine fully one-half are living within the walls of Jerusalem, or in the twenty-three colonies that cluster just outside the walls. This number, 42,500, is an estimate only, but is made after careful investigation by good judges. No house-to-house census is ever taken here. The Jews are opposed to it on the grounds of religion, and on

The Jews in Jerusalem

very good financial grounds also. They fear a new tax, and would certainly prevaricate to avoid it.

Among the number of Jews here can be found citizens of nearly every country on earth. The list of strangers who were in the city on the Day of Pentecost, as described in the second chapter of the Acts of the Apostles, can be duplicated to-day and increased by the names of many lands and nations of which history was not then cognizant. These foreign subjects remain foreigners, their papers of citizenship bring the evidence of their right to protection under some Christian flag, though they dwell in the Sultan's realm. Fully one-half of the Jewish residents owe allegiance to foreign powers. This is, no doubt, a good thing for them, but it is hardly justice to the Turk, nor in fact to the power that protects them. The various Sultans of Turkey have shown great courtesy to the Jews at various times, but just now the Jews under foreign protection seem to prefer to remain there. For political reasons Jewish Congresses may pass resolutions complimenting the Sultan, as we have recently seen, but at the same time and for the same reasons the members passing the resolutions prefer not to transfer their citizenship.

The number of Jews in Jerusalem is slowly increasing. During the last years of the decade previous to 1890 the increase was phenomenal. Cruel oppression in Russia compelled many to look elsewhere for homes and their eyes turned longingly to the land promised to their fathers. They came in large numbers, hoping to better their condition, and, had the free entrance granted at that time been continued, the Hebrew population of to-day would have been at least double what it is. Just why the permission was not continued no one outside of official circles knows. Their coming certainly would have added to the importance and wealth of Palestine. But the Turkish authorities are sensitive and perhaps they felt that a large increase of these foreigners would so complicate matters as to give rise to difficulties of a serious political nature. They would soon present a problem which the Turkish authorities might have great trouble in solving. In order not to have to solve it Jewish immigration was prohibited. Now they do not come in large numbers, but this part of the city's population is continually on the increase. Hardly a vessel puts in at Jaffa, but leaves one or more who has come to live in the Holy City.

The officials of Jaffa frequently exercise their authority against these newcomers and some having made the long journey are not allowed to set foot on shore. However, more land in joy than depart in sorrow. When the strict passport regulations have been complied with, there is little difficulty.

That the prohibition does not prohibit may be easily inferred from the continued increase of the Jewish population in the cities and colonies. In Jerusalem new houses are continually being built, and as soon as they are finished, they are occupied. At the same time it must be noted that many are leaving the Holy City and Land to join the dispersion among the Gentiles. The young men and women, many of them, have a longing to experience a more active life than can be enjoyed here. Reports of business prosperity come to them from friends who have preceded them and a desire to participate in similar successes impels them to desert for a time the quiet, unbusinesslike city of their fathers. Many of these more progressive ones look to the great Republic across the Atlantic, and, as soon as they have means sufficient to pay their passage, thither they go. I have met many of these, but among them have never known one who was leaving without the intention to return. They are going to sojourn for a time in the city of the stranger and then come back and make a home in the city they love. To have a competence sufficient to enable them to live comfortably in Jerusalem is their ideal, and to obtain it they are willing to endure years of exile.

A study of the Jew in modern Jerusalem will compel the honest inquirer to revise some of his preconceived notions of the Jewish race. There is no doubt that as a race the Jews are more clearly defined and of purer descent than any other civilized nation of to-day. Because of their general refusal to intermarry with the people among whom they are resident, and because of their strict adherence to their law, which applies to every department of life, they have remained apart. That this exclusiveness and obedience to law have resulted in racial purity is not to be wondered at. At the same time they have not produced unity in the race, and when we discourse about the Jewish type, we must, in order to be exact, describe what type, for they are many. In the varied experiences through which these people have passed during historical times, foreign elements have been forcibly engrafted upon them and Jewish maidens have become the wives of their conquerors. At least in one instance a whole non-Jewish tribe—the Chazari—became converted to Judaism and were assimilated. The Jew also is no exception to the rule that a person is affected by climatic and social conditions. He comes in time to resemble the people among whom he lives and to partake to a greater or less degree of their peculiarities. This will account for the great variety of Jew, in appearance, in habits, and in intelligence, as seen in Jerusalem to-day. The Occidental Jew differs in every respect from his Oriental co-religionist as much as the American differs from the Arab.

Among the Jerusalem Jews there are several clearly marked divisions, divisions not caused by religious variations, except in the case of the Caraites, but due to the difference in locality. The largest division is that of the Ashkenazim, and includes those from Russia and the countries of Central Europe. These all speak a common language. It is called Yiddish and is a jargon in which German predominates, though Russian and Hebrew words are not uncommon and English has been drawn upon to some extent. The construction of this conglomerate speech is that of the German, but the method of speaking and the accent given to many of the words make it difficult for those acquainted with pure German to understand. The written Yiddish is even more anomalous and hence more difficult.

Among the Ashkenazim one meets a great variety of people. There is the Russian Jew, a man whose ancestors have for generations lived in the land of the Tsar. He resembles the pure Russian in many ways. There is the German Jew, the English and the American, each partaking in some measure of the peculiar traits of the people among whom he lived before coming here. Most of these are of foreign birth and it is only within comparatively recent years that they have begun to be "lovers of Zion" to an extent sufficient to induce them to come and live within her walls. The injustice which they have suffered in Russia has no doubt impelled many to leave that land and to seek the peace they longed for within the Sultan's dominions. From choice and a desire to dwell on holy soil and be buried in it those from America and England have come.

The next division in point of numbers is the Sephardim. These come from the Latin countries of Europe and date their arrival from the persecutions that were inflicted upon them, because of their religion, at the close of the fourteenth century. Theirs was an honorable position in Spain especially, and in Portugal, Italy and France. Spanish injustice deprived them of their honors, confiscated their lands and sent them adrift as homeless wanderers to find dwellings where they could. Many went to Holland, many to Italy, taking with them their culture and abilities in the learned professions. Some wandered as far as Constantinople and found protection under the reigning Sultan, Salim, and gained high positions under him and his successors during the sixteenth century. Some came to Jerusalem, and their descendants are here yet. They brought back with them the culture and refinement for which they were noted even in courtly Spain, and these excellent parts are seen in some of their descendants who have never been outside of Palestine. Many of them are poor, but poverty has not detracted from their manhood or gentility.

In this respect they are generally in favorable contrast to the Ashkenazim. The latter are less careful in their personal appearance and in the condition of their residences. The cause of this is not that the Ashkenazim are poorer, for the opposite is the case. It is due to previous conditions. The Askenaz is the descendant of the Ghetto and the limitations that were then prescribed bind him in a measure still.

It has at times struck me as something surprising how cheaply and how apparently comfortably a Sephardim family can live. In some cases the father by his daily toil earns but two dollars per week. It suffices, and he does not ask that it be augmented by a donation from the charity funds which are contributed for the support of their unfortunate co-religionists by prosperous Jews in other parts of the world.

The next division in point of numbers is the Jews from Persia. These are strictly Oriental in appearance and in habits. With few exceptions they are poor in this world's goods, having come from a country where opportunities for money-getting are limited. They have become victims of a habit very common in the Orient, namely that of begging, and persist in practicing it even when there is no need of doing so. Of all the Jews here they are the most ignorant and, like their ancestors of long ago, have partaken deeply of Persian superstition; in their social life too they are, as a class, degraded.

Another type of Jew has within the past few years made his appearance in the Holy City. He differs as much from the Occidental Jew as the lithe, sinewy Bedouin of the desert differs from the heavy, coarse-featured Russian. Having come from Yemen this people are called, for lack of a better term, Yemenites. In appearance they are very dark-skinned, small-featured and of medium height. Their history is not well known, but they are thought to be descendants of the tribe of Gad, who, after the exile in Babylon, went southward and settled in Arabia, preferring a voluntary exile to a return to their devasted city among the Judean hills. The story of their return now, as it has been told me, has much of the romantic and pathetic in it. Cut off from all communications with the outside world they had become possessed with the belief that their long-promised Messiah was about to make his appearance in Jerusalem. Wishing to be present at that sublime event forty families made the arduous journey from their Arabian homes to Jerusalem. Having no means and no friends their condition was, on their arrival, pitiable. Applications for assistance made to the local rabbis were treated coldly, and in their perplexity these Yemenites camped on a vacant lot on the Jaffa road just outside the city and as the people passed called upon all alike to witness their condition and help them. This appeal aroused the Jewish authorities to activity and temporary homes were provided for them. They were worthy people and have since demonstrated their industry and thrift. Some of them are now well-to-do and own their own little, well-kept homes.

The Caraites are a very small community consisting in all of about fifty souls. They are in disfavor with all the other Jews because of their non-acceptance of the Talmud. They discard all of the Mishnic, or Oral Law, and regard the Old Testament as "the only rule of faith and practice." This sect of Jews was founded at Bagdad, but most of its adherents are now living in southern Russia. Their liturgy is much simpler and more impressive than that used in the orthodox synagogues. While very firm in their beliefs they have but little influence in the social or religious life of the city. They are possessed of but one synagogue, which is located almost in the centre of the town and from its condition appears to be one of the oldest structures. It is almost entirely underground. In it are some rare old manuscripts. The Caraites are thought to resemble the old Sadducean party and are designated by Conder as "low Church" Jews. They are certainly the most liberal Jewish sect here.

To these divisions, which largely follow national lines, there are others which are marked by religious differences. The Chassidim are, as their name implies, the ultra-pious Jews, and are now, as they have been since post-exilic times, the bulwark of Jewish orthodoxy. They first organized themselves to resist the Grecianizing influences that were alienating the people from their pure Jehovah worship. Their present purpose is similar to the ancient one, but the power against which they direct their energies is Christianity. Although arrogating to themselves the special virtues of protecting Judaism and calling themselves "the pious ones" the Jerusalem representatives have been sufficiently active in worldly affairs to obtain a fair share of temporal wealth. As a class they are considered the wealthiest among the Jerusalem Jews, though those from Russia are generally quite poor. Their number in the city is about three thousand five hundred.

From a knowledge of the various divisions of Judaism in the Holy City, and from a study that has proved to me that the Jew represents in appearance and in character "all sorts and conditions of men" I have come to the conclusion that Isaac D'Israeli was correct in saying that, "The Jewish people are not a nation, for they consist of many nations; they are Spanish or Portuguese, German or Polish; they are Italian, English and French, and, like the chameleon, they reflect the color of the spot they rest on. The people of Israel are like the waters running through the countries, tinged in their course with all the varieties of the soil where they deposit themselves. After a few generations the Hebrews assimilate with the character, and are actuated by the feelings of the nation of which they become part. What a distinct people are the Jews of London, of Paris, of Amsterdam, from the Jews of Morocco, Damascus and the Volga." While this is true, it is no less so that amid this great variety there is one strong bond that makes them a homogeneous people. It is the bond of a common religion, stronger than any obligation imposed upon them by the nations to which they have attached themselves; to which they have generously contributed of their energies and talents, and for which, when occasion required it, they have not hesitated to shed their blood.

This bond of religion that holds so firmly is what makes unity amidst such great diversity. It is what has kept the Jews a "peculiar people," and, unfortunately, it has been the real cause of much of the persecution they have endured during their sojourn among the nations. In no place in the world will this religion in its purity be seen to better and to worse advantage than in Jerusalem. To better advantage, because here are living pious Jews who are "Israelites indeed," men who combine zeal in their religion with the highest qualities of genuine manhood, and who would be respected for their sterling worth in any place where honor and real character are appreciated. It can here be seen at its worst, because there are those who, under the pretense of piety and with a show of zeal, practice to deceive, their sole object being to impose upon the charitable feelings of their co-religionists in other parts of the world, and thus to maintain themselves in comfortable idleness. I am sorry to have to record as my belief that the latter class outnumbers the former. I am sustained in this view by the opinions of many of the honorable Jews here.

Rabbi is a very familiar title among the Jews in Jerusalem. How many are deserving enough to have it applied to them is a question. In most instances it is simply used as a term of respect. There are those, however, who exercise the functions of masters and are recognized by their people as acting within their jurisdiction when they do so. Chief among these and the one officially recognized by the Turkish government authorities is the Chachem Bashi, Jacob Saul Elyashur. He is a man of great age, being nearly ninety, and of great power. In a recent test of strength he proved himself a greater force in the community than the Moslem Pasha of Palestine. Other rabbis, such as Joshua Diskin and Samuel Salant, are known, the former for his erudition, the latter for his executive ability, wherever Jews are found.

In every quarter of the city, within and without the walls, small synagogues are located. The entire number is about two hundred. It must not be thought, however, that each synagogue is a separate building. Any room in any building may be devoted to this purpose, provided it has been properly consecrated. It is the ambition of many aged Jews, who come here to die and be buried in the holy soil of Olivet, to provide for the establishment of a small synagogue, in which prayers may be offered.

Any ten adult males—a Jew reaches his majority at thirteen —may petition to have such a room set apart where they may read their prayers and spend their time in the study of their Law. Such a petition is usually granted provided the petitioners pledge themselves to see that their synagogue is properly maintained.

Three large synagogues are located within the walls in the Jewish quarter. Two of these belong to the Sephardim and are known as Beth Yakob, or House of Jacob, and Tiphereth Israel, or the Glory of Israel. K'hal Stambouli, the Stamboul Congregation, is the large meeting-place of the Ashkenazim. There are here really four synagogues in one, which united can accommodate eight hundred worshippers. At all hours of the day men will be found in these larger structures busily engaged in the study of the Talmud and in prayer. Many of these are aged men who have spent their lives in this way, supported by the charity of the pious Jews of foreign lands, who, themselves unable to come to Jerusalem, thus secure a representative whose prayers ascend from the Holy City for them. It may be truthfully said now that "Prayer is made continually in Jerusalem."

Not a synagogue, but a place as holy to the Jew and to the Gentile far more interesting, is a small paved court near the southwest corner of the wall enclosing the Haram area. This is the "Place of Wailing,"—the nearest approach the pious Jew ever makes to the sacred enclosure within which formerly stood the Temple of his God. Here on a Friday evening and on fast days may be witnessed a sight unparalleled for strangeness and pathos. Against the stones of the old wall that were put in place by the masons of long ago Jewish men and women, quaint specimens of a once great nation—stand and read their prayers and weep over their departed glories and their desolated city, just as their fathers wept by the waters of Babylon. The old stones are worn smooth by the affectionate kisses of the faithful and by the touch of reverent hands. It is hard to doubt that these tears are sincere. Surely as a people the Jews have suffered enough to warrant their tears, and here in the shadow of the temple wall the meagreness of their present privileges is sufficient to suggest the bitterness of their experiences.

On a day that permits this small court will be filled with men and women who have come to beseech Jehovah to remember with favor His ancient people. It is a strange gathering, unlike any other on earth. To the frivolous observer the varied and quaint costumes, the peculiar intonations and the unusual motions of the body are amusing, but the serious man considers their motive which lends an air of sanctity to the place. Surely a plot of ground that has been a place of prayer for centuries has some claims to reverence, and a people who through generations have continued faithful to their religious convictions, however mistaken they may be, will be treated with disrespect only by the despicable.

The practice of meeting at the "Wall of Wailing" has continued since the Middle Ages. The same litany has been chanted all these years and the same prayers read. And the end is not yet! In their chant the leader says, "We sit in solitude and mourn, for the palace that is destroyed; for the walls that are overthrown; for our majesty that is departed; for the great men who lie dead; for the precious stones that are burned; for the priests who have stumbled; for our kings who have despised us." After each of these statements the people respond in pathetic tones, "We sit in solitude and mourn." Occasionally another prayer is used. The leader says, "May peace and joy abide with Zion," and the suggestive response comes, "And may the Branch spring up at Jerusalem."

Few of the many annual visitors from Europe and America take the trouble to visit the real Jewish quarter of the city, and they thus miss a lasting impression. There are places of human habitation that are as wretched as some of these, but surely there can be none that surpass them in squalor. More unwholesome residences could not be devised than are some of these underground hovels where no breath of untainted air ever finds its way. From observations made by day and by night in these wretched holes, misnamed homes, I think I have learned one of the secrets of the indestructibility of the Hebrews: they can survive and increase and seem to thrive amid conditions that would be fatal to the average mortal.

It is amazing how many of these people can live in one small room, a room whose only method of ventilation is by the door, which during the night is closed and barred. Ten is not an uncommon number to find thus living. There will be little furniture in such a room and the beds are but heaps of rags on the floor. There are those even too poor to afford such meagre accommodations. Some of these are provided for in places not fit for cattle. I have seen in this quarter of the city deserted wives with their young children sleeping in sheltered corners of alleys and under low arches that span the narrow streets. In winter when the weather is severe, as it frequently is, the suffering among the homeless poor is very great. At such times the synagogues are thrown open and men and boys who have no more comfortable place are allowed to sleep on the floors. How these unfortunates manage to keep soul and body together is a mystery more difficult of solution than that which surrounds the fate of the charity funds that are poured into the coffers of the rabbis.

From the contemplation of such scenes it is pleasant to turn to the Jewish colonies outside the walls, and which nearly surround the city. The houses in these are usually small, but comfortable and sufficiently exposed for the circulation of fresh air. At the same time one cannot avoid the conclusion, after visiting some of these colonies and seeing what they are and what they might be, that their inhabitants prefer to have their surroundings filthy and to see to what extent they can violate all sanitary laws and still live.

In treating of the home life of Jerusalem Jews only the most general statements can be made. There are Jewish homes here just as commodious and as tastefully furnished and as carefully kept as any homes in the city. Israel has always been noted for the purity of its home life. In the true Jewish home there abides a spirit of devotion to religion, often burdensome to be sure, because bound in the fetters of rabbinism. The law provided for the regulation of home life, but at the same time permitted a certain freedom of action. Rabbinism, which descends to minutest particulars, leaves no room for choice. Its followers are slaves to the letter, and thus make a perpetual task of what was intended to be a continual joy. This "joy in the Lord" is what one misses in these homes. One noticeable positive virtue is the respect and reverence which the children have for their parents. This is universal. It is inculcated in infancy and continues through life. Hospitality is also practiced to the extent of the means of the head of the family. In morals the Jews everywhere will be found to compare favorable with any class of people. These domestic and moral virtues, which are Israel's strength, cannot be separated from his religion, for they are part of it. An undutiful child is impious; an immoral person is irreligious; the Law severely condemns both.

In the home the wife is the equal of her husband. She is not so regarded, however, in the synagogue, nor has she any voice in public affairs. She does not count as a member of the congregation, and her place when she attends public worship is in a retired part of the synagogue, usually a small, remote gallery, where she can see and hear, but not be seen. In any question that concerns the community her husband is the one to act. She may advise him, but he alone is responsible for results. I have never heard of a case in Jerusalem of a wife being dissatisfied with this arrangement.

In one particular concerning the family the native Jerusalem Jew resembles his Arab half-brother. He wishes his children all to be boys, and when a girl baby is born the rejoicing over the event is not nearly so marked as it would have been had the little one been a boy. The congratulations of friends are regulated by the sex of the infant. This is a peculiarity which is accounted for because of the religious superiority of males. In one other respect, namely that of education, the boys have the advantage over their sisters here. Boys' schools are abundant. In them the pupils are taught the rudiments of a general education and prepared for a career of usefulness. There are also industrial schools where trades are learned, and Talmud-Torah schools where special religious instruction is given. In the latter years are passed, lives oftentimes, in traversing "the sea of the Talmud." There is just one school for girls. It is supported by the Paris branch of the Rothschild family, and is called the Evelyn Rothschild School for Girls. This institution is ably conducted and has an attendance of three hundred and fifty. It is an innovation not fully approved of by the rabbis. Perhaps it would be unjust to say that these masters do not wish their women to know anything; the fact remains that they do not establish any other schools of this kind.

This failure to provide for the education of his daughters is one evidence of the unwisdom of the Jerusalem Jew; another evidence is seen in the marriage customs that largely prevail. Rabbinical laws regulate these also. To an uninitiated observer the majority of marriages here seem to be mere alliances for convenience. They are arranged by parents or friends and the young couple simply carry out the arrangements. Financial considerations have great weight, and the bride usually furnishes the weightier ones. But such marriages are not confined to Jerusalem, nor to Paris; not to the Jews, nor to the French. Divorce among the Jews here is a very common occurrence and more easily obtained than in Oklahoma. Under certain conditions polygamy is admissible, though it is practiced only by the Sephardim, and very rarely. The Chacham Bashi has two wives, as has also the chief rabbi of the Mughrabee Jews. They seem not to be thought any less of for this indulgence.

In the observance of their great annual religious feasts the spirit of Judaism is manifest. To properly celebrate some of these requires the temple and an officiating priesthood. In the absence of these the impressiveness of the service is lost and the effort to supply something that will make up for the loss is pitiable and in some instances almost ridiculous. The Day of Atonement is still observed in a way. None knows better than the Jews themselves how far it fails to be the solemn impressive day that it once was in Jerusalem. But the modern service could and should be improved upon. It could point in a clearer and more serious way to the necessity of true repentance. The spiritual degeneracy of Judaism is seen in this, that its most sacredly solemn Day has become a subject for ridicule. Twisting the neck of a young fowl is regarded as a sufficient substitute for the requirements of the sixteenth chapter of Leviticus. In preparation for the Day of Atonement some of the Chassidim, those who would be considered of special holiness, gather in the synagogue and submit themselves to the "whip of scourging." As they lie on the floor in the attitude of humiliation each receives the "forty stripes save one."

The Feast of Purim is still kept vigorously. The deliverance of the exiled portion of their race from the massacre arranged by the devices of Haman was a divine intervention not to be forgotten. The name "Purim" is used in irony, perhaps, because Haman was given to casting "lots," and did so on this occasion in order to learn which would be the most auspicious day for the inauguration of the proposed slaughter. Formerly there were certain days on which it was considered improper for this festival to be begun. But now the custom seems to be to commence the celebration as soon as the stars appear on the fourteenth of the month Adar. It will be remembered that the day is considered by the Jews as beginning at sundown. For this feast candles are lit, as an evidence of a lack of fear, and as a sign of rejoicing, and the people assemble in their various synagogues for a short religious service, during which the Book of Esther is read. At each mention of Haman's name by the reader, the congregation stamp their feet and cry "May his name be blotted out." The children present are taught to show their hatred for this ancient enemy. They are provided with stones on which Haman's name is written. These they rub together until the name is obliterated.

Next morning a service somewhat similar to that of the preceding evening is held, at which, after the prayers for the day, the passage in Exodus xvii., from verse eighth to sixteenth, is read. This relates to the destruction of the Amalekites, from whom they believe Haman was descended. The Book of Esther is again read and the synagogue service is over. Then comes the real rejoicing. Presents are exchanged; the children are supplied with an abundance of sweetmeats, and as generous a feast as can be afforded is indulged in. Wine is freely partaken of, as the Talmud enjoins, and he who is not intoxicated by the time the festivities are over is considered as not having kept the feast properly. In this connection we may observe that it is not possible for a religious Jew to be a total abstainer. Talmudic injunctions require the partaking of wine on the Sabbath, at the Passover Feast and at Purim.

The Feast of Tabernacles is kept with something of its original simplicity and rejoicing. It comes at the time of year when grateful thoughts are natural to the recipient of divine favors. It was originally a national thanksgiving, and is yet in a sense, though the conditions for its proper celebration are not possible to dispersed Israel. Two of the former requirements, namely, "joyous festivities and dwelling in booths" are practiced. The third, that of sacrifice, has been discontinued since the fall of the temple. This feast lasted seven days—from the fifteenth to the twenty-first of the month Tishri—and was followed by a day of "holy convocation." During these days all the Jews appear in holiday attire. Booths are built in the yards or on the flat roofs or balconies of every house. In these booths the male members of the family reside during the week. Here the family partakes of its meals and receives friends. At night all except the most rigid religionists occupy their accustomed beds under substantial roofs. As the booths as now constructed afford little protection from the weather this move indoors at night is certainly the part of wisdom. The symbolic meaning of this feast is lost sight of by the Jews. As the feast of ingathering of the full harvest it pointed forward to the final ingathering, "the glory of the latter day," when all nations shall appear before the Lord.

To these practices, which have a Biblical foundation, others with no such basis have been added and are observed as carefully as if there were a "thus saith the Lord" to support them; but to enter into a discussion of these would carry us beyond the limits of a work of this kind.

Among the strictly Oriental Jews there are many practices that seem to be mere superstitions. In common with their Moslem neighbors the fear of the "evil eye" is quite prevalent. Charms are worn to counteract this baleful influence and numerous invocations are used to protect against it. Over the doors of many of the houses will be seen the whitewashed or painted representation of a hand. The resemblance to a hand is generally a very distant one, there being simply five straight lines diverging from a point. These lines are meant to represent "the Hand of Might." This symbol has a significance similar to a horseshoe nailed above the door; namely, to bring good luck to the household and to protect it from the evil spirits. Amulets are resorted to in cases of severe illness and are frequently applied when a physician's treatment does not appear to be successful.

Among the orthodox here, as everywhere, belief in the coming of the Messiah still obtains; Him whom the Christian world recognizes as its Messiah the Jerusalem Jew utterly disregards. Many will not endure the mention of His name without expressions of contempt, and to speak of Him in their presence as the Anointed One of Israel will evoke from them what sounds to Christian ears as the harshest blasphemy. This estimate of Jesus of Nazareth is taught to the children as soon as they are old enough to comprehend it. It is impressed upon them throughout their life until maturity. What wonder, when to this teaching is added the accounts of how Israel has been maltreated among the nations, that Christianity has made hardly any impression upon this citadel of Judaism!

Systematic Christian mission work is done among these people, but the results lead to the conclusion that the time of the "ingathering" is not yet. There are some sheaves, however, for one may see on any Sunday during the year at the services of Christ's Church a fair-sized congregation of Hebrew Christians. Nor is anything to be said against missionary methods as applied by the London Jews Society, the Missionary Alliance and other independent workers who are employing themselves in presenting Christ to the Jews. It is simply a conclusion reached after some years of study and observation on the ground, that the great body of Israel remains untouched by the Gospel. Years of faithful preaching, teaching and medical mission work have failed to break down the wall of division.

That some work is effective may be judged by the recent violent opposition of the rabbis to the hospital of the London Jews Society. A fine new hospital building has just been completed in one of the most attractive parts of the city, and at an expense of seventy thousand dollars. Here Jewish patients were received and treated free of charge. No sooner were the hospital quarters removed from the old building to the new than war was declared by the rabbis. A "charem" was issued against the new hospital and all Jews were warned against applying there for treatment and threatened with excommunication if they disobeyed the warning. One Jewess dared the wrath of the rabbis and entered the hospital for treatment. She died, and burial was refused her by the Jewish authorities in their cemetery. Influence was brought to bear upon the chief rabbi to permit the interment, but he positively refused. Having disobeyed the "charem" she was no longer considered as a Jewess. The hospital authorities brought the matter before the English consul, who communicated with the Pasha. The excitement lasted for three days and in spite of all protests the chief rabbi won. The woman was buried in a secluded corner of ground not in the Jewish cemetery, and had no service of any kind at her grave. This incident has had the effect of so frightening the Jews that they will not go near the new hospital. This opposition will probably be very short-lived.

Nor is this opposition to Christian missions confined to Jerusalem. It seems to be a concerted plan of the rabbis everywhere, apparently due to fears that all the efforts being made to convert the Jew are not fruitless. In Jewish periodicals recently there has been much said against all "conversionists," and much contempt heaped upon the proselyte.

The Jews in Jerusalem

One cannot much blame the spiritual leaders of Israel for seeking to hold their people within the ancient pale of their religion; some criticism is possible of the methods used.

Besides the spiritual terrors which the Jerusalem rabbis have at their disposal, there is also a weighty temporal force which they can make effective. In all parts of the world where Jews are found there are collections made for their brethren in the Holy City. The house of every pious Jew of the Dispersion has a little box in which the members of the family deposit now and then a small coin which is meant for Jerusalem. Collectors are appointed, each one having a certain district, who visit the houses and empty these charity boxes. How much money from these finds its way each year to the old city none but the rabbis who handle it can tell. But that it is a considerable sum may be estimated from the number of people who are supported out of it. It is known as the Haluka, or charity fund, and, with but few exceptions, every family in the city draws upon it. Any one asking can receive; consequently many having no need of charity are sharing that which was intended for the poor. The really poor whose daily bread depends upon this charity fund must obey the commands of the dispensing rabbi or suffer.

A large Haluka is raised in America. I am informed that about forty-five thousand dollars is the annual amount collected there for the Jerusalem poor. I am assured here that only six thousand dollars ever reaches Jerusalem. Where the rest goes is a matter of speculation which does not require much astuteness. In the spring of 1896 some intelligent American Jews residing in Jerusalem concluded to remedy this palpable wrong, which really amounted to fraud, and decided to organize an American congregation. They laid their case before their co-religionists in the United States, informed them how their charity was being dispensed, and proposed the organization of a strictly American society which would see to the collecting and forwarding of the fund in an honorable business way, and promised to see that it was dispensed in the same way to only the deserving poor here. A storm of opposition was raised by the collectors and forwarders in America and by the distributers in Jerusalem, and rabbis in Russia and Austria protested strongly at the proposed innovation. But the innovators had right on their side and there is now in the Holy City an American Hebrew congregation, managed by honorable American Jews, and contributors to the Haluka may be assured that their charity is not lost.

Like their brothers in other parts of the world the Jews of Jerusalem, and of the rest of Palestine, are being moved by the spirit of Nationalism. In numbers the Hebrew nation is respectable; in wealth and abilities it is wonderful. A sense of what it is, is compelling it to think of what it might be and to discuss methods of fulfilling its destiny. In these discussions Palestine is coming into prominence and the formerly indifferent are made "Lovers of Zion." Israel needs a home, a land he can call his own, a city where he can work out his salvation. He has none of these now. His present home is among strangers, people with whom he has little sympathy and who have little for him. The lands in which he lives are not his own, though he has frequently shed his blood for their preservation. The cities he has helped to build are not his; they never can be. Israel's hope of a home land is possible of realization, but it will be realized only in Palestine.

I would not enter upon the discussion as to how the dispersed nation is to be gathered, or when. There are obstacles in the way, which will not be removed to-day or to-morrow; that they can be removed is enough. There is coming a time when Israel shall "no more be termed forsaken" nor his "land any more be termed desolate." Then Jerusalem shall be called "Sought out. A city not forsaken."[1]

[1] Isaiah lxii.

THE CHRISTIANS IN JERUSALEM

Beginnings of Christianity—Christian Affection—Evidences of that Affection and Reasons for It—Historical Experiences—Variety of Religions—Greek Church—Church Statistics—Religious Paupers—Ecclesiastics—Criticism of Missions—Mission Difficulties—Houses of Industry—" Peculiar " Christians—People with " Missions "—The Second Advent—Incidents of Peculiarities—Work of the Oriental Churches—Russian Influence—Greek Church Possessions—Latin Possessions—Schools—The Latin Patriarch—Armenians—Syrians—Anglican Church—London Jews Society—Germans—Children's Hospital—German Colony—American Missionaries.

XVII

THE CHRISTIANS IN JERUSALEM

THE beginnings of Christianity were in this sacred city of Judaism, and since the dark Friday, when by His death on the cross the Son of God sealed His earthly ministry, there have always been some of His followers residing here. While not regarding it with the same feelings of devout veneration as do the Jews, Christians generally have a peculiar affection for Jerusalem, founded upon the hallowed events with which the old city is associated. The words and acts of Christ, the establishment of the Church, the bitter trials and cruel persecutions which the Apostles endured for their faith, the organization of the first missionary band and its starting out into the wide world with its Gospel of love and salvation, these are reasons sufficient for that sentiment. Some of us at this "end of the age," fettered by the iron chains of hard utilitarianism, may refuse to acknowledge the presence of this feeling in our hearts; and thereby we lose not a little that is commendable, and much that would be beneficial. The event is always greater than the place in which it occurred : Christianity is greater than Jerusalem. Still, our high regard for the former should not cause entire forgetfulness of the latter.

That Jerusalem is not forgotten, and has not been through the centuries by Christians, can be known by a perusal of the history of pilgrimages. There have been those "afar off" whose eyes turned longingly to the poor city in which their Lord died. There are those to-day—the number is increasing—who from Christian lands far distant come to see this city which, though still insignificant as compared with the great cities of the earth, is the world's religious capital. It would be otherwise a miserable village, peopled by a few wretched Jews and miserable Moslems.

The history of Christianity in the Holy City has been marked by many scenes of blood. Some of these have been enacted in the name and for the supposed glory of the Prince of Peace, some because of enmity to that Prince and His followers. Perhaps no city of its size has witnessed so much of the horror of religious persecution as this chief city of Palestine. Perhaps none to-day exhibits to the world such a diversity of religions and so many varieties of the Christian religion in particular. Certainly there is none where, because of ecclesiastical intolerance, the unlovely spirit of hatred for each other dominates to such a degree the various confessions. This unloveliness in the name of love is the cause of much grief to the earnest Christian and much of the suspicion with which Jew and Moslem regard the religion of the Crucified.

Since the return of the Christians from Pella, there has been no time when there has not been a resident Christian community. During most of the time previous to the Mohammedan occupation the Christians had been in the majority and held the official positions. Since that time (637), with the exception of the one century—the twelfth—when the Crusaders held the city against the Saracens, they have had no nominal and very little real power. At present the Christians outnumber the Moslems and both together are outnumbered, three to one, by the Jews. And nearly every ordinary Christian sect is here, along with a good many which would not be possible in any other place.

Of the entire Christian population nearly a half are adherents of the Greek Orthodox Church—the wealthiest and most influential of all. Next in order are the Roman Catholics who number three thousand two hundred, and who as a Church are by no means poor in this world's goods. The following list will give a concise idea of the various Christian bodies.

The Christians in Jerusalem

Greek Orthodox	4,000
Roman Catholic	3,200
Armenian	600
Protestants (all forms)	500
Coptic	120
Greek Catholic	100
Abyssinian	60
Syrian	50
Total	8,630

Of this number a great many are practically supported by the various religious societies operating in the city. If every private house occupied by a Christian were destroyed there is room enough in the convents, hospices and nunneries to give every family comfortable quarters. The Greeks and Latins have large revenues from the faithful in other parts of the world who do not forget the "poor saints which are at Jerusalem." They use a great deal of this income to supply bread to their native adherents. In this way they manage to retain many who would otherwise be indifferent to religion. Twice a week each of the two great Churches distributes food to the needy, and it is notorious that some of the recipients are Greeks on the day the Greeks distribute and Latins on the day the Latins dispense bounty. While it is a worthy work to supply the wants of the needy it is a work that is carried on to such an extent in Jerusalem as to make paupers out of many who are capable of self-support. But it is very easy to obtain funds for charity in Jerusalem. The very name of the place appeals to all the Jewish and Christian world and the amounts of money that come in for the regularly organized missionary and charitable societies, as well as for private independent workers, are truly surprising. For the amount of work done, as well as results accomplished, there is more money spent in the Holy City than in any other city on earth. And a great part of that money comes from America. It would be useless to decry this expenditure or to attempt to turn some of this revenue into more useful channels. The charitably inclined wish to send it here and the stewards of the distribution are glad to receive it; and it will continue to come.

The city ought to be "holy" if the presence of rabbis, priests, lay missionaries, religious sheikhs and dervishes be conducive to holiness. At any time of the day and in any part of the city you can see one or other of these "holy men." The Christian priests seem to be the most numerous and it is not an exaggeration to say that there is a priest for every fifteen of the Christian community. Some of these priests are engaged in mission work, some in teaching in the various schools; but the majority do nothing distinctively religious. They enjoy the comforts of life and walk about in their long robes, visiting the holy places and appearing holy themselves. Jewish rabbis and Moslem sheikhs lead similar lives, each guarding their own peculiar beliefs and places and enabled to keep up the best of appearances by means of the generosity of the faithful in other lands.

It would be doing a great injustice to many faithful men and women to criticise without reservation all the mission work that is being done. I shall have to leave that for those professional critics of Christian missions who are all too ready to publish their ignorance and are all too readily believed. If those who criticise these workers and their methods in other parts of the world have as little experimental knowledge of them as has the average critic of the Jerusalem missions what they say is not worth listening to, for it is false.

This must be said of the majority of Protestant Christian workers, that they are faithfully living and preaching the Gospel of the Master as they believe it. They are teaching these people how to live for this world as well as for that which is to come. And if there is one thing the native of Palestine needs to learn it is how to live so that life will be something more than animal existence.

The Christians in Jerusalem 317

It should be borne in mind also that those who are here doing the Master's work as they see it have one of the hardest fields in the world to work. Christianity is no new thing to these people, but the Christianity of Christ is. The Oriental Churches have been on the ground for centuries. They have repelled rather than attracted the non-Christian element. They sadly need a reformation. During all these centuries they have had no converts from Islam or Judaism. Their policy toward the Jew is one of hatred; toward the Moslem one of indifference. To people whose only idea of Christianity is obtained from such representatives the western missionaries come. What wonder that they are not received and have first to break down a strong hedge of prejudice before Jew or Moslem will tolerate them even to the extent of listening to them! It is true that the apparent results are small, but they are substantial.

The "Houses of Industry," where young men are taught some useful trade, are in themselves a blessing. These young Arabs go out to the different villages scattered over the land able to do something more than pass their time in idleness. They also have some idea of what the true religion of Jesus is, even if they do not brave the ridicule and possible dangers that a public profession of it would bring upon them. There are girls in the mission schools who are taught ideas of cleanliness and get valuable lessons in home-making. This is work that will tell in the coming generation. If nothing more were being done than such work as this it ought to silence adverse criticism. And it would if the adverse critics knew it was going on. But they come to the city for a few days, spend those days in seeing the sights, among which mission work is not one, and then go away to answer any who may question them about it that there is very little if any such work being done. All that such people need is an object lesson showing what these boys and girls were when they entered the schools, or Houses of Industry, and what they are when they leave to take their places in the world.

There is another class of individuals making a part of the population who are counted among the Christians and that a mistake is made in so counting them is not for me to say. The name most suited to them is the modern word "crank." If any one in Europe or America has any particular religious vagary, which in his or her diseased imagination is God-inspired and which the whole world must accept or be forever lost, he comes to Jerusalem if he is able. It would take a good sized volume to describe these people and their views. It would make strange, but unprofitable reading. America leads in the number furnished to this class.

They all differ in most respects but in one particular all are agreed; all the world is hopelessly in error as to religion; the Christian Church is either intentionally or ignorantly corrupt and there is no salvation for it. By a dream, or a vision, or some special inspiration God has showed them the only true way and appointed them to herald the truth to the world. The Apostles began at Jerusalem, so must these apostles of a new dispensation. They arrive in the city full of enthusiasm over what they have been "called" to do. One man, the disciple of a new kind of Mormonism, arrived in the city, immediately called at the consulate and requested to be shown the offices of the leading newspapers, as he wished to announce his arrival and give a prospectus of his work. As there is not a single newspaper published in the place this request was easily answered. But he managed to make his announcement. Five years have witnessed no results. He has given up trying, but still retains belief in his divine appointment.

During the winter of 1894-95 a very intelligent gentleman arrived. He looked and acted like an ordinary tourist, but one had to converse with him but a short time to learn that he too had a "mission." "I have come with a message to the Jews," he informed me, "and I want to know if you think

The Christians in Jerusalem 319

there would be anything in the way of my procuring a large tent, setting it up in a vacant lot and delivering my message to the people to whom I am sent."

"No," I replied, "there will be nothing in the way except getting the Jews to come to the tent."

"Oh, that will be all right. The Lord will take care of that."

"Can you speak Hebrew, or Spanish or the Jewish Jargon?"

"No. I cannot." "Then how will you convey the message? Very few of these people understand English."

"Oh, the Lord will take care of that. He sent me here to remain for thirty days and in this time I must get my message to all the Jews."

In about two weeks I saw him again. He had reconsidered the matter of the tent and had decided to issue two addresses in Hebrew, one to the rabbis and another to the common people. This he did and scattered them broadcast. At the end of thirty days, true to his mission, he returned to his home in the United States.

The belief that the Second Coming of the Lord is near at hand, and that His first appearance will be on the Mount of Olives, has drawn many to this place. They are patiently waiting to see their belief realized. Some have knowledge of the exact day of His coming; others only know it is to be soon.

One good old lady, now gone to her rest, went day after day to the Mount and made her afternoon tea. Questioned as to why she did this she replied, "Christ is coming and I want to be on Olivet when He comes and have a cup of tea ready for Him."

The story is told, though the genuineness of it is not vouched for here, that an American of this peculiar stamp had come to the city to announce what he called the New Gospel. Walking down David street he was met by a fellow countryman and a general conversation ensued. Very soon the man with the message was asked how long he intended to remain in Jerusalem, and replied, "I have come here to stay." "Indeed; but what are you going to do here. This is no place to live."

"It may not be the place for you, but it is for me. I have come to preach the New Gospel."

"Is that so? and what, may I ask, is the New Gospel?"

"It is the Gospel that there is to be no more death. Death has controlled long enough and I am to preach that its power is ended from this time on. Death is played out."

This was a revelation to the man who did not feel that he had any special mission in the Holy City and he hardly knew what reply to make to it. Finally he said, "But, my friend, are not all the facts against the truth of your Gospel? People are dying this very moment in spite of your Gospel."

"Yes, I know it; but the Gospel of no death has not yet been announced. I was sent here to announce it and as soon as this is done no more deaths will occur."

"Very well; that is very comforting, but just suppose, after you have published your Gospel, that you yourself should die, what would become of this Gospel then?"

"Oh, if such should happen, if I should die after proclaiming this, the whole blame thing would 'bust up.'" And so it would.

So would many of the other so-called gospels that just now have one or several advocates residing here and doing what they can to propagate them. There was a company of deluded people who came here fourteen years ago and announced that none of them were going to die until the Lord appeared. In as many years thirteen of them have died.

All these religious vagaries, and there are many others, each with its ardent supporter who misses no opportunity to voice his belief, has its deterring effect upon the regular missionary efforts. Moslem and Jew regard them all as phases of Christianity and wonder at a religion that produces them. The city could very well dispense with the presence of all this

SYRIAN BISHOP OF JERUSALEM.

The Christians in Jerusalem

class of its population. The only redeeming thing about them is that they are not numerous.

In this connection it will be proper to speak of the distinctive mission work done by the Christian Church in Jerusalem. Concerning the Oriental branches there is little to be said for they are satisfied to retain their native adherents and make little effort to spread the Gospel among non-Christians. They seem to have forgotten their "marching orders" to "preach the Gospel to every creature." Oriental Christianity is little else than lifeless form, and to "preach the Gospel" seems to be no part of the labor of its numerous clergy. Their work is to care for the holy places, look after their large property interests in and near the city, see that their privileges are not infringed upon by other sects, repeat their prayers and live comfortably. The Greeks are far more active in getting possession of land in and near the city than in anything else. Any piece of property that is at all desirable that comes on the market is soon bought up by those who manage the temporal affairs of this community. Where the money comes from to make these purchases is a matter to speculate about. While this patriarchate has the largest revenue of any in the Church there is a pretty general belief that the property is not all paid for out of this. Russia's desire to number the Holy Land among her possessions is well known, and her diplomats may be using this arm of her established Church to accomplish that desire. In the event of the dismemberment of the Turkish empire these possessions—if they be Russian—would no doubt have considerable weight in deciding to which one of the interested European powers this land would fall. In the event of the land falling to any other power, Russia's claim to her purchased territory would in all probability be recognized, and she would at least suffer no loss.

The Greeks possess the following buildings devoted solely to religious, educational or charitable purposes:—

The Monasteries of St. Helena and Constantine, Abraham

and Gethsemane; the Convents of St. Basil, St. Catharine, two of St. George, St. Michael, St. Theodore, Carolombos, Demetrius, Euthymius, Sectuagia, Nicholas, John the Baptist, Nativity of Mary, Spiridon and Spirito. They have a girls' school, a boys' school and a hospital. Besides these are numerous private residences and stores from which a good income is derived.

The Russian Mission, whose aim it seems to be to Russianize the land rather than Christianize the people, has a fine property just northwest of the city, with a large cathedral church, several pilgrim houses and an extensive hospital. The Russian Palestine Society is making its presence felt and seems to have an abundance of means and great influence.

The Latin Church is a missionary institution and its priests do not lose sight of that fact. Each one of them is a missionary and wherever he is holds in mind his commission to make Latin Christianity supreme. There can be no questioning this fact by any one who takes the time to view their operations in Jerusalem and Palestine. In Jerusalem itself are the following schools and orders for the propagation of the Latin faith.

Sisters of St. Joseph, having under their care the parish school for native girls with an average attendance of one hundred and twenty pupils. This order also conducts an orphanage and hospital.

Sisters of Zion, with an excellent school and orphanage for girls, the school caring for about one hundred resident pupils.

Franciscan Sisters. These carry on an orphanage and have under their care always about fifty little girls.

Sisters of Charity. These do an excellent and much needed work in their quiet, but effective way in supporting a house for aged, infirm men and women and a home for foundlings. There are usually about twenty of the latter unfortunate little ones whom they care for.

The following are the schools for boys carried on by the different orders of the Latin Church:

The Christians in Jerusalem 323

The Franciscans have an institution for the study of theology, an orphanage for boys, a parish and an industrial school.

The Dominicans also have a school for Bible study.

The White Brothers of St. Anne have a home, church and school for the education of Greek Catholics.

The Brothers of St. Peter have an orphanage and house of industry.

Herein these Latins show their wisdom. They are caring for the future by getting hold of the children. This is really the only effective way; and it is very effective. The Church that employs such enginery is bound to progress, and the one that does not is sure to be surpassed. The Latins are caring not only for the children of Latin parents, but are providing education for children of the Greek and other Churches. They are very willing to do this, spending time, and money also, for they are bringing up as Latin Christians the children of non-Latin parentage.

The present Latin Patriarch, Monseigneur Leodovico Piavi, is a broad-minded, intelligent man, whose kindly face is expressive of great power. The position requires such a man, for it demands of the incumbent in the patriarchal chair the exercise of executive powers and political acumen rather than great learning. However, the Patriarch's executive and political abilities have interfered but little with his scholarly attainments and I have wondered how a man whose time is so fully occupied could manage to be so well informed as to current events in all parts of the world.

The Latin Church is by no means poor in worldly goods in Jerusalem. With the same success that they seem to have in other parts of the world they have here found the means to secure some of the most desirable property and have erected substantial buildings. In the school of the Sisters of Zion they possess one of the most interesting sites in the city, even if it be not the place of Pilate's judgment hall where Christ was condemned ; though I see no reason for doubting this claim. In the Fréres' College in the northwest angle of the walls they hold the most commanding position within the city. Add to these the churches, namely, that of the Patriarch, St. Salvator, St. Anne, Ecce Homo, Notre Dame du Spasme, the Chapel of the Agony, the Monasteries of the Holy Sepulchre, the Scourging, the Dominicans, the Brethren of the African Mission, the Convents of the Carmelite Sisters, the Sisters of Zion, the Sisters of the Rosary, the Sisters of St. Joseph, and to these the Hospices for the entertainment of Pilgrims, namely the Casa Nuova, the German Catholic, the Austrian and the immense French Pilgrim building, and it forms a list of possessions in the Holy City well worthy even of that Church to which they belong.

The Armenians have an extensive property on Mount Zion near the Tower of David. The patriarch lives in a large monastery near the Zion Gate, where, when the occasion arises, a thousand pilgrims may be housed.

The other Oriental Churches are rather poor; the Syrians have a quaint old church on the eastern slope of Zion near which their Bishop resides. The Copts have two monasteries. The Abyssinians possess a monastery in the city and a fine church in the new city on the northwest.

The Church of England, represented by the Church Missionary Society and the London Society for the Promotion of Christianity among the Jews, carries on the most extensive mission work done by the Protestants. The former society confines its efforts to the native population and works in the neighboring villages as well as in Jerusalem. Their native adherents number about 130, many of whom derive support from the mission. For the number of workers the results appear very small, and when one compares the amount of money expended with these small results the wonder is that the supporters of the work do not become discouraged and apply the money here used to more appreciative people in other parts of the world. Plainly, Jerusalem is over-missionized. This is saying nothing derogatory to the missionaries, both men and women, for whom one cannot but have the very highest regard. If there is any censure it belongs to the Church Boards of England and America, who keep increasing the number of workers and the amount of expenditures without any intelligent consideration of the conditions. If the object of the Churches is to increase the working force on the mission field it is attained; but if it be to make the best use of time and money—two things which ought never to be lost sight of in this as in all other kinds of work—thorough knowledge of the conditions, and the conduct of affairs in strict accordance with that knowledge, must take the place of the present methods. Until this change is made, the missionaries will continue to be subjects of criticism because of their lives of apparent ease; and conclusions unfavorable to all missionary effort will continue to be drawn by those who have no real interest in the Christianizing of the Moslem and the Jew.

The Church Missionary Society employs in all about twenty workers. These are preachers, teachers, and house to house visitors. Services in Arabic are held every Sunday in St. Paul's Church north of the city. There is a boys' boarding-school, founded by Bishop Gobat, where about seventy boys are educated; it is situated on the southwestern slope of Zion. This society also conducts a day school for boys and girls.

The "London Jews Society" owns the handsome stone church on Mount Zion, just opposite the Tower of David. Services are held every Sunday and are in English and Hebrew. A fine boys' school adjoins the church where children of Jewish parentage are cared for. To the north of the city is the girls' school of this society which is ably conducted and possesses the best equipped school building in Palestine, with the exception of the American Friends' School at Ramallah. Under the care of the society is also a "house of industry" where young proselytes are taught useful trades; and just now there is being erected a magnificent new hospital a short distance north of the British Consulate.

The British Ophthalmic Hospital near the railroad station, which is supported by the English Knights of St. John, is doing a noble work.

The German Evangelical Community numbers about two hundred. These with the English community formerly united under one Protestant bishop, supported by Prussia and England; an arrangement which was not found altogether satisfactory and was dissolved in 1887. The Anglican Bishopric is still maintained and the office held by the Right Reverend G. F. Popham Blyth, D. D.

The German religious and charitable institutions under the care of the Evangelicals are the girls' orphanage, Talitha Cumi, conducted by the Deaconnesses of Kaiserswerth; Schneller's orphanage for boys; the Hospital of St. John; the Hospital of the Deaconnesses of Kaiserswerth. In this connection should be named the estimable work done by Doctor Sandreczky and his family in the Children's Hospital. Though hampered by lack of means, the results accomplished by the doctor in his small institution are beyond praise. Any one has but to see the wretched condition of the native children of Palestine and the children of poor Jews to appreciate what a blessing such an institution is. The hospital is always overcrowded by the little sufferers and their mothers, and were the means provided the accommodations could be indefinitely increased. As it is the doctor and his family serve gratuitously and by doing their very best cannot supply the needs of all the deserving applicants. Their work is done without ostentation and most economically.

Very worthy of mention also is the Lepers' Hospital southwest of the city, which is supported by the Brethren of Herrnhut. The form of leprosy that may now be seen all too frequently in the environs of Jerusalem is not the same as that of Bible times. Hideously repulsive as the victims of it are and fatal as are its results it is not contagious. There is no doubt that it could be stamped out in a single generation if the authorities would seclude the infected ones and prevent any of them from marrying. The disease is hereditary and the children of afflicted parents are sure to have it sooner or later.

The Evangelical Germans own one of the finest pieces of property in the city. This was a gift from the Sultan to Prussia, made in 1869 on the occasion of the visit to Constantinople of the Crown Prince. The property is now called the Muristan. Since the time of Charlemagne Christian buildings have stood on this ground. The most important of these, the remains of which still exist, were the work of Raymond du Puy in 1130 to 1140. In the conquest of Saladin this magnificent property was given as an endowment to the Mosque of Omar. As usual with such possessions in Moslem lands the buildings were permitted to fall into decay. City refuse was thrown in and about the grounds so that when the Prussians came into possession an immense amount of labor and expense was necessary in order to clear away the rubbish. At present the Germans hold services in a temporary chapel which was formerly the refectory of the Hospitallers. The fine new church that is being erected on this site will soon be ready for occupancy, and when completed will be the most imposing structure owned by the Protestants in Jerusalem.

Southwest of the city is the pleasant German colony numbering about three hundred souls. The members of it are Templars and are now engaged in business and useful trades. Their settlement here and in other parts of Palestine was the result of a religious movement in Würtemburg in 1860. The leaders of this movement considered that it was the duty of Christianity to illustrate and embody the Kingdom of Christ on earth; and accordingly they started these Christian social settlements with the avowed object of regenerating the Church and the social life of Europe. They have discarded the doctrine of the Trinity and the Divinity of Christ. Numerous schisms have disturbed them and their object in coming and founding these communities seems a long way from being realized. By their industry and frugality, however, they set a good example for the natives about them, though their community is not "ideal."

Though the first Protestant Mission in Jerusalem was opened by Christians from the United States, the mission representation from that far-away country is now small, and, with the exception of three ladies under appointment from the Christian Alliance of New York, is confined to three or four independent workers whose labors are for the conversion of the Jews. The Spafford Community near the Damascus Gate, originally composed of Americans, cannot be classed as missionaries, as they do not pretend to do any mission work.

After this recital of Christian institutions and laborers, one unacquainted with the place might look for the immediate conversion to Christianity of all the non-Christians. But it must be said that there is no place in the world where indifference and opposition are so manifest. Indifference is the attitude of the Moslem, while opposition characterizes the Jew. The results of the mission work are necessarily small, and will be so as long as there is so much called by the name of Christ that is unlovely and false, and in some instances despicable. Here as elsewhere Christianity is judged by its fruits, and so much of the product is undesirable that the whole is refused. Before the indifference can be changed to interest and the opposition to favor, there must be a radical change in the Christian Church. It must return to the Christianity of Christ, exhibiting less of outward form and more of love. Until that change is made—when dead form will give place to genuine Christian living—the results can be no greater. At present the time given to this work is almost wasted and the money spent well-nigh lost.

THE MOSLEMS

Their Names for Jerusalem—Religious Reverence for It—El Kuds—Mukaddasi the Historian—Early Moslem History—Abu Bekr—Abou Abeidah—Omar's Conquest of the City—Terms of Surrender—Moslem Occupation Previous to Crusades—Christian Pilgrimages—Peter the Hermit—Christian Conquest—Saladin—Frederic II.—The Kharezmians—Crusade of St. Louis—Sulieman—Jerusalem's Governor—Megliss—Moslem Population—The Unwelcome Turk—Arab Aristocracy—Moslem Fatalism—" Children of the Sultan "—Military Service—Domestic Life—Social Life—Masculine Superiority—Female Education—Moslem Toleration—Religious Practices—Indifference—Fasts and Feasts—Nebi Moosa—Moslem Places of Burial—Death—End of Moslem Supremacy.

XVIII

THE MOSLEMS

SOME idea of the position which Jerusalem occupies in the estimation of Moslems may be obtained by a brief consideration of the names they give it. We must first, however, take into account an exceeding fondness for religious expressions and titles which is peculiar to the Oriental. By no people is this fondness exhibited more than by the Arabs; judging by their conversation at times, one unacquainted with them would imagine them to be an exceedingly holy and religious race. Religious they are, but in the majority of cases it would be a mistake to call them holy. They have a fondness, too, for reverencing certain places, because of some real or supposed connection of the place with an event in the history of the nation or with the life of a worthy individual. Throughout Mohammedan lands there are reputed holy places, and as the true follower of the Prophet passes these he stops to breathe a prayer; and if it should be the regular prayer hour he spreads his rug or arbeyyeh and piously prostrates himself.

But of all holy places in Palestine Jerusalem is the most renowned. No pious Moslem comes within sight of it without emotion and some religious expression. All about, on the neighboring hills, where a first view of the city is had are small piles of stones set up as memorials. These are silent prayers of thanksgiving and adoration—thanksgiving because the ones who erected them have been permitted to attain these view-points, and adoration at what they behold. It is the "holy of holies" of Palestine; hence the names they have given it. Many of the natives within a short distance of the city do not know the word "Jerusalem," and if one were to ask them where the city of that name is would not understand. The name would be new to them. To the Moslem Jerusalem is always El Kuds—the Holy. Sometimes he speaks of it as Bait El Mukaddas or Makdis—the Holy House.

Early Arab historians were loud in their praises of the city. In poetry it is occasionally spoken of as El Balat, meaning "the court" or "royal residence," a word supposed to be a corruption of the Latin palatium. Mukaddasi, whose name indicates that he was a native of "the Holy House," writing near the close of the tenth century, says:

"The Holy City, Bait el Makdis, is also known as Iliya and El Balat. Among provincial towns none is larger than Jerusalem, and many capitals are, in fact, smaller. Neither the cold nor the heat is excessive here, and snow falls but rarely. The Kadi Abu-l Kasim, son of the Kadi of the Holy Cities of Makkah and Al Madinah, inquired of me once concerning the climate of Jerusalem. I answered: "It is betwixt and between—neither very hot nor very cold." Said he in reply: "Just as that of Paradise."[1] This quotation is here introduced to show that at the time it was written the name Aelia (Iliya), given to the city by Hadrian, in A. D. 130, was still in use and also that the ancient Jewish name was known.

The history of how Palestine became the possession of the followers of the Arab Prophet while exceedingly interesting can be but touched upon here.

Mohammed, driven from his native Mecca, barely escaping with his life, was soon to return at the head of ten thousand zealous followers, take that city, crush his enemies, shatter the idols of the Caàba, give a new religion to Arabia and begin that marvellous conquest of fanaticism, which was to sweep like a fury over eastern Asia and northern Africa; enter Europe at its eastern and western extremities and retain much of that territory to this day.

Belief in the divine mission of their Prophet sent the wan-

[1] "Palestine under the Moslems," p. 84.

dering Arabs, fired with holy zeal, out from the "parched plains of the Hejjaz," with its wastes of dreary landscape, to the more fertile and much more attractive lands to the west. Abu Bekr, the successor of the Prophet, looked with covetous eyes upon Palestine, and, issuing an appeal to the sheikhs of the various tribes of Arabs, exhorted them to assist him in adding it to his territorial possessions. The response was all that could have been desired, and an army was soon on the way. The Christians made a feeble resistance. One by one the cities of Syria fell into the hands of the invaders. After the battle of Yarmúk, in 636 A. D., where the Christians met a disastrous defeat, nothing prevented the victors from marching against Jerusalem. The Moslems were then commanded by Abou Obeidah. Arriving at the fords of the Jordan this general despatched a messenger to the Patriarch of Aelia demanding the absolute surrender of the city. His message was couched in the following terse but determined words: "In the name of God, merciful and gracious! From Abou Obeidah Ibn-el-Jirah to the Christians of the people of Aelia, health! and to all who follow the right way, and believe in God and in His Prophet! To come to the point. For my part I beg you to bear witness that there is no God but God, and Mohammed is the apostle of God; and that the moment of judgment will come beyond all doubt, and that God will raise men from the dead. And if you will stand to this your blood is sacred unto us as well as your property, and your children, and you shall be to us as brothers; but if you will refuse I will bring down upon you a people more earnest in their love of death than are you in the drinking of wine or eating of hogs' flesh, nor will I ever pass away from you, please God, until I have killed your warriors and made captive your children."[1]

Such a proposal was enough to arouse the ire of all in Jerusalem. It was refused and for four months the Christians in

[1] Ockley's "Saracens," Vol. I., p. 214.

the city held out. But at the end of this time, seeing the hopelessness of resistance, the patriarch from the city wall called the Moslem general for a parley. No terms satisfactory to both could be agreed upon, so that finally the patriarch decided to capitulate. That he was still regarded as a respectable adversary is shown by his refusal to treat as to terms of capitulation with anybody but the caliph himself. His request was granted. Omar was sent for and came. Terms were agreed upon and Jerusalem became a Moslem city. The terms were rather severe on the Christians, but were more favorable than they would have been able to secure had they refused and resorted to the judgment of the sword. The conquered were guaranteed security for their persons and property; freedom to practice their religious exercises in their churches, except that at all hours the churches must be open to Moslem inspection; Christians must always treat Moslems with the greatest respect, affording them hospitality when asked, rising to receive them and granting to them the places of honor in their assemblies. Christians must build no new churches; have no public exhibitions of their religion; not wear the cross or exhibit the sign of it on the street; in no way were they permitted to imitate Moslems. They were to carry no arms; use no bells; not place their lamps in public places, nor enter a Moslem house for any purpose whatever. No Christian should strike a Moslem. Violation of any of these stipulations might cost the offender his life, as he was "deserving of the punishment inflicted upon rebellious subjects."[1]

To accept such terms was an evidence of the weakness of the Christians, and we may be sure that there was a silent determination to better those terms just as soon as the strength was theirs. In the meantime they must make the best of their bad condition.

The Moslem conquerors were not harder masters than they

[1] "History of Jerusalem," Besant and Palmer, p. 81.

had to be, and were probably more lenient in their treatment of the vanquished than the vanquished would have been to them had the positions been reversed. It is true, on the other hand, that the promises of the caliphs were frequently made of none effect by the generals in the field. By many of the latter the Christians were regarded as legitimate prey, whom, to leave "unplucked" was out of the question. Consequently the unfortunate non-Moslems were often roughly treated, beaten and robbed.

During the Moslem occupation previous to the Crusades the Christian population of Palestine were frequent sufferers at the hands of their political masters. Warring tribes of Moslems kept them in fear of their lives, and the result of every change in the caliphate was anxiously awaited. But all the oppressions of all his predecessors were forgotten in the awful persecutions inflicted upon them by El Hakem Biamr Ullah. This madman was the third caliph of the Fatimite dynasty. Hakem ascended the throne in the year 996, at the age of eleven. Four years later Christians and Jews began to reap the harvest of his hatred. Important persons had the choice of embracing Islam or losing all their property, and those who made the latter choice often suffered violent death. On Jerusalem Hakem's destructive hand fell and, in the year 1010, the order was given for the demolition of the Church of the Holy Sepulchre. The order was executed, only to be followed shortly after by one for the restoration of the Church. Various reasons are advanced to explain Hakem's actions, but the only satisfactory one is that he was mad and that this was one of the freaks of his madness.

The restoration of the Church of the Sepulchre was completed thirty-seven years after the destruction. It could not really have been called a restoration, for it was only a partial rebuilding. The Basilica of Constantine was not included in the work, while Calvary and other sacred sites near at hand were covered by small chapels. The persecutions, however, did not cease, nor was the condition of the Christians alleviated by any of Hakem's successors. It became worse, until the sufferings they endured were terrible. The treatment accorded pilgrims from the west was such as would lead one to imagine that the desire to make pilgrimages would cease. On the contrary, that pious ardor could not be smothered. The people still came in crowds. At the same time the indignities the pilgrims suffered were arousing in Europe a spirit of hatred against the Moslems, and a determination to wrest from them the places made holy by their association with the Lord and His disciples. For at least a century before the preaching of the Crusade by Peter the Hermit the patriarchs of Jerusalem and those high in the ecclesiastical position in the west felt that the pilgrimages must cease or the pilgrims be protected. Either seemed impossible. The effort was made to stop the pilgrims and to convince them that it was possible to worship God and venerate the memory of Christ without leaving home. But the tide of pilgrimage kept rising each year.

In the year 1050 (cir.) there was born in Picardy a child who was to be known in history as Peter the Hermit. When over forty years of age he joined the pilgrims to Palestine. What he saw along the route and in the Holy Land itself called up in him a spirit of enterprise that was not to be put down. With the sanction of Pope Urban he went through Europe and with irresistible eloquence summoned the people to take part in the glorious work of recovering Jerusalem from the sacrilegious presence of the infidels.

It does not belong to such a work as this to describe the forces operating in Europe that assisted in the rousing of public opinion, the raising of immense bodies of men, the starting them on that dreadful march of death to the Holy Land. A miserable remnant finally reached their destination, and, on June 7th, 1099, pitched camp before the walls of Jerusalem. It was not until the fifteenth of the following July that an entrance was effected. Then Jerusalem became

The Moslems

a Christian possession and so remained, nominally, for nearly a hundred years, or until the year 1186. It was retaken by Saladin, the Magnificent, after a tedious siege during which the Christian inhabitants fought with the courage of despair, and secured by their heroism much better terms, when they finally capitulated, than they had any reason to expect. No more famous or liberal prince has appeared in Moslem history than this conqueror of the city. He was a man of many virtues, a true knight, and the peer of any prince among the Crusaders.

At Saladin's death the kingdom he had won was divided between his two sons Efdhal and Aziz, the former retaining Syria with his capital at Damascus, the latter succeeding to the throne of Egypt. Aziz dying shortly after, his uncle Aadel became virtual ruler of Egypt. Internal wars marked the course of the succeeding rulers at Cairo and Damascus. These weakened the power of the defenders of Islam and gave some encouragement to Christian hopes that the city of Jerusalem might be recovered by them. The spirit of the Crusaders had not yet subsided.

These hopes of the Christians were realized, but not in a way expected, nor was there any rejoicing in Christendom when the fact that Jerusalem had been ceded to the Emperor Frederic II. was known. The Church was against this prince as he was under the interdict of the Pope, having been twice excommunicated by Gregory. In spite of the pontifical maledictions Frederic went on his Crusade to the Holy Land and soon after landing at Acre, where he was acknowledged as king by the Knights Templars and Hospitallers, entered into secret communications with the sultan Kamil of Damascus. A treaty was soon effected, and Jerusalem was again a Christian city, with the exception of the Mosque of Omar, to which Mohammedans were to have free access and where they might practice undisturbed, their religious observances. Frederic went to Jerusalem, entered the Holy Sepulchre, accompanied only by his trusty retainers, took the crown and placed it on his own head. The clergy of all degrees refused to participate in the act of coronation and without religious ceremony Frederic became the Christian king of Jerusalem. However, he soon returned to Europe; the city was left defenceless and its Christian population were in constant fear of danger from their unfriendly neighbors.

In 1244 a new terror to Christian and Moslem alike appeared. Driven out of their land by Tartar bands the Kharezmians appeared in Syria. Death to all followed the course of their march. To appease them the Sultan of Cairo gave them Palestine as their own on condition that they should conquer it, and the condition was met by the slaughter of nearly all Jerusalem Christians. The Sultan failed to carry out his promise to give them Palestine, thinking to satisfy them with Damascus which they captured and plundered; they were not to be thus put off however, and making war to establish their right were, after ten battles, hopelessly defeated. Four years will cover the period they were known to history.

To encourage the few remaining Christians and, if possible, repeople the depleted land with their co-religionists from the west the Crusades of Saint Louis were undertaken. This was the fifth move of this kind. It was begun in 1250 and was a failure, as was that of Edward, the Black Prince, in 1270. Subsequent attempts at arousing the crusading spirit all failed. Priest and poet used all their powers to this end, but without effect. Repeated disasters had chilled the ardor of the people. They were content to rest quietly at home, regretting that the holy places were in infidel possession, but not willing to undertake the heavy task of displacing the unbelievers.

For the next three hundred years nothing worthy of a place in history happened in this city that once defied the armies of imperial Rome. There were strifes at arms around it, but the contestants were members of Moslem clans little better than highwaymen, and their quarrels were tribal disputes. The

The Moslems 339

ecclesiastics who were permitted to remain, for lack of profitable employment, indulged in theological hair-splitting, wordy contentions unprofitable to themselves and to the world.

At the beginning of the sixteenth century the power of the Egyptian Sultans had so waned that some of their outlying provinces were merely nominally under their control. Such was their authority over Palestine, where the governor was the virtual ruler and carried out the Sultan's orders when they coincided with his own wishes. Outside the city the sheikhs of the various tribes of the Bedouin and Fellahin were beyond the control of anybody and could not be called to account for any of their numerous deeds of violence. It was a condition bordering on anarchy. At this time Selim I., the Ottoman Sultan came into power. Both before and after his conquest of Egpyt he visited Jerusalem. Under his successor Suleiman (1542) Jerusalem again rose to some little importance. Her walls, as they stand to-day, were erected by this monarch.

For the next century and a half the city was too insignificant to command any marked attention from the outside world. During the revolution of Mohammed-Ali it came peaceably into this really great general's possession in 1832, but was restored to the Porte after the bombardment of Acre in 1840. It now enjoys the distinction of being the capital of a pashalic.

The Pasha of the city, called Mutaserif, receives his appointment from the Sultan, and is responsible for government affairs over the entire province of El Kuds, which comprehends all southern Palestine west of the river Jordan and the Dead Sea. The present governor is a Turkish gentleman of high character who admirably maintains the dignity of his office and whose integrity has never been questioned. Nor has he an easy post to fill. The variety of nationalities represented in his district, their amenability to their consular representatives and the rights guaranteed them under treaty, the untrustworthiness of some of the officials upon whom he must depend for the management of certain branches of the government, all conspire to complicate matters and make absolutely necessary a head clear in planning and a will determined in execution. That he sometimes fails to give satisfaction to all parties is no discredit. Any one who knows the obstacles against which the governor has to contend will be sparing in criticism of his failures, and wonder that he accomplishes with so little friction his many duties.

In the management of city affairs the Pasha is assisted by a local council, called Megliss, composed of nine Moslems, one Jew and one Christian. The power of this council, however, is very limited, and its findings are liable at any time to reversal.

The worst sufferers at the hands of the officers of the law are the Jews. These people are not wanted in this city by the government, and those who have government affairs in charge make it difficult for them to get here and still more difficult to remain. But in this respect the various Christian nations have little to say to the Moslem. The records of Jewish oppression in Christian lands are quite as painful as any that the Orient can show. Yet the Hebrew not only endures his many wrongs; wonderful as it is, he thrives in spite of them.

Of the Moslem population, which numbers between seven and eight thousand, not more than three hundred are genuine Turks, but these three hundred hold the chief civil and military positions, and it is true of them, as of Turks in other parts of the empire, that they are an unwelcome minority. The Arabs do not like them and would be glad if some event would cause their removal. The reason for this is not far to seek. As long as the Turks are present they will hold the offices, and the opportunities for advancement that go with them, to the exclusion of the native Moslems, who are quite ready to serve the Sultan in this way. They are certainly right in considering themselves equally competent with their

Turkish brethren, but it will be a discouragingly long time before their turn arrives.

The native Moslems nearly all lay claim to aristocratic origin, that is to say, they trace their descent from the Prophet, or some relation of the Prophet. Guarded as zealously as the greatest treasure is the genealogical tree, a transcript of which, in ornamental Arabic characters, may be seen in the chief room of each of the houses. There is no doubt that the line has been kept unbroken, and that their progenitors did come at the time of the conquest of Omar and settle here. The leading families are the Husseini, Jawani, Khaldi, Jarallah, Ersasi, El Jaberi, El Kelami, Dijani, and Denaf. Some of these are well provided with this world's goods, so that to do any sort of labor is a matter of choice with them; others are quite poor, and though the blood of the Prophet—equal to that of any king—flows in their veins, they are compelled to engage in some remunerative employment. There are tradesmen and storekeepers among them, and the fact that they can do business where the Jew so largely predominates is all the evidence one needs that their abilities in this line are not to be despised.

The real Moslem is a good deal of a fatalist. This is exhibited in even the smallest matters of life. No one is more frequent in pious ejaculations, brief prayers for Divine assistance and thanksgiving for favors. They seem to rise naturally to his lips and, no matter what the surroundings or other matters in hand, must be expressed. When he opens his shop in the morning he invokes Allah's blessing on the new day and the business that may come with it, saying,

> "Oh, Opener of the day, oh, Gracious One,
> Oh, Restorer of property, oh, Bountiful One."

And then with assiduity he proceeds to business, using every effort to make as much as he can, but never complaining. All comes from God.

The soldiers wearing the uniform of the Sultan form a conspicuous part of the population. There are usually from six hundred to a thousand of these "children of the Sultan" stationed in Jerusalem. All are Moslems. To have Christians or Jews in their armies is not thought of by the Turks, or, if thought of, very wisely never put into execution. The Turk well knows that his subjects of other faiths have no love for him and in case of war with a Christian Power would be certain to desert the Crescent and favor the Cross. Consequently his regiments are composed of Moslems only, while his Christian and Jewish subjects are taxed to support them. At first view this looks a little severe, as if it were sort of "taxation without representation"; but it is the only way out of the difficulty. No doubt both Christians and Jews are very glad not to have to serve, for the life of a soldier here is not attractive; his quarters are miserable, his food abominable, the uniform he wears every day was never intended for him, is made of the cheapest shoddy which soon fades to a sickly blue, and is worn until it has become so dilapidated as to be beyond repair. When a special occasion requires it the same careless looking fellows can display neat uniforms and orderly behavior; and when it comes to actual war they show splendid fighting qualities and hardly know what fear is.

There is a resident general in Jerusalem who has charge of all the military affairs of the province, and as the troops are frequently changed from post to post his position is not a sinecure. The bashi-bazouks (military police) form part of the force. They are distinguished for their excellent horsemanship.

The term of service for the soldiers is seven years, and it is an experience entered upon by most of them with great reluctance. Annual conscriptions are made and various are the devices employed to escape the officers. It is only a question of time, however; in the end they are caught, and once in the toils they settle down to serve their time with characteristic resignation. Though in times of peace their duties are light, no one can doubt that their remuneration, thirty piastres ($1.20) per month, with food and clothing, is well earned.

Moslem domestic life has few attractions for an Occidental. Even among the highest classes there is a lack of cheerfulness in the home life, due, no doubt, to the assumed inequality of the sexes and the consequent inferior position which woman is compelled to occupy. Before girls have passed the age of childhood they are denied that freedom of action so essential to the happiness of children; they are kept secluded, and when they do appear on the streets it must be with face hidden by a veil and with the body covered entirely by a loose flowing garment, called jibbé, which conceals any grace of form its wearer may possess. Once the veil is donned no man except father, brother, husband or son must see the face. To allow a stranger to look upon it without its covering veil would be considered a disgrace.

There is no social function ever held at which men and women mingle. At occasional family celebrations friends are invited, but the ladies occupy one part of the house and the gentlemen the other. The amusements consist of conversation, smoking and coffee drinking, in all which the female guests will equal the males.

In earliest childhood the daughters of the household are made to feel their inferiority to their brothers. A girl baby is always unwelcome, and the mother of many daughters is almost sure to lose favor in her husband's eyes, while the mother of sons gains it. The boys soon learn that they are considered superior to their sisters and act accordingly. Before they are very old they do not hesitate to assume supremacy over their mothers. Another cause of woman's inferiority is her lack of education. Within a few years there have been some improvements in this regard, but it is said that as late as twenty years ago there was not a Moslem woman in Jerusalem who could write her own name or read it when it was written.

Now there are a few who can read and write, and within a year a school for the education of girls has been opened by the Moslem authorities. This is a decided innovation and was doubtless done to counteract the influence of the various Christian schools which were attracting the daughters of some of the careless Moslem parents. The authorities saw a danger in these Christian institutions and concluded that the only way to avert it was to establish a school of their own so as to control the teachers and the teaching.

It must be said of the Jerusalem Moslems that they are much more tolerant of other religious beliefs and practices than are their co-religionists generally. In the universal condemnation of Moslem fanaticism this should be remembered to their credit. . Their religion is intolerant. It has little sympathy for the adherents of other faiths. It once advocated an extermination of the "infidels." Perhaps it would continue in that advocacy did its leaders dare. There are evidences in other parts of the Empire that give reasons for such an opinion. But after several years of acquaintance with some of the leading Moslems of Jerusalem I cannot but regard them as gentlemen of very liberal views, who, while they are firm in their belief in their religion, have no desire to interfere with or injure any who differ from them. They are certainly as tolerant of the Jerusalem Jew or Christian as the Jew or Christian is of them. The only exceptions are the Mohammedans who live on Mount Zion and have charge of the Mosque Nebi Daûd. These are very fanatical and lose no opportunity to insult strangers who go too near this, one of their holy places. They resemble in this the Moslems of Hebron and Nabulus.

Of the religious practices of the followers of the Prophet little need be said; they are the same here as in other Mohammedan places. The stated hours for daily prayer are still cried from the minarets: the summons are obeyed by some, but many pay no attention whatever. Indifference is certainly

# The Moslems

on the increase and its growth is one of several grounds for the belief that the doctrines of Islam are losing their power. Other reasons are found in the private life of the people. The commands of the Koran concerning temperance and purity are openly violated. It is true that no saloons or houses of ill-fame where Moslems congregate can be seen, but that they exist is an open secret, and that nameless iniquitous practices are common is well known. Only the uninformed will listen to the ignorant, or intentionally deceptive comparisons of the results of Islam and Christianity in the lives of their respective followers which are unfavorable to the latter.

Like the Jews and Christians the Moslems have their religious fasts and feasts. The fast of Ramadan and the feast of Beiram are the greatest of their kind. These are observed in all Moslem lands and have been often described. A festival peculiar to Jerusalem is the annual procession to the tomb of Moses. Moslem tradition locates this tomb in the wilderness west of the northern end of the Dead Sea. Over the site buildings have been erected capable of accommodating several hundred pilgrims. Just before the pilgrimage is made crowds of Moslems from all over the country and from other parts of the Empire throng to Jerusalem. As it usually comes about Easter-time the city is thronged until the streets are almost impassable. Men, women and children, on foot, on donkeys or camels, and in palanquins, to the music of pipes and drums and cymbals march through the Jaffa Gate and make their way to the grounds of the Mosque of Omar. They are several days in gathering, during which time the spirit of fanaticism runs high. No strangers are admitted to the Mosque area during this week, for the governor cannot control the actions of these visitors from the villages. On Friday, after prayers in the Haram, the procession forms. Accompanied by mounted police and led by the military band the pilgrims file out of the St. Stephen's Gate. The Bethany road for a mile or more is lined on both sides by spectators, who are anxious to see this display. And it is a display! Such varieties of costume, such wealth of banners, such a display of colors can be seen only in the Orient. The pilgrims walk to the tomb of Moses, twenty miles distant, and spend a week in feasting and semi-religious exercises. The entertainment is provided by the Houssani family, of Jerusalem, who have charge of the tomb and grounds.

Moslem women have a special fondness for tomb visiting. On any pleasant afternoon you may see them in any of their three cemeteries, sitting in twos and threes among the desolate graves. There are no more cheerless and desolate places in this land of rather dreary aspects than the Moslem fields of sepulture. And yet the memory of their dead is well preserved. Believing that the spirits of the departed are near and can understand what is said the women come and sit for hours by the grave of a loved one and tell all that has happened since their last visit. It is a wonder that with this belief does not come a desire to have the last resting-place of their dead show some evidences of care. Most important of the three cemeteries is that just outside the east wall of the Haram enclosure. Its importance is not due to its size, but to its alleged proximity to the seat of the last judgment. Those buried here will be the first to rise and the first judged. Moreover, because of their having been buried in this exceptionally holy ground the judgment will be favorable.

The death of a Moslem of distinction is the cause of great mourning, and it is a time when the Orientalism of this people may be best witnessed. Hired mourners are present at the last rites and "go about the streets." The grief of the female members of the family is terrible to witness. Interment takes place as soon after death as possible. The funeral procession forms and is headed by two bearers of tall palm branches. Following these are a number of blind men—professional mourners—chanting some weird death-song and loudly wailing certain portions of the Koran. The body, in

The Moslems

a plain coffin, borne on the shoulders of four men comes next. At every few steps the bearers give way to others from the crowd. Passers-by join the procession to carry the deceased for a few steps and then drop out to give others an opportunity thus to show their respect. The body is buried without coffin of any kind. If the deceased was a rich man, and generous, crowds of beggars assemble round the grave, for money is sure to be distributed. For many succeeding nights a lighted lantern is placed on or near the grave so that the darkness may not be too oppressive to the disembodied spirit.

Jerusalem has now been practically in undisputed Moslem possession for six hundred years. How long it will continue to be is a question often asked. The weakness of the possessors is very evident. In the dismemberment of the Turkish Empire—an event which is delayed only by the jealousies of the European Powers,—will the Holy Land become the property of Russia, France, England or Germany? Any one of these nations would willingly add this land to its possessions, but cannot do so without the consent of the others. And in the present delicate condition of European affairs such a consent is not easily secured. Perhaps a compromise will be effected by the terms of which Palestine will be considered as neutral territory, where the Jew will be given an opportunity to work out his national destiny. The Jew has national aspirations and ideas, and a national future. Where, if not here, will his aspirations be realized and his ideas carried out?

THE FUTURE OF JERUSALEM

Religious Preëminence—Material Prosperity—Wonderful Preservation—Jerusalem not Self-supporting—Barren Appearance of Palestine—Bethlehem Hills—Recent Improvements—Possibilities—Jordan Valley—Jewish Memorial—Colonists—Objection to Foreign Colonists—Conditions Changing—Jews the Future Inhabitants—Biblical Proofs—Jewish Expectancy—Room for City Growth—Undeveloped Resources—Greatest Difficulty—Lack of Public Spirit—Water in Abundance Promised—Certainty of Prophecy—An Indication—Jew and Christian.

XIX

THE FUTURE OF JERUSALEM

IN the preceding pages an endeavor has been made to tell something of the Sacred City's past and present. The facts brought forth must have convinced the reader that Jerusalem, like the Jews, is—as it ever was—peculiar. Its location away from any adequate water supply, on rugged, almost barren hills, is unusual. Its nearly four thousand years of strange, many times destructive, experiences give it an unique place in history. Its religious preëminence is undoubted. Its present material prosperity is a fact in spite of the great and ill-reconciled variety of its people.

What reasons governed the choice of its site is a question neither so difficult nor so interesting as how it has been preserved. Founded it was and it was preserved; there was a Divine purpose in the founding and in the preservation; nor is it rash to go further and say that there was a *special* Divine purpose in both.

Judged by the ordinary standards on which human judgments are framed Jerusalem ought never to have been anything more than a mountain hamlet where a few hardy villagers could live, because their wants were few and their courage great. The land of which it became the capital was much greater in area than in value. On the east and south was the desert, on the west the sea, and on the north the rival kingdom of Syria. The central range, running from north to south, on which the city stands, does not, and probably never did, present a pleasing view to the husbandman. Its hills are rugged, its valleys deep gorges where cultivation can only be affected with great labor. That labor has been available, however, and patient industry, when labor cost almost nothing, has succeeded where to-day it would surely fail.

The land of Palestine does not now alone support the city of Jerusalem as it is; Jerusalem is not self-supporting. By this it is not meant that it differs from other cities, for it is true in one sense that no city is self-supporting; no city is independent in the sense that it produces all that is necessary for the sustenance and comfort of its residents. The people of London and New York would soon starve were they shut off from outside communications. But London and New York are self-supporting in that they produce that which they can exchange for the products of other places. Jerusalem produces nothing, and therefore has nothing to exchange. The land of which the city is the capital now produces little more than its villagers require. The formerly terraced hills are sadly denuded of soil and stand, naked limestone mountains, on which but little vegetation can find room to live.

This barren appearance at first sight puts a damper on any belief in the country's future, and many visitors immediately jump to the conclusion that it has no future. Centuries of negligence, and governmental oppression that encourages negligence, have made a sorry spectacle of a land that once flourished with every form of vegetation that pleased the eye and delighted the taste. But I am satisfied that what once was produced here will, or may be, again produced, and by similar methods of industry and skill. Fifteen years ago the hills near Bethlehem were as void of fields, vineyards and orchards as any in the land; the soil upon them was thin and the rocky ledges very prominent. Now all around this little city are fields of grain, abundant vineyards and grand orchards of fig and olive trees. Industry has wrought the transformation. The terraces have been rebuilt, the earth brought from the valleys into which it had been washed and the result is all that could be desired. There are similar spots all over Palestine, as, for example the grounds of the American

Friends' Mission, in Ramallah, the precincts, the numerous Jewish colonies, and the lands of the Latin Convents. All these improvements, accomplished in a few years, indicate that the land that once supported a population of at least two millions could again do so. The divine conditions of soil and climate are the same as ever, only the human conditions of industry in the individual and encouragement in the government are sadly lacking.

Supposing the latter two conditions to be met, there is no doubt that Jerusalem would become the centre of an agricultural district that could compete with other countries in the great world markets. This may seem a strange statement to those who have depended upon the accounts of casual visitors, or professional writers, who presume to know all about it after a few days' stay, for their information. The Jordan valley is now desert. It has in it the possibilities of a Paradise. East of the Jordan, the land of the homeless Bedouin, is an unknown country to most people. I venture to state that there is no finer wheat land on earth than this. The methods of agriculture are of the crudest, but the harvest that results would abundantly remunerate a more skillful husbandman. The Jewish committee that presented a memorial to Lord Salisbury in 1891 did not prophesy the unlikely when they said: "If at this moment the ground is barren in parts and refuses to yield its increase, we know that it is the hand of man that has wrought the evil. The hand of man shall remedy it."

Certain it is that when the country contiguous is properly cared for, the city will thrive. Temporal prosperity is in sight. Societies of colonization have been formed in recent years in Roumania, Southern Russia, Germany, England, and, quite lately, in America. Agents have been sent to purchase lands and have succeeded in acquiring possession of desirable tracts along the maritime plain in the neighborhood of Jaffa and near the base of Carmel. The majority of the colonists thus far have been Jews, and when they have had some previous knowledge of agricultural life have been reasonably prosperous. It has been learned at the same time that the attempt to make tillers of the soil out of shopkeepers and petty artisans is a waste of money. The German colonists have been uniformly successful, because of their ability and willingness to work. One cannot help admiring their neat villages and comfortable looking homes at Haifa, Jaffa and Jerusalem; they are like little bits of the prettiest of German rural life.

It is impossible to foretell the future of colonization plans, because of the uncertainty of the political horizon. Naturally the present rulers do not wish to see these foreigners coming and settling here, bringing their foreign ideas, habits, and religions, and retaining their allegiance to their governments in Europe and America. They are small foreign states in the land of the Turk, and the Turk is aware that the longer they remain the more determined and intelligent will be their opposition to him. Thus it will be readily understood that intending colonists will hesitate to come, not wishing to risk their all in the face of present opposition and future uncertainty.

Conditions are changing. Even the unprogressive Turk is submitting gradually to modern improvements. If a prophet twenty years ago had predicted as many changes for the better as have been made in Palestine during that time he would have been treated as a dreamer. There are now some good carriage roads, where then there were only miserable paths threading the land. Now there is a railroad from Jaffa to Jerusalem, and another is building from Haifa to Damascus, passing through the rich valley of Jezreel, by Lake Galilee and across the fertile Haúran. These improvements, continued as they surely will be, are the presages of a future for that city which is destined to be the capital of the land. It needs no prophet to foretell this now, but the majority may need some one to recall to them the fact that present conditions and future improvements were foretold centuries ago.

The Future of Jerusalem 355

My own belief is that the time is not far distant when Palestine will be in the hands of a people who will restore it to its former condition of productiveness. The land is waiting, the people are ready to come and will come as soon as protection to life and property is assured. I am ready to go further and say that the coming inhabitants will be Jews. This must be accepted or the numerous prophecies that assert it so positively must be thrown out as worthless. The subject of Israel's restoration I freely admit is not a popular one now; but the unpopular of to-day is the universally accepted of to-morrow.

It certainly will not be considered out of place to introduce in this connection a few of the many prophetic passages that assert this return of the dispersed of Israel: "He that scattered Israel will gather him" (Jer. xxxi. 10). "He shall assemble the outcasts of Israel and gather together the dispersed of Judah" (Isaiah xi. 12). "Like as I have watched over them to pluck up and to break down and to destroy and to afflict, so will I watch over them to build and to plant, saith the Lord" (Jer. xxxi. 28). "For I will take you from among the heathen and gather you out of all countries and will bring you into your own land" (Ezekiel xxxvi. 24). Now this gathering has not yet taken place; it must be made or prophecy counts for nothing. The present movements among Jews in many parts of the world indicate their belief in the prophetic assertions. Their eyes are turning toward the land that once was theirs, and their hearts are longing for the day when they as a people can dwell securely in it. With every improvement of the country the city must improve. It will always be the centre of Palestine. Should an independent nation arise and occupy the land as it once did we should see history being repeated and Jerusalem a city of prominence. There are physical obstacles that would have to be overcome, but they are not so great as has been often assumed and asserted. There is room for a large city. The Plain of Rephaim as far south as the Convent of Saint Elias—half way to Bethlehem—is admirably adapted to city construction. The broad plateau on the north, now being rapidly built over, is all that could be desired for residence sites. There is ample room for a large city.

There is something more needed than room, however; there must be means of support for the people. These means are at hand, but, as already mentioned, they are undeveloped. Rich mineral deposits have been discovered, but work upon them has been abandoned because of the paralyzing policy of the government. Copper and tin have been found; coal exists in paying quantities in the Lebanon and near Sidon; at the former mines the coal is of good quality and 12,000 tons were at one time mined, then the works were abandoned. With the introduction of railways these fields would all be worked and made to pay. There are large mineral deposits in Gilead and Moab and along the shores of the Dead Sea. Petroleum is said by experts to exist in abundance in the southern part of the Jordan valley. There are salt deposits in and near the Dead Sea sufficient to supply the world's demands. All this wealth of minerals is of no value now, but once capital is assured of safe investment the present death will give place to activity. In such an event Jerusalem would be the natural manufacturing centre and could not only supply her own demands, but be able to compete with other manufacturing cities in the markets of the world.

The greatest difficulty in the way is the lack of water. No doubt this was always a difficulty, but one which in the former days of prosperity was met by great skill and great labor, which were applied in devising and building the great aqueducts that led from distant fountains into the city. Many of the early kings made the providing of water for their capital their chief concern. Large pools—as Upper and Lower Gihon, Hezekiah, Bethesda, Siloam—collected and preserved for public use large quantities. Cisterns were then much more numerous than now. And it is more than probable that the Virgin's Fountain was a much more copious stream.

The Future of Jerusalem

Whether added to these was another natural source springing up in the midst of the city or in the temple area is a question on which the authorities differ. The inhabitants of the modern city do not enjoy the blessing of an abundance of water, but they have omitted the efforts to obtain it and preserve it put forth by their predecessors. It really is not so much a question of lack of water as lack of energy and public spirit; an honest capable city government would soon have it. The money necessary for the work was once offered by an English company, but as the capitalists stipulated that an English superintendent was to oversee expenditures, the local authorities declined the offer.

But in the city that the prophets beheld in moments of inspired vision this great lack was to be supplied by natural means. There will be an abundant supply in the very midst of the city. Perennial streams shall issue. Zechariah (xiv. 8) tells us, "And it shall be in that day that living waters shall go out from Jerusalem, half of them toward the former sea and half of them toward the hinder sea; in summer and in winter shall it be." That this great change is to occur in the millennial age is generally conceded. To speculate any further about it, to attempt any description of the changes physical and spiritual that must attend it would be going too far for this work. At the same time it may be said, and repeatedly, that the city of prophetic assertion must be realized or prophecy be relegated to a position on a par with fictitious literature.

Any one desiring to know the millennial future of Jerusalem can find it described on many pages of the Inspired Word. The only legitimate method for the interpretation of the various allusions to that future city is the natural one, *i. e.*, to take just what is there said as it is said and attempt neither to add to nor detract from the statements.

Forgetfulness, or rather, disregard, of this has led to many fanciful and some foolish conclusions. The result has been that serious-minded people have come to believe that there is no interpretation of these passages that can lead to any certainty. There may be some grounds for the belief, they are due however to fault, not in the prophetic narrative, but in our methods of treating that narrative. Better take the narrative as it stands and believe that what is there said of the future of Jerusalem will come to pass, or believe, as many do, that the city can have no future that will make it sufficiently important to command the attention of the modern world. For my part I see no reason to question the Bible statements about the future of Jerusalem and believe there are many signs in the present pointing to the fulfillment of what the Scriptures say about it.

It is very certain that Mohammedanism will have nothing to do with the city's future. Its six hundred years of possession and its present deplorable condition warrant the assertion. Jerusalem has been ground under the heel of Moslem oppressors, in spite of the fact that as a holy city it is with them second only to Mecca. It would still be in the same deplorable condition were the Christian nations and their many Jewish subjects not becoming so much interested in it. Quietly the Jew and Christian have been getting possession of desirable building sites and erecting substantial structures. Less than half of the city within the walls is owned by Moslems, while hardly any of the new city outside the walls is now in their hands. This desire to acquire Jerusalem real estate, a desire that animates Christians and Jews, gives a strong indication of what the city of the future is to be. Its destiny is bound up with religion. For similar reasons Christian and Jew love it; to each it is holy for what it has been; it will become holier and greater still.

It has already been said in this chapter that the coming inhabitants of Palestine will be Jews. The fact that Christians now hold a goodly portion of the city and land counts for nothing against this. The time has come when Jew and Christian can live together without persecution on either side.

The "wall of partition" still stands. It is higher and stronger in Jerusalem than any place else on earth. But even here it is crumbling. There is at least tolerance for the narrowest Christianity in this capital of the severest Judaism; and this tolerance must grow into something more friendly. Christianity and Judaism are radically the same religion. We believe that Christianity has the real life—the life of the Spirit —a stage of development to which Judaism has not attained, but Judaism will advance; that when it has reached the spiritual stage, the "wall of partition" will be broken down and a union will be effected in a religion nearer the divine ideal than this world has yet witnessed, whose adherents shall be "Israelites indeed."

These maps are from "The Holy Land in Geography and in History," and are used by the kind permission of the author, Mr. Townsend MacCoun, M.A.

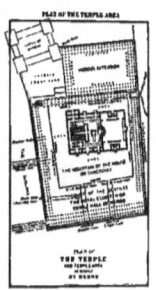

Selections from

Fleming H. Revell Company's

Missionary Lists

New York: 158 Fifth Avenue
Chicago: 63 Washington Street
Toronto: 154 Yonge Street

MISSIONS, AFRICA.

The Personal Life of David Livingstone.
Chiefly from his unpublished journals and correspondence in the possession of his family. By W. GARDEN BLAIKIE, D.D., LL.D. With Portrait and Map. *New, cheap edition.* 508 pages, 8vo, cloth, $1.50.

"There is throughout the narrative that glow of interest which is realized while events are comparatively recent, with that also which is still fresh and tender."—*The Standard.*

David Livingstone.
His Labors and His Legacy. By A. MONTEFIORE, F.R.G.S. Missionary Biography Series. Illustrated. 160 pages, 12mo, cloth, 75c.

David Livingstone.
By Mrs. J. H. WORCESTER, Jr., Missionary Annals Series. 12mo, paper, net, 15c.; flexible cloth, net, 30c.

Reality vs. Romance in South Central Africa.
Being an Account of a Journey across the African Continent, from Benguella on the West Coast to the mouth of the Zambesi. By JAMES JOHNSTON, M.D. With 51 full-page photogravure reproductions of photographs by the author, and a map. Royal 8vo, cloth, boxed, $4.00.

The Story of Uganda
And of the Victoria Nyanza Mission. By S. G. STOCK. Illustrated. 12mo, cloth, $1.25.

"To be commended as a good, brief, general survey of the Protestant missionary work in Uganda."—*The Literary World.*

Robert Moffat,
The Missionary Hero of Kuruman. By DAVID J. DEANE. Missionary Biography Series. Illustrated. *25th thousand.* 12mo, cloth, 75c.

Robert Moffat.
By M. L. WILDER. Missionary Annals Series. 12mo, paper, net, 15c.; flexible cloth, net, 30c.

The Congo for Christ.
The Story of the Congo Mission. By Rev. JOHN B. MYERS. Missionary Biography Series. Illustrated. *Tenth thousand.* 12mo, cloth, 75c.

On the Congo.
Edited from Notes and Conversations of Missionaries, by Mrs. H. GRATTAN GUINNESS. 12mo, paper, 50c.

MISSIONS, AFRICA.

Samuel Crowther, the Slave Boy
Who became Bishop of the Niger. By JESSE PAGE. Missionary Biography Series. Illustrated. *Eighteenth thousand.* 12mo, cloth, 75c.

"We cannot conceive of anything better calculated to inspire in the hearts of young people an enthusiasm for the cause."—*The Christian.*

Thomas Birch Freeman.
Missionary Pioneer to Ashanti, Dahomey and Egba. By JOHN MILUM, F.R.G.S. Missionary Biography Series. Illustrated. 12mo, cloth, 75c.

"Well written and well worth reading."—*The Faithful Witness.*

Seven Years in Sierra Leone.
The Story of the Missionary Work of Wm. A. B. Johnson. By Rev. ARTHUR T. PIERSON, D.D. 16mo, cloth, $1.00.

Johnson was a missionary of the Church Missionary Society in Regent's Town, Sierra Leone, Africa, from 1816 to 1823.

Among the Matabele.
By Rev. D. CARNEGIE, for ten years resident at Hope Fountain, twelve miles from Bulawayo. With portraits, maps and other illustrations. *Second edition.* 12mo, cloth, 60c.

Peril and Adventure in Central Africa.
Illustrated Letter to the Youngsters at Home. By BISHOP HAMMINGTON. Illustrated. 12mo, cloth, 50c.

Madagascar of To-Day.
A Sketch of the Island. With Chapters on its History and Prospects. By Rev. W. E. COUSINS, Missionary of the London Missionary Society since 1862. Map and Illustrations. 12mo, cloth, $1.00.

Madagascar.
Its Missionaries and Martyrs. By Rev. W. J. TOWNSEND, D.D. Missionary Biography Series. Illustrated. *Tenth thousand.* 12mo, cloth, 75c.

Madagascar.
By BELLE MCPHERSON CAMPBELL. Missionary Annals Series. 12mo, paper, net, 15c.; flexible cloth, net, 30c.

Madagascar.
Country, People, Missions. By Rev. JAMES SIBREE, F.R.G.S. Outline Missionary Series. 16mo, paper, 20c.

MISSIONS, CHINA.

Chinese Characteristics.
By Rev. ARTHUR H. SMITH, D.D., for 25 years a Missionary in China. With 16 full-page original Illustrations, and index. *Sixth thousand. Popular edition.* 8vo, cloth, $1.25.
"The best book on the Chinese people."—*The Examiner.*

A Cycle of Cathay;
Or, China, South and North. With personal reminiscences. By W. A. P. MARTIN, D.D., LL.D., President Emeritus of the Imperial Tungwen College, Peking. With 70 Illustrations from photographs and native drawings, a Map and an index. *Second edition.* 8vo, cloth decorated, $2.00.
"No student of Eastern affairs can afford to neglect this work, which will take its place with Dr. William's 'Middle Kingdom,' as an authoritative work on China."—*The Outlook.*

Glances at China.
By Rev. GILBERT REID, M.A., Founder of the Mission to the Higher Classes. Illustrated. 12mo, cloth, 80c.

Pictures of Southern China.
By Rev. JAMES MACGOWAN. With 80 Illustrations. 8vo, cloth, $4.20.

A Winter in North China.
By Rev. T. M. MORRIS. With an Introduction by Rev. RICHARD GLOVER, D.D., and a Map. 12mo, cloth, $1.50.

John Livingston Nevius,
For Forty Years a Missionary in Shantung. By his wife, HELEN S. C. NEVIUS. With an Introduction by the Rev. W. A. P. MARTIN, D.D. Illustrated. 8vo, cloth, $2.00.

The Sister Martyrs of Ku Cheng.
Letters and a Memoir of ELEANOR and ELIZABETH SAUNDERS, Massacred August 1st, 1895. Illustrated. 12mo, cloth, $1.50.

China.
By Rev. J. T. GRACEY, D.D. *Seventh edition*, revised. 16mo, paper, 15c.

Protestant Missions in China.
By D. WILLARD LYON, a Secretary of the Student Volunteer Movement. 16mo, paper, 15c.

MISSIONS, CHINA AND FORMOSA.

James Gilmour, of Mongolia.
His Diaries, Letters and Reports. Edited and arranged by RICHARD LOVETT, M.A. With three photogravure Portraits and Illustrations. 8vo, cloth, gilt top, $1.75.

"It is a vivid picture of twenty years of devoted and heroic service in a field as hard as often falls to the lot of a worker in foreign lands."—*The Congregationalist*

Among the Mongols.
By Rev. JAMES GILMOUR. Illustrated. 12mo, cloth, $1.25.

James Gilmour and His Boys.
Being Letters to his Sons in England. With facsimiles of Letters, a Map and other Illustrations. 12mo, cloth, $1.25.

Griffith John,
Founder of the Hankow Mission, Central China. By WILLIAM ROBSON. Missionary Biography Series. Illustrated. 12mo, cloth, 75c.

John Kenneth Mackenzie,
Medical Missionary to China. With the Story of the first Chinese Hospital. By Mrs. MARY I. BRYSON. With portrait. 12mo, cloth, $1.50.

The Story of the China Inland Mission.
By M. GERALDINE GUINNESS. Introduction by J. HUDSON TAYLOR, F.R.G.S. Illustrated, 2 volumes, 8vo, cloth, each, $1.50.

From Far Formosa:
The Island, its People and Missions. By Rev. G. L. MACKAY, D.D., 23 years a missionary on the island. Well indexed. With many Illustrations from photographs by the author, and several Maps. *Fifth thousand. Popular edition.* 8vo, cloth, $1.25.

China and Formosa.
The Story of the Mission of the Presbyterian Church of England. By Rev. JAMES JOHNSON, editor of "Missionary Conference Report, 1888." With 4 Maps and many illustrations, prepared for this work. 8vo, cloth, $1.75.

MISSIONS, INDIA.

In the Tiger Jungle.
And Other Stories of Missionary Work among the Telugus. By Rev. JACOB CHAMBERLAIN, M.D., D.D., for 37 years a Missionary in India. Illustrated. 12mo, cloth, $1.00.

"If this is the kind of missionary who mans the foreign stations, they will never fail for lack of enterprise. . . . The book is withal a vivid and serious portrayal of the mission work, and as such leaves a deep impression on the reader."—*The Independent.*

The Child of the Ganges.
A Tale of the Judson Mission. By Prof. R. N. BARRETT, D.D. Illustrated. 12mo, cloth, $1.25.

Adoniram Judson.
By JULIA H. JOHNSTON. Missionary Annals Series. 12mo, paper, net, 15c.; flexible cloth, net, 30c.

Once Hindu, now Christian.
The Early Life of Baba Padmanji. An Autobiography, translated. Edited by J. MURRAY MITCHELL, M.A. 16mo, cloth, 75c.

William Carey.
The Shoemaker who became "the Father and Founder of Foreign Missions." By Rev. JOHN B. MYERS. Missionary Biography Series. Illustrated. *Twenty-second thousand.* 12mo, cloth, 75c.

William Carey.
By MARY E. FARWELL. Missionary Annals Series. 12mo, paper, net, 15c.; flexible cloth, net, 30c.

Alexander Duff.
By ELIZABETH B. VERMILYE. Missionary Annals Series. 12mo, paper, net, 15c.; flexible cloth, net, 30c.

Reginald Heber,
Bishop of Calcutta, Scholar and Evangelist. By ARTHUR MONTEFIORE. Missionary Biography Series. Illustrated. 12mo, cloth, 75c.

Heavenly Pearls Set in a Life.
A Record of Experiences and Labors in America, India, and Australia. By Mrs. LUCY D. OSBORN. Illustrated. 12mo, cloth, $1.50.

MISSIONS, PERSIA AND INDIA.

Persian Life and Customs.
With Incidents of Residence and Travel in the Land of the Lion and the Sun. By Rev. S. G. WILSON, M.A., for 15 years a missionary in Persia. With Map, and other Illustrations, and Index. *Second edition, reduced in price.* 8vo, cloth, $1.25.

Justin Perkins,
Pioneer Missionary to Persia. By his son, Rev. H. M. PERKINS. Missionary Annals Series. 12mo, paper, net, 15c.; flexible cloth, net, 30c.

Women and the Gospel in Persia.
By Rev. THOMAS LAURIE, D.D. Missionary Annals Series. 12mo, paper, net, 15c.; flexible cloth, net, 30c.

Henry Martyn, Saint and Scholar.
First Modern Missionary to the Mohammedans. 1781-1812. By GEORGE SMITH, author of "Life of William Carey," "The Conversion of India," etc. With Portrait, Map, and Illustrations. Large 8vo, cloth, gilt top, $3.00.

"This excellent biography, so accurately written, so full of interest and contagious enthusiasm, so well arranged, illustrated, and indexed, is worthy of the subject."—*The Critic.*

Henry Martyn.
His Life and Labors: Cambridge—India—Persia. By JESSE PAGE. Missionary Biography Series. Illustrated. *Eleventh thousand.* 12mo, cloth, 75c.

Henry Martyn.
Missionary to India and Persia. 1781-1812. Abridged from the Memoir by Mrs. SARAH J. RHEA. Missionary Annals Series. 12mo, paper, net, 15c.; flexible cloth, net, 30c.

The Conversion of India.
From Pantænus to the Present Time, A. D. 193-1893. By GEORGE SMITH, C.I.E., author of "Henry Martyn." Illustrated. 12mo, cloth, $1.50.

The Cross in the Land of the Trident.
By Rev. HARLAN P. BEACH, Educational Secretary of the Student Volunteer Movement. *5th thousand.* 12mo, paper, net, 25c.; cloth, 50c.

MISSIONS, JAPAN.

Rambles in Japan,
The Land of the Rising Sun. By Rev. Canon H. B. TRISTRAM, D.D., F.R.S. With forty-six illustrations by EDWARD WHYMPER, a Map, and an index. 8vo, cloth, $2.00.

"A delightful book by a competent author, who, as a naturalist, writes well of the country, while as a Christian and a humanitarian he writes with sympathy of the new institutions of new Japan."
—*The Independent.*

The Gist of Japan:
The Islands, their People, and Missions. By Rev. R. B. PEERY, A.M., Ph.D., of the Lutheran Mission, Saga. Illustrated. 12mo, cloth decorated, $1.25.

This book does not pretend to be an exhaustive treatise of an exhaustless topic; it does pretend to cover the subject; and whosoever is eager to know the "gist" of those matters Japanese in which Westerners are most interested—the land, the people, the coming of Christianity, the difficulties and prospects of her missions, the condition of the native Church—will find it set down in Dr. Peery's book in a very interesting, reliable, instructive, and condensed form.

The Ainu of Japan.
The Religion, Superstitions, and General History of the Hairy Aborigines of Japan. By Rev. JOHN BATCHELOR. With 80 Illustrations. 12mo, cloth, $1.50.

"Mr. Batchelor's book, besides its eighty trustworthy illustrations, its careful editing, and its excellent index, is replete with information of all sorts about the Ainu men, women, and children. Almost every phase of their physical and metaphysical life has been studied, and carefully noted."—*The Nation.*

The Diary of a Japanese Convert.
By KANZO UCHIMURA. 12mo, cloth, $1.00.

"This book is far more than the name indicates. It is the only book of its kind published in the English language, if not in any language. It is something new under the sun, and is as original as it is new. It has the earmarks of a strong and striking individuality, is clear in diction, forceful in style, and fearless in criticism."—*The Interior.*

A Maker of the New Japan.
Joseph Hardy Neesima, the Founder of Doshisha University. By Rev. J. D. DAVIS, D.D., Professor in Doshisha. Illustrated. *Second edition.* 12mo, cloth, $1.00.

"The life is admirably and spiritedly written, and its hero stands forth as one of the most romantic and inspiring figures of modern times, a benefactor to his own country and an object of tender regard on our part; for it was to the United States that Mr. Neesima turned for light and help in his educational plans."
—*The Examiner.*

www.ingramcontent.com/pod-product-compliance
Lightning Source LLC
Chambersburg PA
CBHW030356230426
43664CB00007BB/622